7/9

Dawson, George,
Life is so good
LT B DAWSON

1/02 12x 6/02

W9-DCZ-448

LIFE IS SO GOOD

LT
B
DAWSON

GEORGE DAWSON AND RICHARD GLAUBMAN

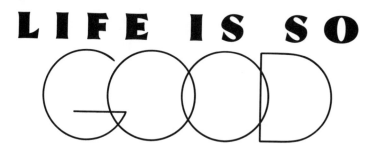

LIFE IS SO GOOD

COMPASS PRESS
AN IMPRINT OF WHEELER PUBLISHING, INC.

Copyright © 2000 by Richard Glaubman
All rights reserved.

Published in Large Print by arrangement with Random House, Inc. in the United States and Canada

Compass Press Large Print book series;
an imprint of Wheeler Publishing Inc., USA

Set in 16 pt Plantin.

FRANKLIN TOWNSHIP PUBLIC LIBRARY
485 De MOTT LANE
SOMERSET, NJ 08873
873-8700

Library of Congress Cataloging-in-Publication Data

Dawson, George, b. 1898.
  Life is so good / George Dawson and Richard Glaubman.
    p. (large print) cm. (Compass Press large print book series)
  ISBN 1-56895-937-0 (hardcover)
  1. Dawson, George, b. 1898. 2. Afro-Americans—Texas—Marshall—
Biography. 3. Afro-American aged—Texas—Marshall—Biography.
4. Centenarians——Texas—Marshall—Biography 5. Afro-Americans—
Texas—Marshall—Social conditions. 6. Marshall (Tex.)—Biography.
7. Conduct of life. 8. Large type books. I. Glaubman, Richard. II. Title

F394.M36 D39   2000b]
976.4'.192—dc21   00-058986
[B]   CIP

FROM GEORGE DAWSON,
this book is dedicated to
my teacher Carl Henry,
and to my son, George Jr.

FROM RICHARD GLAUBMAN,
this book is dedicated to
my wife, Jody,
and to my children, Jessie and Casey

ACKNOWLEDGMENTS

As with any good story, this one would never have come about without the help and support of many people. From the beginning, I had the support of family, friends, and colleagues. As the story progressed, I had the good fortune of meeting some wonderful people who were there at each critical phase of my work and helped me move on to the next level. The opportunity to meet some of these people has been for me the best and most unexpected reward of doing this book.

On the day I finished my final revisions, I received a call from Larry Bingham. In the category of Best Short Feature for man of letters, he had won the Missouri Lifestyle Journalism Award, the oldest feature-writing contest in the country. That same article, along with a photograph by Carolyn Bauman, in the *Fort Worth Star-Telegram* is what inspired me to begin my endeavor. I will always be grateful that Larry encouraged me to go and meet Mr. Dawson.

Carl Pech from my writers' group was enthusiastic from the beginning. Tony Pryor guided me to let go of writing a book and instead to begin a journey. Karen Tangorra read the early chapters and took a genuine interest in the story at a time when a discouraging word would have had immense power. Later, Andy Meyer was also kind enough to critique a few early chapters. Frank Brou, my principal, supported my efforts and at the right time encouraged me to take a leave of absence in order to complete the book. I appreciate the confidence my superintendent, Gene Medina, and the school board showed in me when they granted the request.

When I got to Texas, I met a man of integrity and dedication, Carl Henry, Mr. Dawson's teacher. He took the time to talk with me and welcomed me into his school community in such a way that I often felt more like a participant in his classroom than a visitor. Mr. Dawson, and particularly his son George Jr. and Junior's wife, Sallie, took me in as family— I felt that welcome.

My agent, Harriet Wasserman, showed faith in me by accepting a partially completed manuscript. Her unflagging interest in the story and her support for my endeavor were always there. When I realized midway through the book the enormity of the task I had taken on, she helped keep things in perspective. Always at the right time, whether it be an editing suggestion or a willingness to listen, she was there.

Kate Medina (no relation to my school superintendent), my editor, gave me excellent suggestions for the big picture while her enthusiasm for the story gave me encouragement. Meaghan Rady, her assistant, was always there for day-to-day questions and kept things on track. Dennis Ambrose, senior production editor, and copy editor Karen Richardson were very helpful. I learned that there are many unsung heroes who work behind the scenes to bring a book to a final conclusion. My thanks to them all.

My wife, Jody, read through the first draft and helped with the cuts I needed to make. Instead of a painful process, it became an enjoyable collaborative effort. Yet during a period approaching two years, I know that it wasn't always easy. I was gone on my travels or, at times, even when at home, my mind would wander to some incident of sixty or seventy years ago, but not today. With good humor, she put up with a great deal.

Tanya Jimenez helped with historical research. I would also like to thank Jim Oliphant from the Marshall Historical Society. Back home in Washington, Beth DeJarnette helped me find some resources from my local library. And as my demands on my computer increased, Mary Stolaas gave me assistance along the way.

Even now, I know that the excitement of finishing a book will fade. Mr. Dawson is a remarkable man. What will always matter is that getting to know and become friends with George Dawson has changed my life.

I humbly offer this book as a tribute to George Dawson for the life he has lived.

—RICHARD GLAUBMAN

CHAPTER 1

Wanting to enjoy every moment, I stared at the hard candies in the different wooden barrels. The man behind the counter was white. I could tell he didn't like me, so I let him see the penny in my hand.

"Take your time, son," my father said with a grin. "You did a man's work this year."

Putting his hand on my shoulder, he said to the store clerk, "He's all of ten years, but the boy crushed as much cane as I did." Since the age of four, I had always been working to help the family.

I don't know if it was pride from Father's words or the pleasure from a piece of hard candy that beckoned, but I felt so good I thought I would burst. I had been thinking of those hard candies since my father woke me before daybreak and said, "Hitch the wagon. We gonna take some ribbon syrup into town and you comin'."

When I went back inside, the stove was going and Ma had a pot of mush cooling. We ate quiet-like so as not to wake the little ones that were asleep on the other side of the room.

I was happy to see they was still sleeping for it was uncommon to spend the day alone with my father. We never had much time to talk and I just liked to be with him.

Two barrels of cane syrup were tied down in the wagon. We sat up front. My father clucked toward the mule. I wanted to tell him that I was glad he was taking me and it was going to be just him and me together all day. Trouble was, I didn't know how to say that in words. So under the shadow of my straw hat, I just looked over at him.

Solid is what I would say. He took care of us. We had potatoes and carrots buried in the straw and salt pork hangin' from the rafters. We was free of worries. Papa was a good provider. Someday I would be just like him.

Must have been a couple of hours toward town when my father nudged me. He handed me the reins and unwrapped some burlap. I took a piece of cornbread with a big dab of lard on it. When I commenced to eat, he started talking.

"With this ribbon syrup, we be out of debt and have some left for trading. We gonna have seeds for cotton, some new banty chicks, and the fruit trees that are gonna bear fruit next year. No one has the fever and we all be healthy.

"Life is good." And with a grin, he added, "I do believe it's getting better." I liked it when Papa talked to me as a man.

The morning haze had long ago burned off. The wagon stirred up a lot of dust that kind of settled over everything like a nice, smooth blanket. It was good for the mule as the dust had a way of keeping the flies off. Nothing else was said for the next hour, till we came around the last stand of trees and to the rise above Marshall.

In those days, I had in my mind that Marshall was maybe about the biggest and the best place there could ever be. The hardware store had big windows that I liked to look in. I had never been inside since I knew they didn't appreciate black folks with no money. I was partial to the general store, but I liked to walk by the livery stable too. Once a man gave me two bits to rub down and watch his horse for the afternoon. It was 1908, and I hadn't yet seen a car. I had heard of them, but nobody I knew owned one. Papa said that they didn't do too well when the rains came and the roads was deep in mud. Besides, they scared the horses. Mostly, I just liked seeing all the folks from the big ranches and the little farms like ours that was out on the boardwalk.

The cafe and the barbershop was whites only, but I knew a boy that worked in the cafe. And I knew some folks that shined shoes at the barbershop. I liked to look in those windows too.

We never had no cause to go into the post office. But I pictured that one day someone would say there was a letter waiting for me. I would walk past all the folks sitting in the town square beneath the big oak tree. When I was inside, I would say, "I'm George Dawson. I'm here to get my letter." I don't know when that was gonna happen but maybe someday it would. Marshall was a busy place and good things could just happen. It was the county seat and that had to count for something too. At least, that's what I thought then.

But at that moment, in the general store, when my father told me that I could do a man's work, anything seemed possible. I remember everything. I saw the white man frowning, my father grinning at me, and those barrels of candy to choose from. I also remember everything my ears told me that day.

As I picked up a piece of peppermint, I heard a commotion from the street. My father's gaze followed mine. It was dark and cool in the store and the hot light through the doors caused a confusing picture. There were people running, harsh words, and a lot of shouting. Papa set down a kerosene lamp he was inspecting on the counter and run to the door. I followed with the counterman behind me.

At first, out on the boardwalk, in the bright sunlight, I couldn't see the faces on the street. I heard Pete's voice before I saw him.

"It wasn't me. I didn't touch her," Pete screamed. "Lord, let me go."

I would of backed off from what I saw, but by then we was crowded up against the rail. First time in my life I saw the white folks and the colored folks together in a crowd.

It scared me. There was no more frown on the face of the white counterman that was beside of me. His lips were set in a smile. Hate was in his eyes. Across the street, in front of the barbershop, I saw three colored men frozen in place. The white folks surrounding them had red, twisted faces.

They were screaming. I had done nothing, but I felt them screaming at me.

"Kill the nigger boy, kill the nigger. They can't be messing with our white women."

Six men had Pete by the arms. The toes of his boots dragged in the dust. His face looked up to the sky as he screamed, "I didn't touch her."

I knew Pete and knew that was so. I shouted, "Pete, I'll tell—"

My father's hand clamped over my mouth. His other arm crushed the air right out of my chest. I read his eyes and then he slowly let me go without saying a word. I knew it wasn't so, though. The Rileys' cook had heard the whole thing; she just kept on working in the kitchen and watched Betty Jo and her father. She was right there, but they didn't even notice she was alive.

She was scared about what they said and I heard her talking to my mama about it. Betty Jo had gotten herself in trouble. Folks already knew that she had a thing for one of the Jackson boys and was spending a lot of time with him. When her daddy found out she was with a child, she had a whipping coming sure enough. Her daddy was steaming mad and of short temper anyhow.

"Who's the boy that done this to you?" her daddy shouted. Sally looked at the belt in his hand. She was crying but wouldn't say nothing. She was scared, and afraid to tell the boy's name, because she figured that her daddy just might go off and kill him.

"Well, if you did this 'cause you wanted to, a good beating will teach you right."

She cried even harder then.

"Well, you got it coming unless maybe this happened against your will."

Her crying slowed and seeing a way out of a beating she listened close.

"Is that what happened?" he said slowly.

Scared as she was, Betty Jo could tell that the safe answer was yes. Not wanting to tell a whole lie, she just nodded her head.

"Damn. Was it that Jackson boy from across the ridge?"

Betty Jo, she loved him, or at least thought she did, shook her head no.

Her daddy looked at her hard. His face turned angry and he said, "Was it our hired boy, Pete? That worthless, lazy nigger! Did he rape you? Did he do this?"

To each question, she just nodded in the smallest way. The tears still flowed, but he threw the belt down and stormed out the door.

"There is one nigger gonna pay for this."

Pete was seventeen and the hired boy around their farm—picking cotton, cutting cane, chores like that. He was a good worker. But he was smart and he knew enough not to even look at a white woman.

I knew Pete since we were little. He was older than me, but he treated me well. Pete was the one who swum out and saved Jimmy Blake at the swimming hole. Jimmy had smacked his head on the corner of the raft when he was showing off for us little kids. Everyone was afraid to swim out that far, but he done it. Pete, he would do anything for anybody.

As I was growing up, I didn't have any toys, but I did still own a baseball that Pete had given me a year earlier. We had been at the pasture on a Sunday afternoon last summer. I had helped to cut the field. A team from Tyler had come over to play some of our boys from Marshall. We didn't have a real stadium, but we would go out and mow the pasture, and set up table for a big Sunday feast and get together afterward. Pete played shortstop. He was good too. If you wanted fast, you should have seen Pete run the bases.

The score was tied and went to extra innings. In the eleventh Pete came up with a man on first, two outs. He took their pitcher full count. And then...and then he almost hit a cow. It would of been a home run if we had fences. As it was, he got a triple and drove in the winning run. I cheered and cheered for our Marshall boys, especially for Pete.

I was proud of him when the team gave him the game ball. He gave me that ball and said, "You practice with it, George. You'll be a hitter someday too." I was awful pleased but I could barely mutter thank you when my mama nudged me. Pete was my hero.

The colored couldn't play in the big leagues, but if they could I know Pete would of made it.

Yeah, someone had committed a sin and Pete was gonna pay for it. I looked down the boardwalk. They was dragging Pete in the direction of the post office. Sheriff Tate stepped off the boardwalk up ahead from where the mob was. I let out a big breath of air. The sheriff was a big man. I had heard it said that, on a bet, he had carried a barrel of molasses on his back from the general store down past the saloon. They say that once when things got out of hand at the rodeo and the crowd threatened an official, the sheriff took care of it himself. He laid six men out cold before the crowd settled down. I knew he could stop this. People was spilling off the boardwalk and cursing Pete something terrible.

"We gonna keep our women safe."

"Make that boy pay and show all the niggers that they can't get away with this."

Pete was kicking and thrashing, but the mob was still hauling him farther down the street. Taking a few steps along the edge of the road, the sheriff stopped. He kicked the dust and planted his feet. He had big, shiny-looking boots that dust didn't want to stick to. His pants, tucked into the boots, had a stripe down the sides. A big pistol hung off his belt. He pulled the pistol out and crossed his arms so that the pistol set against his chest.

He turned and looked back toward the boardwalk. The sheriff was in front of a group of colored that was pressed into the crowd. He scowled and sent them a message that gave me a chill on a hot day. I had heard tell that the sheriff ran with the Klan at night when they would come through the colored section or out to the colored farms. They would leave a burning cross or shoot some windows out. That's what people said about him and now I knew it was true.

Behind us, a man was pushing his way out of the store. The sheriff walked toward us and waved his pistol. We opened up some space and let the man through. I saw the big coil of rope slung over his shoulder. I wanted to cry, but I held it back. He ran along the edge of the street and a couple other men stepped down to join him. Some of them were farmers I recognized from when we delivered our cotton. They looked like ordinary farmers with overalls and farm work boots. But that day, their hateful faces made them different.

As they caught up alongside Pete, the mob seemed to get inspired. Pete had been twisting and screaming all get-out, but those men seemed to double their strength when they seen the lynching rope coming. Up by the post office, the old oak tree, the Confederate Tree, they called it, was going to be a gallows.

As the rope got closer to the tree, more men arrived to help. One of them tried to throw it over a big limb, but it fell short. It kept falling short. Some in the crowd jeered as if it were a contest at the county fair. Finally a man tied one end around a horseshoe. It sailed over the big limb, causing a small cloud of dust when it landed. Some cheers and laughter followed as if the spectators was at a picnic.

I looked down at the boardwalk. I saw the

gouges and grooves worn over time. I focused on one rough spot that almost had the shape of a half-moon. I would of studied it forever, but I couldn't help but look up. It had seemed as if we were all in slow motion and now everything was happening so fast. Someone had pulled a wagon into the shade under the rope. The horse was whinnying and nervous. A couple men were up front giving it some kindness and making it calm.

Pete was closer now, could see the rope and the wagon. His shouts and protests had changed to cries for mercy.

"I swear to God it wasn't me. Have mercy, you've got the wrong man. I didn't touch her."

Pete's eyes had a wild look as more men began milling around him. He was up on his feet now, but it was more that they was holding him up. Pete was swaying, as if he was about to faint. His face was all bloodied, but his eyes could see clear what was going to happen.

His arms were pinned behind him and someone had bound him around the wrists. One of the men in the buckboard said, "Get that boy up here."

As they reached to grab his legs Pete started to kick wildly. His boot kicked one of them under the chin. A farmer, actually a moonshiner, by the name of Norris staggered and went down as blood spurted out of his mouth and onto his overalls.

"Damn."

Spitting out a tooth and a mouthful of blood, he said, "That nigger hurt me!"

Some men went over to help him but Norris waved them off and regained his feet. It had gotten awfully still and you could hear his boots scrape across the hard dirt as he pulled himself up. He walked, kinda punch drunk from the kick to the head, till he was maybe two feet from Pete. He was swaying a bit and trembling from his anger. Now it was Pete that stood steady and still.

Some men were still holding Pete tight from behind so that he couldn't even budge. But if Pete knew he was gonna die, the fear had left his face. Though Pete was just a boy, he must of been four to five inches taller than Norris. He just looked down at Norris, looked him in the eye. Most always we was supposed to look down at the ground when a white man was talking, and this seemed to set Norris off even more.

Norris was a squat man but he was powerful and broad across the shoulders. The first punch was so hard to the stomach that across the square we could hear the air push out of Pete's chest. Even the two men who held Pete was pushed back a step by that blow. They seemed to brace their legs for the next blow, and Pete sagged. I didn't want to look, but I seen it all.

The gunshot took me by surprise. I saw the smoke drifting out of the crowd and followed that to see where it came from. The sheriff didn't say nothing, he just walked slowly toward Norris and holstered his gun. My heart lifted. It was like the reverend told us: All had been darkness and now there was light.

I watched Norris and saw that all the bluster was gone. I turned and looked up at my father. His lips were set, but there was a questioning look in his eyes. Mostly, I looked at Pete. He wasn't smiling, but I could see there was hope in his eyes as they followed the sheriff.

It seemed like forever came and went till he stopped in front of Norris.

It was like a low whisper, but the sheriff's voice carried across the crowd.

"This ain't your show, Norris."

People talk about white trash around here. My mama and papa wouldn't let us call anyone white trash, but it seemed that's what the sheriff was saying to Norris, the way that he talked to him like he was a dog that better get himself off the porch. While lots of white folks would buy moonshine from Norris, you could tell that at the same time everyone thought he was shiftless and no account.

Pete was watching the sheriff, but the sheriff, he didn't even take no notice of him. He nodded to the half-dozen men gathered in front of the buckboard and walked back toward the crowd. It was as if he had given his blessing.

Pete had taken the best that Norris had to offer, but you could see that it was the sheriff that had delivered a crushing blow. Pete's legs buckled. He moaned as those men dragged him the remaining few feet around to the back of the buckboard.

"I didn't do nothing," Pete cried in a voice that rang without hope.

I buried my head against my father's chest.

When I heard the whip snap and the buckboard lurch forward, I looked back. Pete's neck broke instantly; his head rested at an awkward angle. His eyes were open and he looked out at everyone.

As he swayed from the tree, the crowd hushed and tried to look away from his accusing eyes. Not till Pete's body stopped swinging did anyone move. The crowd broke up in silence and went their separate ways.

I didn't want to, but as we left Marshall I turned 'round in my seat and looked. Pete was still looking at me and I knew that he always would be. Pete would stay till morning. When they did a lynching, they made us leave the body hanging, to put a terror in the colored folk.

His face looked different than I had ever seen it, but Papa still hadn't said a word. First time I looked up from the wagon, I noticed that we were already passing Miller's Swamp. We was halfway home and I hadn't wanted to raise my eyes to the world. I had always looked closely when we passed the swamp, see if I could see any muskrats or water moccasins. Now I didn't care. I would never care again, I promised myself.

I had been thinking hard, though. We lived just three miles from the Johnsons, a white family. And since I was eight, I had been feeding hogs at the McCready and Barker farms. They always paid like they promised, or most often sent home a slab of beef or salt pork in exchange for my work. But after what I saw, I decided that life was different now. I figured I owed that to Pete.

"I will never work for or talk to a white person again," I said with anger.

My father, who had seemed lost in his own thoughts, jerked his head and looked at me.

"That was wrong what they did," I said. "Those white folks are mean and nasty people."

Papa swallowed hard and pulled up on the reins so that the wagon stopped.

He turned toward me. "No. You will work for white folks. You will talk to them."

"But, Papa, what about Pete? He didn't do nothing and they killed him."

"Yeah, I know they had no cause for that, but—"

I cut my father off short, something I had never done.

"But they made Pete suffer so."

"His suffering is over, son. It's all over for Pete. You don't need to worry for him."

"They took his life. Pete was still young. He should of grown to be a man."

"That's so," Papa said. "It was Pete's time, though. His time had come and that's that."

My anger still had some hold on me and I swallowed hard.

Papa looked at me and said, "Some of those white folks was mean and nasty. Some were just scared. It doesn't matter. You have no right to judge another human being. Don't you ever forget."

14

My father had spoken.

There was nothing to say. I didn't know it then, but his words set the direction my life would take even till this day.

A year earlier, I had been kicked by the mule. It hurt like all get-out. I couldn't work for three days, but I didn't cry. I was proud that I was man enough to take it. But this hurt worse. I cried and my daddy wrapped his arms around me and held me to his chest. Then something broke loose deep inside. I didn't know a body could have so many tears.

I cried for me. I cried for Pete. I cried for the little ones and for Mama and Papa. I cried for all the pain that there was in this world. Papa had his own tears and he just held me.

When the tears slowed, Papa told me, "This morning, I said that you did a man's work. But you was still a boy. Now you are learning to be a man."

After we got home, I found my peppermint was still in my pocket. I scraped off the lint and the dirt. I gave it to one of my little sisters. My taste for it had disappeared. Ninety years later, I still don't like peppermint.

About six months after the lynching, Betty Jo had her baby. It was a boy, a little white boy. No one said nothing. I guess by then most folks, white folks anyway, had all forgotten. I didn't forget. Mama said that maybe where Pete is now, if they have a team, colored could play in those big leagues. I think Pete would be starting at shortstop.

I'm one hundred and one years old now. But

I still remember. Though that was over ninety years ago, I see it in my mind like I was there today. I can't let loose of my memories, even if I wanted to. Yeah, I've seen it all in these hundred years, the good and the bad. My memory works fine. I can tell you everything you want to know.

CHAPTER 2

I would pull out a handful of cotton from the bale. At first, I used to rip it with my hands, just for the sheer fun of tearing something apart. Grandma would give me a look.

"Child, there's a way to comb this cotton. If we are going to have cloth for this winter, you better pay attention."

She showed me how to pull the cotton apart, but just right so it didn't tear. She gave me my own comb to work with. I was only four years old when I started, but I was the first child and the family needed my help.

Along with yams, sugarcane, and potatoes, we grew cotton on forty acres. In east Texas, soil was poor and rain was in short supply. But in the back room of our cabin, there was always cotton. Combing cotton hour after hour was wearing, and being young I would get tired. When I would ask to stop, Grandma Charity would tell me her stories to keep me going.

16

"George, I know you're tired. But President Lincoln, he didn't free us to be lazy and no good. He freed us to work hard and improve ourselves."

Her mother, my great-grandma Sylvie, would be there too. We didn't have a spinning wheel, so she used a drop spindle to make thread out of the clumps of clean cotton that Grandma Charity and I pulled. Great Grandma Sylvie was born in 1812, so, of course, she had also been a slave.

Grandma Sylvie mostly listened, but sometimes she would add something too, kinda like to fill in for what her daughter, Charity, had missed. I loved to listen as Grandma Charity would tell of freedom day.

"Master Lester called us down to the big house. Even the field hands were told to come. Usually, they didn't bring the hands in and lose the work time. They would send a messenger out to the fields. So, we knew something was up.

"Master Lester didn't look too happy."

Great-grandma Sylvie broke in with a laugh, "No, he looked plain miserable."

Grandma Charity said, "He just stood there for the longest time. Master Lester had a powerful voice. I was up front, but even so, on that day I had to strain to hear. His voice had lost its strength. He never took his eyes off that paper as he read.

" 'The Confederacy,' " Master Lester said, " 'has lost the war. Robert E. Lee accepted terms of the defeat at Appomatox.' "

"Funny thing is, in a way, I felt a little sad when I heard him say we lost."

Grandma Sylvie snorted. "We had nothing to lose, daughter. It wasn't our war."

"Yeah, I knows. But I didn't feel no excitement in me till he went on," Grandma Charity said.

" 'Under terms of our defeat, according to President Lincoln, slavery is abolished. You are free,' Master Lester said.

"I had hopes that one day Charity would be free, but I didn't dare hope for my lifetime," said Sylvie. "Yet there it was. The words we had waited for had been spoken. I would of thought there would be screaming and shouting, but it stayed still and quiet."

"That's right," Charity said, "but people were smiling now, even the little ones. It was like the air had changed.

"When Master Lester started up again, he was talking to a free people.

"He said, 'You can stay or go as you choose. If you decide to stay and work, you will be paid wages as free men.' "

Charity nodded. "We all watched him walk his way back to the big house before a word was said. Then there was a buzz, all right.

"John, one of the field hands, said, 'Me, I'm going north. Ohio be a better place, I hear.'

"Ezra, who worked in the big house, said, 'You don't know where this Ohio is. How you going to get there?'

"Mac, he said, 'Well, if John going, so am I!' "

"It went on and on," Grandma Sylvie said.

Charity laughed. "It sure did. We drifted off into small groups. Through the night, there were fires blazing out front of our shacks. People was talking about the new freedom and what they gonna do."

"That's so," Sylvie said. "But for Charity and me, our course was set. We would stay and wait for my man to come back. He had escaped two years earlier and gone off to join the Union Army to fight for freedom. News moved slow but we would wait. I had faith."

I always listened. It was a story that was told and retold. But each telling only made it better. Every time I heard, I had more questions.

"What did you do while you waited?" I asked.

Both grandmas laughed and gave me hugs.

Charity picked me up in her arms and Grandma Sylvie put her hands on my shoulders as she talked. "Only one thing to do," she said. "We worked."

"But that's what you did before there was freedom," I said in confusion.

"That be so," Charity said, "but with freedom we had hope. Hope is what kept us going then. We worked from sunrise till dark, and in the moonlight we tended our own garden patches. It was two years before we learned that he died in battle. Colored was on the move in the South then. A field hand that just arrived, Tom Dawson, told us the story as we chopped cane.

19

" 'Your man,' Tom said, 'he be like a father to me. I was young and so green then. I had escaped from the plantation, but I didn't know nothing about fighting. We was in the same unit, a colored unit. I was in front of Reggie when we got our uniforms. He put his hand on my shoulder and said, "Son, don't you worry. Just stick by me and I'll make sure that you be all right."

" 'We marched together. When we were on watch, we took turns, one sleeping and the other on guard. Sometimes, food was scarce, but when we had it we always shared alike. We took some fierce fighting but I never felt like I went into battle alone.

" 'We fought under the white generals, but we was really on our own. Most colored didn't even have guns issued to us. We had to pick them up on the field from the Rebels that fell. Leastwise, that's how it was for us. Most of us didn't have a weapon except maybe a knife or a club. The general sent our colored unit up first to draw them out. Those Rebs were smart and nothing doing. They didn't budge.

" 'They stayed behind their fortifications of logs and mounds of earth. Our own generals didn't believe in the coloreds as soldiers then. We still had no guns, most of us. Still, he sent us across the open field to take on the Rebs. They mowed us down and we kept going, wave after wave. I got sick just looking, but your father, he got me to shelter. We lay low behind a dead mule and some dead soldiers.

" 'We was there for hours till more soldiers followed up behind. We advanced and could see that some had made it over the top, even climbing over the bodies of our own men to do it. Those that made it might take out some Rebs but they too was sure to die. Only good thing was that after that battle, no one could say that the coloreds couldn't be good soldiers too.

" 'I stayed right with your father and was next to him when he took a bullet. He was hit in the chest. I pulled him down in a ravine with me. He was breathing hard and I gave him water and told him not to die on me. He nodded and I leaned close to listen to him as his voice had become weak. "Master Lester's plantation, Mississippi, go there and tell my wife, Sylvie, and daughter, Charity, that I died in the fight for freedom."

" 'We fought all through the day and when darkness came we broke through and over the top. We didn't kill too many Rebs 'cause we had few weapons, but we put them on the run. I heard one of the generals say that he never saw no unit, white or colored, fight as fierce as we did.

" 'When the war was over, I walked from Delaware down to Mississippi. Seemed like it took forever. Of course, I had to stop and work the fields sometimes to get some food for the body. But I made a promise and I kept it!' "

Grandma Sylvie said, "Don't you ever forget that your great-grandfather died for us to be free."

"That's right," Grandma Charity said. "We

learned how much freedom cost. With the news finally coming, it hurt too much to stay. We packed what we owned in a bedroll and set a pot and frying pan beside it, all set for the next morning. It didn't sound like much but after the war you would see colored folks traveling the countryside just like that. There was hurt inside, but we were ready to test our freedom."

Grandma Sylvie laughed. "I guess you could say we failed the first test."

The story always lifted my spirits and gave strength to my arms. Without noticing, Grandma Charity and I would have combed a big pile of cotton while Grandma Sylvie was busy turning it into ball thread. She would pull it through her fingers while the drop spindle, a big top, was spinning on the floor.

"That's so," Grandma Charity said. "It was just a shack that we lived in, but it had been home for all our lives. We was slow to leave. Had to see it one more time for the mind's eye to set the final picture. It was already mid-morning when we went with our bedrolls to find the overseer and tell him we were leaving.

"He took in our gear but only said, 'You is late. You supposed to be at the big house at dawn.'

"We laughed and said, 'No bother, we are heading north.' When the overseer grinned at us, I had the feeling that we were in trouble.

" 'Well, now,' he said. 'Why don't we just go settle the books before you leave us.' "

Charity continued. "The store used to be

a bunkhouse, but when slavery was over, there were fewer hands and no need. The store was stocked with flour, beans, dried meat—most of what a body needs but not much more. It was owned by Master Lester, but a white man named Jake Henson ran the store and kept the books. In midmorning, except for us, it was empty.

"Whenever we bought something, it would go against our pay. Since we couldn't read or do numbers, he might also been cheating us."

"Might have, daughter! Ain't no *might* about it and you know it."

Charity laughed. "Well, anyway, we went in to look at those books. We each of us had a page. It wasn't good. Mr. Henson said that we was still in debt to Master Lester."

"Or so he says." Grandma Sylvie grinned. "I asked him how much and he started scribbling with his pencil.

" 'Sylvie, you are behind eighty-seven dollars, and, Charity, you owe Master Lester one hundred and five.' "

"Of course," said Charity, "we had less than five dollars in our pockets. Henson knew without us saying it.

"He grinned. 'You can leave Master Lester's plantation when you have paid off your debt.' "

"What did you do, Grandma?" I asked.

"What else? Master Lester had dogs and guns. We walked back, unrolled our blankets, and went back to work like before."

"Except," said Sylvie, "that we was docked a half-day's pay."

Charity smiled. "That's exactly right. Seems like they had us coming and going."

I heard the story so many times, I knew it by heart. But I would ask, "What did you do then?"

"Child, we worked harder and bought less food. We caught catfish in the river, grew our own potatoes and tubers. That helped. But mostly what saved us was Tom. He was a field hand, but he knew his numbers and soon he started helping us each month to pay off our bill, adding some of his own wages against our debt. Mr. Henson, he didn't like it and he would check the books with us each month."

"I guess you could say that Tom had taken quite a liking to Charity."

Charity laughed. "I guess you could say that. I was still in my teens when he first arrived. It was two years before we got married. George, your Grandpa Tom was a good man. He worked hard. All of us working together, we paid off our debt. That be 1875. That's when our freedom became real, ten years after the war ended."

"And we earned every penny of it!" said Sylvie. "I still remember when we gave Mr. Henson our last payment. We watched him write 'zero balance.' "

Charity said, "When we tore up that page into little pieces, he had a scowl on his face. It was a sight to see. We was dancing and laughing in his store. He was mad as all get-out.

" 'I suppose you be leaving, even after all Mr. Lester done for you.'

" 'I suppose so,' we said, trying not to laugh.

" 'All he done,' I said, 'was give us a ham each Christmas and a paycheck each month that was too short. We leaving and we are gonna better ourselves.'

" 'You'll see,' Henson said. 'You won't find it so easy as you think.'

"I have to admit, Henson was right. Leaving was the easy part. It was a good thing we didn't know how hard life was ahead of us."

Grandma Sylvie said, "Finally we were free. But we didn't have a plan. We just figured that anywhere had to be better for us than Mississippi had been. By then, ten years after the war, word had filtered down that life up north was not so much better, just far away and cold. Your father, Harrison, he was just three years old then. So, with some flour, bacon, and potatoes in our bedrolls, we started walking west toward Texas. We had heard talk of work at the lumber mills.

"We didn't know it then, but we walked over one hundred miles, probably more than two hundred. We set down outside of Marshall because they was taking on workers at the new lumber mill. Your grandfather got work pulling logs through the saws. It was hard and dangerous and didn't pay much. But our journey was over."

"Just the journey, not our troubles." Sylvie laughed. "As freed slaves we were given forty acres and a mule. It was a start."

"Yeah, the work was hard and the pay was

little. We saved as best we could with the dream of improving ourselves. When your grandfather died, almost twenty years later, we still didn't have much. But I took our savings and bought another forty acres; cost fifty cents an acre and we could pay it over time. Harrison, your father, was married by then and he and his new wife stayed with us."

CHAPTER 3

The story of the Dawsons: that's my story. Even without both grandmas here today, I know the Dawson story by heart. I'll tell you the rest of it.

There was no money for wood, but my father, he hauled slab ends from the scrap pile at the mill. Since we owned a mule, it didn't cost nothing. The cabin had three small rooms with an outhouse in back. There was a kitchen, a room for sleeping, and a room in back to store cotton and weave cloth. I was born there in 1898, the first of five children.

We owned almost nothing. But we had each other and nobody told us we were poor. I never felt lonely. Ever since I remember, even on the cold mornings when the fire had burned down, I would wake up under a blanket, always with some brothers and sisters next to me. We were warm and cozy.

I was the oldest, but I liked to be up first anyway. In the winter, the dirt floor felt cold, but I would shuffle over to the stove. Mama would give me a hug. When I had warmed myself, she would nudge my shoulder and say, "Are you just gonna watch that fire all day or we gonna get some breakfast going?"

She was right. When the cabin was still dark, I did love to just look into the fire. It warmed me inside and out. But I laughed when she would hand me the bucket. The well was out back.

To me, the best time of year was winter, for it would still be dark then. If it was clear, the stars were out or sometimes the moon was up. Papa would be out by the barn or maybe already out in the fields. The well wasn't so far, but I would stand by the house till my eyes could see in the dark. Since early morning was prime hunting time for the coyotes, I would look toward the chicken house. I also stayed away from the woodpiles, for on cold nights, the rattlers slept in them.

I knew enough to watch out for snakes. Grandma told me a story of how a field hand got bit once. She would spread her hands out big to show me how his leg swelled up just overnight. She says that they had to cut the leg off and then he still died. I could tell that she didn't like snakes.

I told my grandma that I would stay away from them. They don't scare me, though. Fact is, I found that when I saw one and hadn't surprised it none, I could just stay and watch it. I liked to do that, study those old snakes. As long as I minded my own business, they never bothered me. I never told that to Grandma, though.

Most folks, if they saw a rattler, and had a gun, they would try and shoot it. People always say that it tastes like chicken. But I swear, some folks will say anything tastes like chicken. No one ever says that a chicken tastes like a rattlesnake, though. Go figure that one.

On the dark mornings, I couldn't see the bottom of the well. Setting the kitchen bucket down, I would drop the bucket with the rope. The splash was always the loudest if it was dark. I don't know why. But that was so.

The well was dug even before they built the cabin. They all worked on the well. Papa would be down digging. Then Mama or one of my grandmas would haul up the dirt a bucket at a time. They took turns. And when Papa wore out, Mama would go down and take his place.

Of course, getting down was easy, but when the well got deeper, hauling someone back up was hard work. It was twenty-five feet deep. We had some rough summers but it only went dry a couple of times as I remember. Then we had to haul water from the creekbed.

When I was little, the bucket kinda pulled me over to the side and would bump against my leg. I would have to stop on the way to the house and rest. But I always did it by myself. There would be no one to help me anyway. Mama always smiled when she took the bucket from me and would say, "Now you go back out and help your father with the chores. Breakfast won't be ready till first light."

I would always be hungry by then, but I knew that Papa needed my help. By the age of four, I collected the eggs and knew how to look for signs of raccoons and coyotes. (Nowadays, people say those animals are cute, but we figured they was critters that was fighting against us for our food.) As hard as I worked, it seemed that I was always hungry. Sometimes, probably about once a week or so, when food got low, my folks would send me over to the Coals' farm. Always with a pail in my hand I would walk across the fields to get some milk. Grandma never forgot to say, "Keep a watch out for snakes when you going through the field."

Mama Coal first thing would give me something to eat. I never had to ask, but I would never say no. Might be an apple, or might even be a biscuit and a piece of salt pork. Often as not, there would be a glass of milk to wash it down. My folks taught me to be respectful of people. Even when my mother wasn't there, I always said, "Thank you, Mama Coal." We always called them Mama and Papa Coal. I never did even know their first names.

There were three Coal children. Johnny was about my age, Aden was older than me, and Jimmy was younger. So, things were such that I could play with any of them. They were white. But since we were little it didn't matter and I never gave it much thought.

Their barn was much bigger than ours. It had a big loft up above. There was a rope that swung out from the peak of the roof. The barn was open at that spot. Felt like, from up there, a person could see forever. It was actually three stories high 'cause the other end of the barn started on a hillside and this side was at the bottom of the slope. Sometimes when a hawk would fly by it seemed we was just eye to eye.

If there was a breeze and clouds was floating by it felt like the earth was spinning. It could make a body sick if you looked straight down. Aden, who was nine and had been going to school, said it felt like that because the earth was a round ball and it was spinning. Aden was the only one going to school yet, and Johnny would get tired of Aden's showing off. He would say, "If we are on a round ball, how come the folks on the bottom side just don't fall off?"

That would make Aden all mad and red in the face. "I don't know how they hold on like they do, but Mr. Spencer said that China is on the other side and that's what they do there. You should just be thankful that you live on this side, on the top."

And we were, for it was clear to tell that those folks had to work so hard just to hold on. Aden even said it was all in a book and it was so. His teacher had it at school. Well, if it was in a book, even Johnny couldn't argue no more. Even back then, I knew that someday I wanted to go to school so I could learn to read such things for myself.

Down below there was a mountain of hay. The rope had always been there waiting for us, but we never talked about it. Aden, being the oldest, was the first to answer the challenge. One day, when we were sitting in the loft, Aden just got up and said, "I'm going now."

The rope was looped around a cleat that was inside the barn. No one said a word as he wound it off the cleat. I don't know why, but at that point we all stood up. When the rope was free and in his hands he turned and looked toward us. We just said nothing and stared back. Even Jimmy sensed something was up. He got a worried look on his face and took my hand.

Just like he was stepping off the porch, Aden stepped out from the loft like it was no big deal. The three of us walked over to the edge for a better look. I thought he would look like an angel floating in the sky. But it wasn't so pretty. Aden swung out like a turkey vulture that goes in big, looping circles. When the circles got smaller he let go. There was a whoop and then he was buried in the hay. After that, Aden seemed different. The rest of us wanted to try it so bad, but we couldn't even talk of it.

Next day, at the kitchen table, I told Mama and Papa what he did. "I wish I could do that," I said.

Mama, she said, "No, you don't even need to wish it! We ain't raising you to be no fool. We need you here on this farm all in one piece." Nudging my father, she said, "You talk some sense into him."

Papa laughed. "Your mother's right. It don't make no sense to do such a thing." Mama nodded. But then Papa went on. "Of course, sometimes there's moments in life when a body is just bound to do what it's got to do. Sounds to me that's what happened to Aden."

Mama said, "Well, thank you much, as if that's gonna be any help to raising the boy."

Papa grinned. "I don't know about that, but no sense worrying about what may never be. But I don't expect there isn't any boy that ain't never, at least, thought of swinging from the barn."

I saw Mama frowning. She and Papa almost always got along well and I thought it best to leave that talk, but I just had to know something. "Well, if I can't do the swing now, how will I know when the right time has come?"

Papa nodded toward me. "If it happens that way, something will tell you. And if you're listening, you'll hear it."

So, mostly, except when Aden had to show off, we played cowboys and Indians if we were playing in the barn. Aden and Johnny, 'cause they was the oldest, always got to be the white settlers. Jimmy and I were the Indians, and that meant we could attack them. We all had sticks that were supposed to be the guns. Since I was an Indian and had to lose anyway, I liked most to be shot when I was up in the loft. That way I could tumble off into the hay down below. I never really saw the point to it, though, 'cause most times somebody was bound to insist they wasn't shot even when it was clear as day that they was. Of course, that would be the end of the game then.

Wherever we went on that farm, their dog, Roof, would follow us around. I liked him so much, I figured that we ought to have a dog too. In fact, I once mentioned that to Mama.

She said, "Can a dog pull the plow?"

"Of course not," I said.

"Well," she said, "can a dog lay eggs like a chicken?"

I said, "Not that I have ever heard of."

"Tell me, can you milk a dog like a cow or a goat?"

"No," I said. "It doesn't work that way."

"Can a dog be like a pig and become bacon or ham?"

I got smarter and didn't answer. Instead, I asked her, "Can a chicken bark like a dog?"

"No, honey, it don't." She laughed. She gave me a hug and said, "But unless you find us a dog that can pull the plow, or lay some eggs, or turn itself into bacon, we don't need it."

When we walked over to the creek, Roof would follow us across the fields. I think he liked the fields 'cause if he saw a fresh cow pie, he was in heaven. I can still remember that old dog rolling in a fresh cow pie. His black and shaggy fur was matted with manure. He stunk something awful, but he was so pleased with himself that it was hard to fault him.

The Coals' creek was a good one. We could find crawfish under the rocks. For fishing, we made our own poles out of willow branches. Almost anything made good bait. In my mind, chicken livers was the best. I don't believe there was a catfish in that creek that could resist. But we could lift up a log and take some grub worms and do quite fine too.

It was nice on a hot summer day because the catfish liked to collect in the cooler waters that was under the shade of the big willows. Seems that we always caught something for dinner and some of them catfish were pretty decent size too. But I remember one day in particular.

Jimmy hooked one good. His pole bent way over. He was tugging and getting nowhere. It was early spring, and there had been good rains so the water was unusually deep. I figured it could be a big one. But when Jimmy called, "Help, he's pulling me in!" I had to laugh.

But sure enough, it looked like Jimmy was being dragged toward the bank. At that moment, I felt a tug on my own line, and so I just watched as Johnny came running over. Johnny grabbed on just above Jimmy's hands. Soon they were both being pulled toward the creek.

There was a back eddy from where the water came around the big tree roots and such hanging down. It made for a nice pool of deeper and still water. When I saw that water ripple with a huge tail, I just left my pole with the fish still on it. I was eight, and though I was strong by then, I was getting nowhere. Aden came running up and saw that. He jumped in to push the fish from behind. That seemed to help and so I jumped in too.

He was too slippery to hold on to, but with both of us, we could push him against the bank as we stood on some tree roots to keep our footing. And that's where it stayed. That old fish couldn't get away, but we couldn't move him out. Aden called out to Johnny to get their dad.

When Johnny and their daddy came on the mule, Jimmy was still on the bank pulling and Aden and me were still in the water pushing. Their daddy was laughing and said, "I'm sorry, Johnny. I have to admit, I just couldn't believe it. I brought this rope more to be funny, but it's a good thing."

He chopped off a strong piece of root with a curve to it. Then he hopped down in the water with us. He slid the root through the fish's gills and then tied the rope tight. He started barking orders.

"Aden, you hop out. Help Jimmy tie up to the mule. Johnny, you and George get back and hold the tail still. I'm going to guide the rope from here."

When we got all set, their daddy said, "Okay, now, boys, walk the mule back till the rope gets tight."

Aden and me, we could feel that take the pressure off our arms. "Good, now keep it tight and guide the mule downstream to the low point in the bank."

I could see what he was doing. There was a path their cows had carved into the bank and it made the sides fall off to nothing. At that spot, the water was too shallow for that old fish to swim anymore. It fought some on the way in, but once it was in the shallows and mostly out of water, it just gave up.

Besides being the biggest, it must have been the ugliest fish that I'd ever seen. Its head was huge and the whiskers was bigger than a cat's. It was an old fish with ugly spots. After we pulled it up on shore, their daddy took the mule to fetch the wagon.

The four of us stayed and just looked at it. "I dare someone to touch an eyeball," Aden said.

It gave me the shivers when I got close. We went and touched the skin on top of the head and touched the tail, but even so nobody touched an eyeball. I'm glad he didn't call a double dare. I don't know what I would of done.

We tried but couldn't lift it into the wagon. So, we had to gut it first. What you saw in there would almost make you stop eating for the rest of your life. The fish was so big that there was little fishes inside that he had eaten whole and a frog too. There was some fish hooks in him too. So I guess we weren't the first to mess with him. But the strangest thing was, there was a whole squirrel in him. We figure he must of fallen out of a tree even though Papa Coal tried to convince us that maybe that catfish climbed out the bank and up the tree.

It was so good covered in flour and then fried in lard. Next day, I took home as much as I could carry and told everyone all about it, except my arms wouldn't stretch big enough to tell it right.

Folks that heard me tell that story claim the fish gets bigger every year. Well, I'll tell you, for the last ten or twenty years, instead of digging, I been buying my bait at a fishing store. I see the pictures on the bulletin board of the prize fish and I see the big fish mounted on the wall. We never thought to stuff the fish, we just ate them. But what we used to take out of that creek in those days would put them all to shame.

Even if I didn't have catfish to carry home, Mama Coal always put some milk in the pail for me and the little ones. I had fun at the Coal farm, but I remember many a day when we would be following behind Papa Coal's plow putting kernels of corn in the rows. If I was somewhere and they needed help, that's what I did.

That same spring that we caught the big catfish, all four of us was sitting up in the loft one afternoon. I remember clearly how the winds were blowing the clouds across the sky. Maybe it was those clouds that moved me to get up. I don't know, but, fact is, I went over to the rope and said, "I'm going."

I figured to be nervous when I was unwinding the rope from the cleat. I remember everybody watching, but, fact is, it didn't bother me. I felt the rope in my hands, I looked out, and then stepped off.

At that moment the rope swung me out into the sky, I was free. Nothing held me to earth. There was just me and the rope and the sky. I knew then why Grandma so loved her freedom.

Turned out that I never got back to the Coal farm too much more. Jimmy, the last of the Coal children, was to be starting school in the fall. I was eight years old and that's about when children started being just with their own color. Besides, I was getting too old to play anyway. That spring, I started working full-time for the McCreadys.

CHAPTER 4

I could see then that Ma was right. I never would have had time to take care of a dog. Seemed like I just had time to work and sleep.

It was a fair walk over to the McCreadys'. I would leave early enough so as to reach their farm when the sun was coming up. Even in the dark, I couldn't help but know when I was getting close: There was more hogs than a person could ever count, and the racket they made was something terrible.

But even if I was deaf, the smell would of told me I had arrived. The smell was heavy and hung low to the ground. When I started walking down the last hillside it was something else. The McCreadys never noticed it. I can't say as much, but after a little while, I did get to where the smell didn't bother me no more.

That fall, they started the first school for colored children near Marshall. More than anything, I wanted to go. I had started working for the McCready farm in the summer, though. They treated me well. They said I was a good worker and school could wait. Besides, the money, I believe $1.50 a week, was a big help then.

So, the little ones went off to school and I kept working. Sometimes, at work, I tried to think of what school must be like. But it was hard to get a picture in my head. It wasn't real to me like the hog farm. I figured I would just have to see when my turn came.

I had heard white folks say that colored didn't need school, that school would be a waste 'cause the colored couldn't learn their reading anyhow. No one in our family knew how to read. But sure enough, one night my little brother Johnny, he pulled our Bible off the shelf. It was the only book we had. I remember it was in the spring when the days was longest, for the light was coming through the window and there weren't no lantern going.

When slavery was over, colored could go to church. And since mothers and fathers couldn't be sold off and separated, they could even marry then, something they weren't allowed during slavery. According to Charity, a colored preacher that had learned his schooling up north came through and gave her that Bible. Each time someone was born or died, we had the preacher put it inside the Bible. Grandma

Charity, she called it the Dawson Bible. She could never read it but was awful proud of it.

"The Lord is my shepherd, I shall not want," Johnny read.

I looked around the table. Mama had tears in her eyes. Papa had his eyes closed but kept nodding his head as Johnny read. I was smiling. I knew those white folks was wrong and someday it would be my turn to read too.

Around that same time, Papa came home with a dog. I was out by the chicken coop when Papa pulled up and stopped the wagon. He was grinning so that I knew something was up. Pulling back an old blanket off the seat beside him, he said, "Take care of this and then help me unload this feed."

He put a puppy in my arms. It was white with black spots. I still remember, the fur was soft and smooth. It wasn't big but did have good-sized paws. Having sold some ribbon syrup in town, Papa headed toward the cabin with some store-bought cloth for Mama to make a dress with.

When they both came out, Mama asked, "Where did this...?"

"A white man gave it to me and said—"

"How we gonna feed it?" she asked him.

"The man said it's a good duck-hunting dog."

"Duck hunting." Mama laughed. "You are just as bad as this boy!"

"What's its name?" I asked.

"The man said he didn't know, we would have to guess."

We tried lots of names but could never

seem to get it. But that dog would always come to the name "Guess" so that's what we called him. He slept outside the cabin, right in front of the door. He was supposed to be Papa's hunting dog, but from the moment I stepped out, he would follow me over the farm wherever I went. That dog never left my side.

At the McCreadys', I worked hard. But except at slaughtering time, they didn't have enough money for me to be there every day. That was a good thing for it seemed there was getting to be more work to be done on our farm too.

Our soil wasn't so good, though: dusty on top with hard clay underneath that. Papa always said that our soil produced a good harvest of rocks and stones. It was tough to raise enough cotton for clothes and grow enough food for all of us and the mule.

Our neighbors, the McKenzies, had the same problem. They had eighty acres and couldn't make it either. They was white, though, and Mr. McKenzie could get a job in town; I think it was down at the stables. We needed to grow more food and cotton so Papa bought Mr. McKenzie out. Cost us fifty cents an acre and we could pay on time. Till the day he died, Papa always said, "It's a good thing there was some nice folks like the McKenzies that would lend, because a bank was never going to let colored folk have any credit." We paid directly to them.

The Blakes ran some cattle on the other side

of the McKenzies. Their cattle died in the drought in the summer of 1907. In the spring, rain had been scarce. Summer held no rain. Summers are always hot, but that year holding ponds dried up, even some wells went dry. Of course, the creek just disappeared.

I heard tell that Blake's cattle just done lay down and died. Those old buzzards circling in the sky made him go out and check. They was already down with bloated stomachs. The ones that were still alive were so bad off that Blake and his men just put a gun to them on the spot. That's right, he had to shoot his own cattle. They was just too far gone for anything else.

Cattle can make some good money, but we didn't have no money to start up raising cattle. It was a lot more work, but our cotton did all right. It got us by, at least. And that summer, we would have lost it too if we had been able to go to cattle. They couldn't help but notice that we were doing better than them.

Blake and some men rode over one night toward the end of that summer. I still remember, as it was uncommon for white folks to ride out to the colored farms. It did happen, but often as not it meant trouble. The dust they stirred floated up and hung in front of the sun that was dipping behind the hills. It made me stop. For years to come, I never saw a sunset with colors as pretty. It was just like the sunsets in Dallas now. On a hot day, the gray smoke from the cars makes for sunsets with the strongest colors. We never had many visitors on horseback that came so late in the day, and I had never seen anything like it.

But more than anything, I knew enough to be worried. I could tell as much by looking at Papa's face. I had been walking the mule out to the barn and slowed my walk so as to be close enough to see and hear but not look to be nosy. Besides, when I watched his shoulders tense, I figured Papa might need me close if there was to be trouble.

I saw Papa glance toward the cabin where Mama and the little ones were. They was looking out the window but disappeared when they got his look. Even from a distance, I could see his mind working. The white men and the horses were getting closer. The shotgun was in the cabin leaning up the wall alongside the door. If there was going to be trouble, Papa might of stood a chance with the shotgun, but he didn't want to bring the little ones closer to it neither.

I watched as he looked back and then walked toward the men to put more distance from the cabin. Of course, even I knew that if trouble was coming, we was still too close. I had seen Papa glance in my direction and I even seen him nod his head slightly toward me—his way of saying to get away. I started working on the mule some more and pretended I didn't see that.

There were three men. Two of them had rifles alongside their saddles. Each of the men carried a pistol by his side too. Their guns were holstered. In those days, guns were common, especially for white men. But I sensed that Papa was counting their guns, just as I was.

Even so, as the men approached, he kept walking toward them. If he was worried, he didn't show it. To me, Papa was a big man, but as the horses pulled up sharply in front of him, for a moment, Papa was lost in the dust that they kicked up. If Papa had been white, to keep the dust down they would have slowed their approach from a trot to a walk, just to be respectful-like. With a colored man, it probably never even crossed their minds.

While Papa was almost hidden in their dust cloud, I could clearly make out the men that was up on horseback. I recognized Mr. Blake up front and it was clear to see that he was in charge. The other two men were hired hands.

At that point, everyone had all but forgotten about me. I could see that and instead of heading toward the barn, I angled over toward the cabin. I tied the mule up and went inside.

Mr. Blake nodded and said, "Evening, Harrison. I came to talk with you."

"Yes, sir, Mr. Blake, that be fine," Papa responded in the tone that the colored talked to a white man. It was a way of talking that stated who was boss, who was in charge. The white folk expected that. It wasn't unfriendly, but wasn't warm like the talk between two coloreds. I don't think they even knew that we had two ways of talking.

He dismounted and handed his reins to

one of his men. "Good. Well, I hear that your farm is bigger now. People say that you been working to improve yourself."

I held my breath. Coming from a colored man, those words were nothing but good. But such words from a white man... Hard to say, but could be a bad thing. If he was meaning to say that my father was stepping out of his place or such, then we was in big trouble. My uncle Henry always said, "A white man enjoys his success, a colored man has to pay for it."

I looked at Mama, who was with me at the window. I squeezed the shotgun till my knuckles hurt. In the cabin, I was suddenly the man there, the one to protect the family, if things went wrong.

Lately, things hadn't been too good in the county for the colored. After dark set in, the Klan was out riding. I had heard my papa and Uncle Henry saying that right in Marshall, they set burning crosses in front yards. Out on the farms they did that too and they torched some barns. It was an awful thing to see them riding through in white robes with torches burning, guns shooting up the sky. If it was someone they felt had stepped out of his place, they shot out the windows. Matter of fact, that summer, a little girl was hit by a bullet when she was sleeping. She lost her arm. I hadn't forgotten how they had lynched Pete.

Papa looked closely at Mr. Blake to try to get the meaning in his words. I could see that Papa was measuring his words closely, before he talked.

"Well, sir, I have been working hard. Our crop wasn't great, but we did all right. We are thankful for that."

Mr. Blake said, "Well, I went to cattle and you know what happened to me."

Papa nodded. "I'm most sorry about that."

Some of the tension had left, but I was still wondering. Mr. Blake said, "Well, I guess that's what was supposed to happen. Harrison, is there a place we can sit down and talk?"

Still not sure where things were going, my father motioned toward the barn, which was a bit farther from the cabin. We couldn't hear them any longer, but we watched as they sat down on some hay bales in front of the barn. The hired men had stayed back with the horses.

We was far enough away that Mama and I didn't have to shush the little ones. I had relaxed my grip on the shotgun. It was Mama's expression that I most recall. She wore a look of utter amazement. I followed her gaze.

I couldn't hear a word, but Papa was talking and gesticulating with his arms. He swung his right arm wide and Mr. Blake was laughing. They was just talking like two people, not like a colored and a white talking. Matter of fact, they was both laughing and talking up a storm. I leaned the shotgun back in its usual place against the wall and came back to the window.

Mama looked like she had just seen snow in July. I had never seen anything like it either. Mr. Blake handed some papers to Papa and pointed at some parts with his finger. They talked a little more and then shook hands. Mr. Blake walked back to the horses, and Papa toward the cabin.

He couldn't hide a grin. Soon as he opened the door, Mama said, "What did he want? What did that man say?"

Papa shook his head. "You ain't gonna believe it."

"Enough already. Just try me. Now, don't you drag this out, Harrison."

Papa smiled. "Okay. See these papers here? They say we can buy eighty acres that Mr. Blake has next to the McKenzie property we bought."

"How we going to pay for it?"

"He told me it says fifty cents an acre, same as the McKenzie property. We can buy it on time and fill out the terms that will work for us. We just got to be quiet so his own people don't hear that he treated us so fair. That wouldn't sit too well for him with his own people. I figure the preacher could read this for us and help to fill out the numbers too."

"Why is he doing this?" I asked.

"He had a bad time on that eighty acres. Besides, he's got plenty of land where his home sits and he don't need the aggravation. But I believe that's only part of it."

"Well, I'll be; him being the son of a slave owner and all," Mama said.

Papa shrugged. "I don't know. Maybe that is the reason why. I guess there is good and bad white folks, just like there is with colored."

After the preacher helped with reading the

papers, he showed Papa where to put his *X*. Our little farm had gotten bigger. If we had ever been lacking for work to do, there would never be a shortage again.

Matter of fact, if you asked me if it was a good thing having a bigger farm, I wouldn't have known which way to answer. There was never enough daylight to match up with all the work we had in front of us. Besides cotton, the new land went to potatoes and root crops for us and some more corn to feed livestock and ourselves. With enough feed, we figured to get some milking cows when we saved enough from selling more ribbon syrup.

Taking that extra ribbon syrup to sell in town was a good idea, but it meant crushing more cane. At times, it seemed that all I did was cut cane. Generally, I would do the morning chores early so as to be out in the field at first light. Within minutes of swinging that old machete, the morning chill would leave my body. It felt good, though. I would keep my eyes out for snakes. The snakes liked to curl up in the cane and didn't take kindly to being disturbed, so I wore boots.

The shoe man made them with brass toes. As soon as the leather wore off the front, you would see the shiny brass toes. We called them brassies. People would bring them back to him when they got too small. He would put on new heels and new brass. So we would buy an old pair with the closest fit. He sold them to us for two bits.

But cutting cane only got us partway to

48

ribbon syrup. Crushing the cane was the next step. I would hook up the mule to a long bar that was attached to the crushing machine. We worked together. All day long, the mule would walk in a circle to move the gears. I would feed the cane into the machine. I had to keep pace with the mule. As we worked, cane juice would run down a trough into a barrel. We called it ribbon syrup. It was good.

It was just the thing on a little mush or with some hominy and grits. Since money was scarce, ribbon syrup also made for good trading stock. At the general store we could trade a barrel for just about anything; nails, shotgun shells, and, if times was good, store-bought cloth and such things. We could even trade for flour if we had a mind to, but we generally took our corn to the mill to be ground. The mill kept half the flour, and the other part was our share. I guess they could sell flour to folks that didn't have a good crop.

So, we was never wanting for anything. We always had hot days and warm nights. When we had some decent rain, life couldn't of been any better. I don't think I ever saw Papa worry. But I would see him watching the clouds, particularly when we was planting corn. Papa would be guiding the plow and I would be right along putting in corn kernels. Sometimes, there wasn't a cloud in sight. The earth would be so dry, the mule would be kicking up dust. Looking up at the sky, Papa would say, "We could use some rain and if you was to send it our way, we would be most thankful."

Seems like, often as not, God was listening, for most times the rains would come when we needed them. Cornbread was always on the table. But I think it was parched corn that I liked the most. Just put those ears in hot water and scrape the kernels right off the cob. It was nice to eat fresh corn and just pick it as we needed it. But we always harvested a good amount for the mule and the pigs and some to set aside for seeds for next year.

We put more land into cotton. Cotton wasn't afraid of poor soil, but we found that we could only keep up with so much cotton. My grandmas still cleaned, spun, and wove it. With more farm work, I couldn't help them so much. I was always there to help when it was time to dye the cotton, though.

There was a big old tub that we would fill with water and then add some bark from the oak trees. I would help them fill it with water. Then we would go out barking. I would keep adding bark till Grandma Charity nodded to stop. We let it soak for two or three days. Grandma always knew how much bark to use and how long to soak the cotton. There was no recipe, but she taught me and I can still do it today. The white cloth came out as a nice reddish-brown color.

I would say by the second spring since the farm got bigger, we traded some ribbon syrup for a couple of milk cows. It meant growing more corn for their feed. But there was nothing like fresh sweet milk, the milk you get before it separates to milk and cream. I don't see it in the stores that way today. Milking the cows became one of my morning chores before I could get to work out in the fields.

I always liked to get out early because of the heat, particularly with cotton picking. Wasn't never that hard to start with, but when that sack starts getting full, it is heavy. I would start off carrying the sack and pretty soon it was a burden just to drag it with me. Don't know why, but it always seemed hottest at cotton-picking time.

With some of that new land in cotton, we had some extra to take to the mill. In a year or two, we had enough cotton to trade in for some cattle. We left some land open in grass for them, and hoped to have enough beef for the family and some to sell. Papa said that it was a good idea, except it didn't work out that way. Just when things was going good, we was visited by another drought. We watched as the pond and then the stream dried up.

I could see that Papa wasn't too worried. Even I had seen that before. But one day when we was out in the fields, he said, "Look here, George."

He pulled up a clump of grass. All the grass had gone brown, long ago, but he was looking at the roots. "Feel how dry those roots is."

I touched them and could feel the soil fall off. "Grass is already brown, but these roots are too dry to hold water. Pretty soon, any rain that comes is going to be too late."

The summer passed with no more rain. Like everyone else, we slaughtered the cattle early. Uncle Henry, who was over helping, said, "You always got to take something over nothing and be grateful to the Lord for that." Papa nodded, but for the first time that I had ever seen, it looked to me like he had lost heart.

That fall, the harvest was thin too. We got our crops in, but I noticed they would have done better with more rain. When Papa and I were digging out the last of the potatoes, he said, "Put your fork down and rest a spell."

I did, but it was uncommon for him to say such a thing and as we sat with our backs against a mound of potatoes, I waited. We looked out at the rest of the potato field and Papa said, "Even the potato crop is low this year."

"That be the rain?" I asked.

"Yeah. Seems like it hurt everything. Some years, one crop is down and another is up. This year everything is down."

I nodded in agreement. "I expect I can work harder," I said.

"No, that ain't it, son. You're a good worker, but I guess we need to talk, you and I."

I always wanted for Papa to talk to me like a man, but right then it wasn't feeling so good. "Like I said," he continued, "crops is down, but prices is too."

"Why is that?" I asked.

"I don't know. Usually with a poor crop, we at least get the higher prices. Only thing that staying the same right now seems to be the mortgage payment." He laughed. "We gonna need your help."

"Papa, you know that's no problem," I said.

"I know, George, and here it is. I was talking with Mr. Little down at the flour mill a couple weeks ago. He's heard that you are strong and can do a man's work."

I felt awfully good when Papa said, "He's right about that and I told him so. He said that if I was ever disposed to your doing some work at his place, he could always use you there."

"That would be fine, Papa, I've already worked for the Barkers and the McCreadys."

"Yeah, I know, but this is different. The Littles' place is too far for you to walk back and forth each day. You gonna have to stay there and board. He would send me a payment each month, and one less mouth to feed right now would help the family too. I expect it would just be a short while until things turn around for us here."

"I'm twelve years old now," I said with pride. "I can do that. I can work hard and help the family."

Papa looked at me. He swallowed hard but didn't say nothing.

CHAPTER 5

Marshall was where I grew up, but since I left, there hasn't been much reason for me to visit. Fact is, friends I grew up with done passed away. The homestead is still there, but I am the only one still alive that has memories of living there.

I've never been that keen on visiting, but lately I been talking a lot about my days in Marshall with this man that be coming to see me now. His name is Richard. He has lots of questions, thinks he wants to write a book. He comes with a tape recorder and we just sit and talk all day.

He's different than other people that I know. I don't mean because he's white or because he's younger than me. Most folks that I know don't read so much and don't have great book learning. This man Richard is different that way. He's read a lot of books and knows about things I never heard of. At the same time, for all his reading, he didn't even know what chitlins is. I had to tell him. He didn't even know how to slaughter a hog. I had to tell him how to do that too. So, at the same time, I know about some things he is ignorant of.

Lately, there be lots of folks coming to ask me questions. It's always the same questions. They want to know what I eat, what I do to stay healthy. I've done what I want and never gave it much thought. But now so many folks keep asking me why, at 101 years old, I walk just fine without a cane, I eat what I please, I have all my teeth, and my memory is fine. I even got a letter from a little boy that said he was glad that my brain still works. Well, I'm glad too, but folks have asked me about it so often that now I wonder too.

Richard, this writer, reads a lot of books. So one night I asked him some questions. I've never spent much time philosophizing and such, but I do wonder, "Why am I still here and so healthy too? And why is it that after all these years everybody wants to listen to what I have to say now?"

Richard couldn't answer. I laughed and gave him a bad time and said, "Well, when you ask *me* questions, I've always got some answers for *you*."

So, I said, "Just think on it some, and if you see the answer or find it in a book, let me know."

I think reading those books does help him when we are watching *Jeopardy!* though. He doesn't try to help me too much like most folks do when they find that I am over a hundred years. One night he cooks dinner, the next night I cook dinner. Afterward, we do some dominoes and the loser does the dishes. Some nights we watch *Jeopardy!* and some nights we just talk. Matter of fact, that is how he got me back to Marshall. One night, a question on *Jeopardy!* was "What newspaper has the logo 'All the news that's fit to print'?"

Richard answered, "What is *The New York*

Times?" I admit, he beat me on that one. But that wasn't all. He got so worked up, he knocked his cornbread off his plate.

I told him, "Take it easy. I don't have no dog to clean up the carpet."

"How about the Marshall newspaper?" he asked.

"What about it?"

"Did Marshall have a newspaper when you were growing up?"

"Sure, Marshall had its own paper. When I was growing up, it came out once a week."

"We should go over and read some of the old newspapers and see what the town was like then."

I figure, I grew up there, I already knew what Marshall was like. I didn't need to see it, but the next day I was in a van with Richard, my son George Jr., and his wife, Sallie. It was early morning and we were going to make a day of it. We had hardly left the house before I saw the weather ahead of us. "Might as well turn back," I said.

"Why?" Richard asked.

"See that cloud ahead? That's a thunderhead. Bad weather be coming in real quick."

Sallie said, "That's only one cloud. The forecast is for a ten percent chance of showers. I just heard the weatherman."

"I've seen weather for one hundred years. I know what I see."

But people today go with what they see on TV when all they need to do to check the weather is open the window and put their head out. We got on the freeway. In five minutes some drops hit the window. "Just gonna be a shower. It will pass," Junior said.

Richard kept driving. Five minutes later we had the headlights on to see a little better and traffic was almost stopped, the rain was so heavy. And five minutes after that we had to get off the freeway. We went to a restaurant and waited for over an hour before we headed home. We hadn't gone far, but we had to make some detours on the way home because the roads were so flooded.

Still, all those years and I had never read a Marshall paper. The idea stayed in my mind. The next day things had dried out. We left, just Richard and I this time. Straight off, I could see that things had changed. I walked right in through the front door of the paper and somebody called me "sir." That's not the Marshall that I knew. It wasn't just talk either. The people wanted to be helpful. Before long, they had us set up with a mountain of old newspapers starting at 1908.

Richard, he kept getting stuck in the ad section. "Look at this," he'd say. " 'Three-year-old Ford, runs good, needs new crank, $150.00 OBO.' And '3-bedroom house, with elec., $975.00/terms.' "

Did all my growing up in Marshall but was always on the outside. I couldn't read in those days and never even looked at a newspaper. I would listen when people would tell me the news. In those days, it seems like everything had two stories, the white story and the colored story.

I started to notice that this paper was not about the Marshall that I knew. All the pictures, at the fire hall, the school yard, the grange, and the rodeo, only had white people in them. It made me wonder and I started working back to see what I could find.

I had worked so hard to learn how to read and I was seeing lies, all lies. It brought tears to my eyes.

"What is it?" Richard asked.

I couldn't speak and just handed him the paper.

PARKER WARNS MEMBERS KLAN NOT TO THREATEN THE STATE'S WITNESSES

With troops on duty in Morehouse parish in connection with the state's investigation into the activities of hooded and masked men...it was learned on good authority that if any of the state's witnesses were threatened in any way...martial law may be declared immediately.... Counties in southern New York are being searched for Harold Teegerstron, desired as a witness [in the investigation of hooded bands].

REWARD IN WACO KILLING GROWS; K.K.K. ADD $250

Waco, Jan. 24—...the reward offered for arrest and conviction of persons involved in the double murder (Holt and Denecamp)

and in the Skipworth and the Holton murder mysteries was constantly growing tonight. In addition to several citizens who contributed to the fund the local KKK sent Mayor Richards a note today offering to pay $250 into their reward fund.... They [J. T. Williams and his son, Gilbert] were testifying at the habeas corpus hearing of Ivory Clay, a negro, charged by complaint with the murder.

—*The Marshall Morning News*, January 25, 1923

I had never really talked to any other white folks about such things as the Klan and so I watched to gauge Richard's reaction. An odd look came across his face as he read. He stopped and looked at me. I looked back and said nothing. He went back to reading. When Richard was done, he said, "The Klan was big?"

"We didn't see them every day, but we could always feel them about. We always knew they was there. They could do whatever they wanted and nothing was going to happen. They could do the worst things and no one was going to be punished. If they didn't want a witness to talk then that was that."

"Then why pay for a reward?"

"I remember that case. There was some thought they could prove the murderer was a black man, though a lot of folks thought that he was framed. So then they come up with reward money, but if it was a black man that was killed you could forget it."

"Like when they lynched Pete?"

"Yeah, I don't even find that in the newspaper. They didn't talk about those things. I guess I am the only man alive that knows the truth about Pete Spillman."

We looked at each other. Then I said, "I guess this answers my question."

"What question do you mean?"

Sometimes, with all his schooling, I would like to know what he does with it. "The question that I been wondering on and you was supposed to answer for me."

"Oh, yeah," he says. "That question."

I said, "Why am I still here? I can see that I'm going to have to answer the question myself."

He nodded at me to go on.

I said, "I am a witness to the truth. That's why I am still here. I can't let the truth die with me. That's why you're here: to help me get the true story down, before it's my time."

There was nothing else to say and we sat till the newspaper lady asked if we had found what we needed. "We're getting closer."

"You all come back, then."

"Thank you. We might just do that."

Marshall has changed some, but the truth is still hidden. Now I can see that maybe just telling my story of how things really was might help folks today. It could maybe change some misunderstandings and help folks to get to know each other better. Mostly I have good memories, but even if I wanted to I can't make the truth good or bad. It's just what it is.

When I was twelve, there was no misunderstanding back then as to how things was.
Things was real clear. I remember Mama as
she handed me a sack with cornbread and
lard. When she gave me a hug, she said,
"Lord, I told myself I wasn't going to cry, but
there is only so much that a mother can do."
I hugged the little ones and then Papa cleared
his throat. "Mr. Little be expecting us by
afternoon, and with him giving you a job and
even a place to live, it wouldn't look proper
to be late."

I climbed up next to him on the wagon and
worked hard not to cry myself. The baby was
already asleep in Mama's arms but Johnny and
Odessa stood with Mama and watched till
we were out of sight. I didn't know when I
would be back, but as we went over the rise
and headed down, I was already missing them
and the farm.

Most days, heading off with just my father
was something special since it didn't happen
too often. But today was different. While we
was in the wagon, I worked hard not to let Papa
think that I felt anything but good about
leaving. It wasn't till years later that I realized
that for my sake, Papa was keeping up a good
front too.

He actually talked more than usual just to
keep things going for us. "Should be about a
month or so that your uncle Henry and aunt

Mary going to have another baby. Your mother is going to go over to help with the delivery and stay for a bit to help out. I guess that be number eight for my brother. How about that. Looks like my little brother gonna have more children than I will."

I know Papa was only trying to pass the time, but he was making me think of what I would miss while I was gone. "I wonder if it will be a boy or a girl," I said. "If it's a girl, then they would be even with four boys and four girls."

"That's so," my father said. "But with another boy they could get further along with the farm work, and Henry's farm does need more help."

I nodded. Nowadays eight children sounds like a lot to most folks. But back then it was common. It took a big family to run a farm. And besides that, most families I knew lost some of their children. God came and took them early. Seems like when the children was young they got the fever or if it was a rainy winter, they got the cough. None of us could afford a doctor so the children survived it or they didn't. Sometimes the prayers was answered, but often God had other plans. So, with never knowing about tomorrow, a big family was a blessing. I was happy for my uncle Henry.

They had their farm about an hour's ride from us. So we had get-togethers. I always enjoyed that. I didn't play so often since I had gotten too old to play with the Coal children. We both raised pigs, and when it was slaughtering time we would get together and help each other. Most often we had already shot and hung the pigs to drain the blood before they would come over to help. Or they would do the same if we were going to their place.

First thing after that was to dip them in hot water so as to be able to scrape the hair off the hide. That took more people. After that, it didn't take so many people to gut them. Fact is both Papa and Uncle Henry would each be doing one at the same time. My cousins and I would help take out the entrails. Nowadays some people throw them away. We would take the liver, and the kidneys, and the heart, and some intestines, rinse off the blood real good, and give them to Mama or Aunt Mary. They would boil that till it was hard. Then they would melt some lard down in a big skillet and fry it up good. That's what chitlins is. Grandma Charity and Sylvie say that in slavery times, that's the only parts they got. The hams always stayed in the pantry of the big house for the masters. If any slaves got caught with a ham or some bones, they would be in big trouble. Since freedom, of course, things are better. We can have both the chitlins and the hams. The hides we nailed to the barn to dry.

But it wasn't all work. After the regular chores were done, my brother Johnny and my cousins and I, we would head off fishing or go swimming. We had some good times together. And we did the same at my uncle's farm. They weren't as prosperous, though. We had glass in our windows and their barn wasn't the size of ours neither. There was lots of folks like that and I wasn't saying they were poor. But I watched things and I took notice of what I saw.

I asked Papa about that. "Do you think their farm will get better off with more children out working in the fields?"

"Can't but help, but that's only part of it," he said.

"How do you mean by that?" I asked.

"Well, our soil, it's all rocky and got more than its share of clay. But we're still a heap better than at Henry's farm. At least we are mostly flat. He's out there plowing up one hillside and then down another. It doesn't hold water and then when the rains do come, the water runs through those gullies and as likely as not just washes out the crops. He'll get a good year, but then you never know about the next. After the war, it was a nice thing when Lincoln gave the colored forty acres and a mule. But nobody said it had to be decent acreage. Matter of fact, though, a good number of freed slaves never got the forty acres or the mule that had been promised to them anyway.

"Yeah, son, not everybody be as fortunate as we are. That's a good thing to remember."

We were approaching Mr. Little's place by then and I tried to keep that in mind. For some reason, thinking that way did make me feel better. I didn't want Papa to feel too bad about what we had to do either and as we were clearing the rise above the Little place, I said,

"It looks like a nice farm and I hear that Mr. Little is a nice man."

My father seemed relieved to hear me say that. He looked over and grinned at me. "That's right," he said. "Folks around here, white and colored, say that he's more than decent."

It wasn't a big hill that overlooked the farm, but at the rise he pulled up on the reins. We looked down. They had a real house. It wasn't no cabin. It was big—part of it was two-story and it even had some nice porches. The old, weathered look that most places around here had was missing, for this house was whitewashed and clean-looking.

"Lot of work to whitewash a house that big," I said.

"I imagine that's so. But look at that barn. It's big and they been prospering."

I looked in the direction of the barn, but when Papa cleared his throat I turned in my seat.

"Son, don't forget where you come from. You will grow up to be as good as any man. But there's white and there's colored folks. They weren't meant to mix together and when they do there will be trouble. That just the way it is and it's never going to change. You are colored and you always need to take heed of that. It's when you don't take heed that you be asking for trouble. Sometimes, problems come anyway, so don't be asking for more than your share."

I nodded. In one way or another, that was the talk that all colored fathers had with their sons. It was a part of growing up. Papa didn't say to remember what happened to Pete. He didn't have to.

As we rolled in, Mr. Little came out from the barn and started walking toward us. Papa pulled up on the reins and climbed down. The men stood right alongside the wagon. I wasn't quite sure what to do so I just stayed up on the seat. I actually looked down on them, but I felt kind of small.

I wasn't sure I should be listening, but there was no way not to.

"Mr. Little." Papa nodded and looked down. He had turned from me and was talking in that colored-to-white way of speaking that we used.

Mr. Little nodded, but in a more confident way. "Trip over here okay?"

"Yes, sir. It was just fine."

"Good. And everything going all right on your farm?"

Now, I couldn't help but think that things weren't going so well or I wouldn't be there just to leave more food for the family. But Papa said, "Oh, yes, things be just fine with us." That's what he was supposed to answer.

"Glad to hear it. I understand your boy here is a good worker. You can come and take his wages at the end of each month."

"That be just fine, sir."

I heard them talking business. I didn't have much learning of numbers, but it seemed like they was saying the wages to be $1.15 or $1.50 a week. And beside that, they was gonna feed me too. I knew they were talking about me. So as not to be in the way, I sat real still-like to fade into the woodwork.

I was watching, though, for I knew this was going to be home. I noticed white folks, only white folks. In the way people did then, the Little family included a few generations. So there was a fair number of them to sort out too. But it wouldn't be till a while later that I would get them all sorted out. At that point, I only knew Mr. Little. I had met him a few times when we were taking some corn to the mill.

Mr. Little's son came up to us. "I thought I should move the cows out of the south pasture and back with the main herd."

He nodded. "Yeah, good idea. I want you to meet Harrison, though."

"This is my son, Harold. He and his wife, Barbara, live here with their children, Jacob, Ashley, and Johnny."

Papa and he nodded toward each other. Mr. Little pointed at me and said, "That's Harrison's boy, George. He is gonna be a farm-hand here. Why don't you go take him to get settled. He can stay in the shed behind the main house. I suppose it's best for you to be leaving soon, Harrison, as the afternoon is wearing on."

We all knew what he meant. The roads were safe in daylight, but the Klan were out riding strong after dark set in. I hopped down off the wagon and grabbed a burlap sack with all my stuff. Papa came around and shook hands with me. "You be good now, son. I'll be stopping by toward the end of the month."

In front of the Littles, it didn't seem that there was much else for us to say. I was glad that Papa and I had already talked before we reached the farm. I turned and followed along behind Harold. The shed was about forty or fifty feet behind the house. It was a hot day but when he opened the door there was a blast of hot air escaping at us. I guess that's because it was out in the open sun and there was no windows. There was no furniture except for a wooden platform with a corn husk mattress on top. The shed wasn't big at all and I leaned in through the doorway and dropped my sack in front of the bed.

Harold motioned for me to follow and we headed out toward the pastures. "You ever worked with cows before, boy?"

"Yes, sir."

"Fences?"

"Yes, sir."

"Good. That's what we do here along with crops, and pigs, and such things."

By then we had opened the gate and the cows were following us back. "I'll just do whatever it is you want."

"Fine." We had stopped and he said, "Why don't you start with cleaning the stables here. Tomorrow, I'll show you what your regular chores will be. Right now, I could use a break."

We were inside by then and I looked around. Seemed clear enough: shovel out the manure to the pile out front and put in new straw.

Harold spread his arms out and said, "Any questions?"

"No, sir. I think I see it."

"Good, good. There'll be a dinner bell in a few hours. When you hear that, you can wash out by the well and then come in through the back door."

CHAPTER 6

Between 1882 and 1901, nearly 2,000 blacks were lynched. By 1910, blacks were caught in a degrading system of total segregation throughout the South. Through "Jim Crow" laws (named after a black minstrel in a popular song), blacks were ordered to use separate rest rooms, water fountains, restaurants, waiting rooms, swimming pools, libraries, and bus seats.

The United States Supreme Court gave its approval to Jim Crow segregation in the 1896 case of *Plessy* v. *Ferguson*.

—*Free at Last,* by Sara Bullard

For me, in 1910, it didn't make any difference about voting and I didn't know any of what was happening. I was twelve years old and beginning my time at the Littles'.

The whole time I was there, I never did go

into the Littles' house through the front door. But they treated me fair and I have no cause for complaint. They fed me regular like they told Papa that they would. The back door entered into the kitchen and that's where I ate.

The way it was that first night and each one to follow was that they left a plate on the kitchen table for me. The Littles ate at a big table in the dining room, which was the next room over. I noticed right off that they ate more meat than I got at home, but then again the biscuits weren't as good as my mama made for us. Still, they had hominy and grits and ate pretty much as we did.

First night after dinner, Jacob Little showed me how to bring the cows into the barn, or, if the weather was good, to leave them be but check on the fences. He was younger than me, but on that farm everyone was my boss. It was understood that I took orders from him or anyone else there. That first night, it didn't take long to settle in. I had a couple of pairs of socks in the sack and an extra shirt and pants. I pulled out the baseball Pete had given to me three years earlier when I was nine. I set that down on the two-by-four that went across the wall behind the head of my bed.

The shed was small enough that I could cover it in five paces one way and only two paces from the edge of the bed to the other wall. They had a blanket for me too. It was thin, but it was clean and didn't have any bugs. I had worked till dark, but when I lay down sleep didn't come easily.

I was twelve but had never been alone like that before. In our cabin, I shared a bed with my brothers and sisters. And back when I used to visit at Mama and Papa Coal's place, they just squeezed me into a bed with their little ones. I guess that must have been crowded, but for me it was warm and cozy, and as nice as being in a litter of puppies.

I didn't find any fault with the Littles. So I know they meant well. I don't know if that was the difference between white and colored or how the rich and the poor lived. But I would have given anything for a crowded bed with my brothers and sisters sleeping and breathing next to me.

And then I thought of Mama's biscuits. It would have been okay in the daytime when I was working. But somehow out there by myself in the shed, thinking of her biscuits only made me cry. Mrs. Little made good biscuits, but they weren't Mama's. I wanted to be strong, but I couldn't help myself. I just wanted someone, Mama or Papa, to say it would be okay, or even for one of the little ones to ask, "What's the matter, George?"

I didn't need any answers, just someone there who cared about me. I wanted there to be people that would be safe to talk to, people that looked like me. But I knew Papa had warned me that the colored always paid a price when the races got too close to each other. I knew it wasn't right to feel that way, but it was the first time in my life that I ever felt sorry for myself.

There weren't no windows but the wind blew in between the boards. When the wind slacked off, I could hear the coyotes howling. We would hear them at night on our farm too. But when I was snuggled in with my brothers and sisters, their howling never bothered me. I knew they couldn't hurt me. That night, their sounds added to my loneliness. I knew that folks with enough money didn't have to share a bed and I should be happy in my new home. But that first night, even under the blanket, I shivered and I cried till I fell asleep.

The next morning was the beginning of a better day. Not knowing what was expected of me, I was out waiting behind the big house before the light came up. Someone had a lantern going in the kitchen, but I just waited outside figuring that to be the safest thing. Jacob was the first one out. I could tell he had forgotten about me, but he nodded and said, "Come with me, I'll show you the chicken shed."

It was bigger than our shed, but still, once inside it felt familiar to me. We collected eggs and then stopped at the well on the way back to the kitchen. Harold's wife, Barbara, and Mrs. Little had breakfast going. For a breakfast, they ate pretty fine. There was oatmeal and toast, hominy and grits, and milk too. They had coffee brewing. I liked the smell of the coffee, but I never did drink coffee.

I had walked in behind Jacob. Then I just stood and waited. My first night, I had eaten in the kitchen, but I was separated because the rest of the folks was in the dining room. That morning it was clear they were going to eat their breakfast right at the kitchen table. I know if I was a white boy working for them, I could have just pulled up a chair and sat down. But I wasn't and I didn't know what to do. I didn't like just standing in their kitchen and causing a scene. I felt downright uncomfortable. But I knew it could be a lot worse than that if I sat down in the wrong place. Safest thing was to wait.

So, I stood and waited. Seemed like forever to me, but it wasn't so long before Mrs. Little waved me over. She handed me a plate and a glass of milk and said, "Boy, you can take it over to that chair along the sideboard."

A sideboard is the same as what folks nowadays call a counter. The food was good but I had never eaten in a room with whites before. I was real careful to use the manners that I had been taught. They had been decent to me, but I knew I was the only colored and I didn't want anyone to judge badly of me. I didn't say anything and no one expected otherwise of me.

More folks came. I set over to the side and ate. I didn't know if it was proper to listen to white folks, but I couldn't help that. I sat apart, but on the other hand we really was close together. With some folks, that first night, I never did get a real introduction. As folks came down and sat at the table, I learned their names by listening.

Barbara was sitting at the table now, next to a baby in a high chair. She was spooning

73

him some oatmeal, but it looked to me like most of it ended up on his face. "Come on, Johnny, you've got to eat more of this or you'll be hungry later."

At our house you didn't have to ask someone to eat. We had to share, but we knew enough not to waste food. Still, I grinned inside to myself because Johnny was the name of my younger brother too. For some reason, that made me feel good.

"Ashley, we got some syrup to go with these grits," Mrs. Little said.

I had noticed that girl last night. She had red hair and some freckles across her nose. She was about the same age as me. But it was the first time I had heard her name. I would have liked some syrup for those grits too, but since no one had asked me, I kept quiet.

No one said anything, but when Mr. Little kind of nodded, folks pushed their plates aside and started getting up. It still wasn't light yet, but Harold said, "It's getting late and this would be a good day to check on fences before we move the cows to another pasture this week."

I had been watching closely so as not to make any mistakes and I got up then too. Mr. Little beckoned toward me and I hoped he was pleased that I was all ready for work. If so, he didn't say nothing except, "Follow me."

By the time we were outside, everyone was already going their separate ways. Mr. Little said, "I'm going to show you the chores that need doing here. I hope you can watch and think for yourself so I don't need to spend time each day showing you what to do."

He looked at me and I figured that I was supposed to say something.

"Yes, sir, that be fine."

He nodded. "We'll just have to see."

I could tell that he doubted my thinking abilities, but without being disrespectful, I hoped to show him wrong. As he walked me over the farm, I started feeling better. There wasn't any work here that we didn't have on our own farm. I had already seen the chicken shed. The barn was big, but horses is horses. He showed me how he wanted the horses stabled and groomed. They had cows too, with enough milk to sell the extra. Although we only had one milk cow then, it was nothing new to me.

There was a lot more fences than we had. The barbwire could come loose and the fence posts would rot out and need replacing. I could see that they had plenty of trees to get rails for splitting. Thing was that those fences always needed checking and fixing.

After checking on the chickens and collecting eggs each morning, it was to be my job to milk the cows. They had a lot of cows, but I didn't mind. I've always liked working, even then. The milk went up to the house. Besides milk they got cream and butter from it. A man would come with a wagon for the extra milk and take it to town.

Then for the rest of the day, I did the things I was told. Some days it seemed like I was forever digging post holes or splitting rails.

Other times, it was just cleaning out the stables. I kind of got the feeling that I got the jobs that nobody else wanted to do. But, no matter, like Papa would have wanted, I always did my best and gave no cause for complaint.

I had more chores every day, but in a short while, I could see what needed to be done without being told. Mr. Little saw that and I guess he trusted me, for he didn't bother with me no more. There was enough to be done that I always worked till dark set in even without being told what to do.

I spent a lot of time in the stables. At the Dawson farm we just had a mule but no horses. So caring for them was new to me, but I liked the horses. They used them for plowing and pulling their wagons. They was of a different nature than a mule. If a person treated a horse right, I found that you could talk to a horse and it would listen.

I would bring them oats and rub them down and always talked to the horse when I was working with him. Matter of fact, some days I hardly saw any people so I was glad the horses knew me and would listen when I talked to them. In the stables, I always knew where things stood. The horses were happy to see me and I could never say the wrong thing to a horse and see any trouble for being out of place.

I would set the horse in its harness for the plow, but I rarely did the plowing. I know that if I could plow with a mule, I sure could do it with a horse. But I noticed that working with horses seemed to be one of the things that whites thought they was best at. Not to be disrespectful, but I could see the horses didn't think so. Still, I knew enough to keep such thoughts to myself.

I would follow along planting corn or potatoes in the furrows. At day's end, when we were done, I would take the horses back and rub them down. At harvesttime, the horses were mostly used to pull the wagons. We would load up with potatoes or corn or beets. I would harness the horses, but someone else rode in the wagon while I loaded the crops.

At harvesttime, we were in the fields all day. At midday, Mrs. Little would bring some food from the house. We would all stop then. I made sure that I never stopped working before everyone else did. Though I never got any complaints, that seemed like the safest way to me.

I had been through two harvest cycles. They had added more stock and a few more acres to crops. I kept growing and by the time I was fourteen, I was strong enough to do as good a day's work as any man. Though Papa still got the payments, I understand that I had gotten a raise that put me over $1.50 a week. I got to feeling pretty good. I had been there for a while and was pretty sure about myself and about where I stood with the Littles.

At harvest, it was the custom for both white and colored schools to close, for children were needed at home then. Jacob would be with us out in the fields and Ashley stayed at home to cook for the harvest crew. Jacob wasn't much younger than me, but he wasn't nearly as strong nor as willing to work. He made it clear he'd rather have been in school. But everybody worked then.

One season, Mrs. Little took ill. In those days, we just called it getting old. Probably got the arthritis real bad or some such thing. It got harder for her to bring the food out to the fields. Harold's wife, Barbara, had another little one in the house and another on the way. So, Ashley started to bring out the food—chicken and biscuits, maybe some milk.

When Mrs. Little brought us food, she set it in a hamper in the back of the wagon and headed back to the house. It had been two years and I hadn't given no cause for complaint. Still, I would wait until everybody had served themselves and then I would take some food too. Everyone was comfortable and it seemed best to leave it like that.

Having always worked in the house, Ashley didn't know any of that. She stayed and filled up the plates for us. As always, I worked a little longer and was the last one at the wagon. I had expected an empty wagon and was taken aback to see Ashley there extending a plate toward me.

I didn't know what to do. By then, I had been there more than two years, but I had never talked directly to her. She was usually gone at school or else working inside the house. I felt awful uncomfortable to see her at the wagon, but it would of been disrespectful to let on about that. I took the plate from her and kinda looked down.

As I began to head toward the tree where everyone was sitting, she said, "Everyone else had come for their food and you were still working, George."

I stopped. People talked to me every day. But it was always an order about some work to be done. No one meant me any harm, but they never gave no notice of me besides that. I didn't know what to say or even know if I was supposed to say anything. I kind of muttered, "Yeah, I guess, I was out there working."

I felt kind of dumb because she had just said the same thing, but she let it go and asked if I wanted some milk. It was a normal enough question, but when I looked up to answer, I just nodded yes, for all of a sudden, it wasn't so easy to talk. I took a glass of milk but noticed that, somehow, Ashley had become awfully pretty. I barely remembered to say my thank you.

Harvest work never changed much. That didn't bother me. I knew what was expected of me and I was a good worker. The field work remained the same, but the time passed differently. It used to seem that there was the early morning hours when it was cool and then the rest of the day when the sun came on strong and beat down on us. Now it was the morning hours of work and then the midday break for supper.

I looked forward to suppertime, although

we didn't say much. Mrs. Little had been kind to me and I hoped that she would be doing better. Still, I now had something to think about. In the mornings, I wondered if Mrs. Little or Ashley would be coming to bring some food to the wagon. No one told me, but I guess Mrs. Little had let go of her job delivering food because she didn't make it out to the wagon anymore.

There wasn't much said, and at first it was always about the chicken or the biscuits, or maybe the day's weather. But it had been a few years since someone had asked me how I was and meant it. It was a small thing, but I noticed when, instead of just serving and leaving me a plate of food, Ashley asked what I wanted. She even asked once if I liked her cooking.

No one had asked me anything for over two years. So sometimes I had a hard time answering even if I did appreciate the questions. I couldn't help but notice how good-looking Ashley was. Of course, I worked hard to make sure that no one could tell that I would think such a thing.

As good as things might feel in the daytime, I always picked up Pete's baseball and looked at it each night before going to sleep. It let me know how things were and kept me safe. The Littles always treated me fairly, but I knew that it was not safe to forget how things were.

Sometimes, maybe two or three times a month, usually on Saturday, my father would come and pick me up and I would go home and visit. I couldn't see as how the farm had really changed, but somehow I didn't feel the same there. Mama was so happy to see me and my brothers and sisters would crowd around the wagon.

Of course, there was always work to be done at home. Most often, I would fix fence posts or join Papa and my brother Johnny in the fields. On one of those visits, we were out in the field picking cotton. I remember everything. The sky was blue, not a cloud in it. We were working on a slope and I could look down toward the cabin. Wasn't quite midday so the heat wasn't overbearing and there weren't no heat waves across the fields to make the eye see things funny.

Anyways, we all heard the sound before we saw it. I had never heard anything like it. There was this steady hum of the largest hornets' nest except that it kept getting louder and louder. It was coming from up in the sky but there wasn't nothing there. Papa and Johnny had put their cotton sacks down. I could see that Mama had come out of the cabin with her apron still on.

We all looked up and could see this speck in the sky start to grow. It clearly weren't a bird and we just kept watching. I didn't know whether to be scared or what. I looked out toward Papa and Johnny. Papa's hand was shading his eyes but I could see that a smile was coming across his face. At that point, Johnny had his hands cupped around his mouth and was shouting at us, except I

81

couldn't hear a word. A dust storm kicked up from nowhere.

It was the first airplane we had ever seen. It was beautiful. It dropped down so low that I could see the two men inside. They had on leather helmets, but there wasn't no window over them. The airplane came down so low that I could see those men were laughing. They were white, of course.

Our mule was running in circles, the cow was running toward the barn, and even the chickens took notice when the dust swirled around them. The plane got smaller but then circled back. It came in so low, it had to climb at the last minute to clear the barn. I thought it might get stuck on the roof. This time, they waved to us and then tipped their wing. The dust was so strong that we had our hands over our mouths, but I kept my eyes open so as not to miss a thing.

Papa said those planes wouldn't amount to much, but within a few years we saw them at the county fair. Folks with money could go up for a ride and you could see your house from the sky.

On Sundays after church, Uncle Henry and Aunt Mary's family would come over to visit more often now. They had a bigger family than ours and it was a fun time. Uncle Henry said that he already knew about those airplanes from the newspapers. He and Papa would talk politics. We always listened because he could read the papers. Uncle Henry said, "The world is changing. Things will be different. Life is going to get better for us. You'll see."

If things were getting better, it wasn't enough that the family could both feed me and live without the wages from Mr. Little. So, on Sunday afternoon, Papa would drive me back to work. Leaving was hard at first, but it was what I did and I got used to it.

Matter of fact, sometimes I didn't see home for more than a month. During slaughtering time, things was too busy for me to take off. In the fall, some years, there was a lot of pigs and hogs for butchering. Seemed like then they needed me every minute of daylight and every day of the week. They usually had me skinning hides and I got to be pretty good at it. During those times we had both dinner and supper out in the field area.

You would think that with all the blood and entrails about that we wouldn't have any appetite. That wasn't so. Ashley always brought the meals now. I don't know if anyone else noticed, but she stayed longer than her grandma would have. Sometimes, I was sure that when she was smiling, she was smiling at me.

That caused me some confusion for I couldn't be sure. I felt like smiling back, but I figured that the best thing was to ignore it all. At least, that's what I would try to do. Sometimes it was hard to remember. One day she said, "George, how come you never talk to me?"

I shrugged. I didn't know what to say.

"You don't want to talk to me?"

83

Looking back, I appreciate how much courage it must of took to say something like that. But I didn't know what to say, and I just nodded. "Yeah, I guess that's it."

I could see I hurt her real bad. Before she turned away, I thought I saw tears in her eyes. I wanted to say, "Wait, that's not it at all. I don't want to cause pain to anyone, especially you."

But I kept my mouth shut. That night, I held Pete's baseball tight. I knew that saying too much could cause trouble, but then I wondered if saying nothing could be just as bad, maybe worse.

I was scared, but besides that, I felt downright awful. I could see that somehow I had hurt Ashley. I liked her and that made it worse. Still, I knew that to have such thoughts was dangerous right there.

I didn't know if I should say something. But next day, though she still brought out our food, she set it down and left even faster than her grandma used to do. It seemed like she did that from then on, so while I wondered on what to say, there never seemed to be much chance anyway.

My own family couldn't afford to feed us all and the Littles had been good to me. But now, I could see that things was all different. At night, I rubbed the stitching of Pete's baseball and knew how bad it could be. I didn't want to die, but I didn't know what to do either.

I was always happy to go home for a visit,

but even that didn't help. I would do my chores, but things weren't the same at home. Mama saw it right away and had Papa talk to me. "Have you been doing your work and keeping yourself out of trouble?"

I wanted to ask for help, but said, "Yes, sir."

For the first time, I felt as if I couldn't talk to anybody, colored or white. Thing was, I just didn't know anymore. I hadn't told nobody anything. But Uncle Henry looked at me and must of figured something out. He said, "It's a white man that will decide when a colored man is in trouble."

Papa, he said, "No, Henry. We make our own way. Trouble is out there. More trouble is set aside for colored, but a person can leave it alone and just do the right thing. Then, if trouble still finds you, you've done the best you can."

I figured they was right. It was true that Pete didn't cause no harm and he still had his troubles. But mostly, folks could stay out of trouble if they had a mind to do that. Still, after talking to Papa and Uncle Henry, I decided I would do the right thing every day and leave trouble alone. There wasn't nothing more than that I could do.

CHAPTER 7

GIRL ANARCHIST TAKES BLAME
OF KILLING EDITOR

Paris, Jan. 24—Germaine Bertom, the girl anarchist who last Monday shot and killed Marius Plageau of Royalist newspaper *L'Action Française,* was examined by an investigating magistrate today in the hospital where she is being treated for the wound in the breast which she inflicted upon herself after killing Plageau.

—*The Marshall Morning News,*
January 12, 1923

Richard handed me the paper and asked, "Some historians say that, in 1914, political conditions were so tense that the assassination of Archduke Ferdinand by an anarchist started World War One. What did you think of World War One at the time?"

The paper in my hand had yellowed with time, but I read the article with interest. I had to say, "I don't know anything about an archduke; don't even know what an archduke is."

Richard said that he was a history major in college and studied World War I and read about his assassination in some books.

Well, I never thought of it, but I guess you could meet someone in a book and get to know him that way.

"I remember the year 1914 all right, but don't recollect any archduke or much about the World War," I said to Richard. "People must of liked that archduke a whole lot for the world to start going to war."

Richard said, "It was more about honor and power and politics."

I told him, "Sounds like what white folks would do then!"

"What do you mean?" he asked me.

"I mean all this killing over someone's honor. Seems like, especially back then, folks were going to die if a white man is put off too badly. They was too ready to kill each other. For colored folks, it was different. We didn't have the time to worry about honor and we didn't have enough power to lose. Staying alive, keeping food on the table, that's what counted for us. That's what I remember about 1914."

I remember, during slaughtering time, there would be some talk about the war. No one ever asked my opinion, but it sounded like we were not going to join the fighting. People, white folk anyway, would sit around waiting for news to come about the war. They kept talking about how we weren't going to join that war, but they was always wanting to hear more about it anyway.

For me, the news that mattered came that fall of 1914. I hadn't been home for several weeks, when one day I saw Papa coming over toward us on the wagon. He had never come over like that during the middle of the workday.

I was skinning a hide and I dare not just put my work down. But I kinda stole glances as I kept on working.

Papa and Mr. Little were talking. Thing was, usually it would be the white man talking and the colored man listening and nodding. That day, it was different. Papa was talking and Mr. Little was listening and nodding every now and then. They shook hands.

I had just finished that hide when Mr. Little came over. He said, "Son, you are a good worker, but you need to go with your father."

I set my tools down and walked over to the wagon where Papa stood. I was still covered in blood, but my father didn't seem to notice and gave me a big hug. He still didn't say anything when I climbed into the wagon. The wagon started forward and then Papa seemed to think better of that and pulled up on the reins. I had never seen Papa like that and I looked over at him. There was pain in his eyes and I could see that he was struggling with something.

Usually, I waited for Papa to speak, but this time I said, "What's the matter?"

"Your uncle Henry and aunt Mary."

"What about them?"

"They passed on."

I had just seen them on my last visit home. They were healthy and fine and I was confused. "You mean they both died?"

"That's right."

I was too surprised to cry. "What happened?" I said.

"They took sick and died, both of them within a day."

I didn't want to believe it. "Why, what did the doctor say was the matter?"

"Son, times are tough. You know that. We can't afford a doctor. We don't know what they had. Your mama and I were with them the whole time, did the best we could. We kept bathing them with cold cloths, but they was consumed with fever."

Scarlet fever was taking away a lot of folks at that time. I expect that's what took them.

Papa brought the wagon over to the pump. I washed up and then we went over to my shed. The burlap sack that I came with four years ago was still there. It didn't take long to collect my belongings. We tossed it in the wagon.

Word travels fastest when someone dies. In those days, death was more common and people knew what to do for each other. The Littles, all of them, were waiting by the wagon. Mr. Little said, "George, you been a good worker, as good as any I've ever had."

Funny how death can bring out the nicest side in some folks. Mr. Little wasn't given to praise. Any other day I would have had to work hard not to get too prideful from such words coming from him. That day, I heard the kindness in his voice toward me, but the words didn't do much. That moment was as close as we could ever get to all of us just being people—not colored and white people, just people.

Mrs. Little, who wasn't doing so well these

days, was there too. She had tears in her eyes, but said, "Good-bye, George. We'll miss you."

Mr. Little's son, Harold, stood beside his wife, Barbara. She was shook up. Harold had his arm around her, but she was crying. "I'm sorry, George."

She didn't even know Uncle Henry and Aunt Mary, but I could tell she really meant it. Harold extended his hand and we shook hands. " 'Bye, son. You be good now. There'll always be a place here for you if you need it."

I wasn't used to hearing such kind talk and muttered, "Thank you."

Jacob stepped out and said, "Maybe we go fishing sometime." I didn't feel like it, but I liked him saying that to me and I nodded.

Johnny, who was just a baby at the time I started at the Littles', was now four years old. He didn't really understand. "You going, George?" he said.

I didn't try to explain. I just said, "Yeah, I be going, Johnny."

"But you didn't break the Big Red yet!"

Even as low as I was feeling, that made me smile. When I was working with horses, Johnny liked to follow along. I would keep him back so as not to see him hurt, but I got to where I did like him to come. Johnny was talking about a red colt that was pretty wild. Still, I had it in mind to break that horse and had just started working with him. When Johnny was sitting up on the rail, I told him, "When I'm finished with this horse, he be gentle enough that you can ride him."

That seemed to please Johnny so much that he didn't talk about nothing else, except as to how George was going to break Big Red for him to ride. I saw people smile when he would say that and it made me feel good too.

I was hurting, but I felt bad about leaving a promise like that. "Johnny, I meant to do that and I am sorry."

Johnny seemed to understand. He said, "That's okay, George." Then he caught me by surprise when he jumped up and gave me a big hug. He squeezed me tight like we was best friends. I guess he was still young enough that he could do that.

I was feeling a little funny being at the center of things and was kind of caught off guard when Ashley came up and put her hand on my arm. It didn't rest there long, but it drew my attention from Johnny. She lifted up the hamper that served to supply supper out in the fields. It was full of chicken and biscuits, probably ready for the supper that would of been coming up shortly.

This time she didn't just set it in the wagon and walk away. She said, "Your mama won't feel like cooking tonight, so you can have this for dinner when you get home. There's some napkins on top. I embroidered them myself. You give those to your mama too."

"Thank you. That's mighty nice of you." I felt like I should say something more, but she just nodded at me. Anyways, I could see that she wasn't mad at me anymore.

Mr. Little and Papa had been talking over

by the side of that group and they walked over. "Harrison, I'm sorry about your little brother."

Uncle Henry was a head taller than Papa, but he was five or six years younger. Papa always gave him a hard time about that and he always was Papa's little brother, even to us kids. Mr. Little continued, "But if you need something, just let me know."

They shook hands and Papa made to climb into the wagon. So, I did the same. It was rare to see Papa shake hands with a white man and now I saw it twice in one day. Any other time, I would have pondered on that, but right then it seemed natural. I never bothered with a calendar, but I heard them saying it was the middle of the month. Even so, Mr. Little was going to pay for the whole month. I was proud to hear Pa say, "We can't do that. The boy didn't earn a full month's pay."

Any other day I would of been burning inside if I heard Mr. Little say, "Yes, he did. He works twice as hard as any worker I've ever had and that boy earns his pay by the middle of each month." That day, I just listened as he went on.

"Besides, it's not just for you or for George. You've got a big family now and it wouldn't be right of you to take away my pleasure in being of some help, however small that might be."

Old Mr. Little didn't talk much, but that day he had a way with words. Papa just shook his head and grinned. "Thank you. That is much appreciated."

He shook the reins and we started rolling. And I was glad too for if we was there any longer it would of been hard not to cry. The Littles had been good to me, treated me fairly. People talk about "good folks," that was the Littles, all right.

We didn't head to our farm but went straight off to Uncle Henry and Aunt Mary's place. Their cabin was just full of people. I kept hearing everybody saying that they was there to help. There was lots of food and lots of talking. Even the preacher stopped by and ate with us. Still, as much as they wished it, no one could make it any better.

Their cabin was familiar to me for I had spent a lot of nights there. But it had a different feeling then. When everyone left, the quiet got real powerful. During the night, each time I would hear some crying, I heard Mama whispering in a comforting way. I guess I felt like crying too, but the little ones needed her most.

Some friends had worked through the night to finish the coffins. We had a lot of pine forests in East Texas then and the coffins were made of pine. We went out to the cemetery the next morning. Papa carried the coffins in the back of our wagon, and I followed behind with Uncle Henry's wagon. Mama and most of the children that could fit were with me. There were other wagons too—actually quite a line of wagons—behind us. It was so quiet in the wagon that you could hear the wheels squeaking. Funny thing to think of, but I still remember thinking they needed some axle grease. As we passed by the thickets, the birds broke into the quiet, not caring what we was about that morning. By the time we got to the cemetery, the sun was warming things and more people were waiting to pay their respects.

In my time, I've been to a lot of funerals, so many I couldn't count. There was such a crowd of people that I haven't seen at any funeral before or since. I expect that might of been because Uncle Henry and Aunt Mary were so young, and because of their children. When I tossed a clump of dirt on the coffins, Papa put his arm around my shoulder. "They are at peace now, son. Their suffering is over."

But I could see the pain in his eyes, could see that there was a whole lot of hurt.

There wasn't a plan. No one ever asked or even talked about it. Their children just moved in with us. Suddenly, there were fourteen children instead of just five.

The cabin seemed much smaller. Meals were crowded till we built a bigger table. Even then, it took some time to serve up for fourteen children. I never heard my mother complain, but I know it wasn't easy to cook for that many either. And there was always a little one that needed something.

I got back to my old routine of doing chores and field work. My dog took me back like I had never been gone. No one ever had to be lonely. They was more like brothers and sisters than cousins. It was good to have them with us. But with fourteen of us, the farm felt different. And after almost four years, I had gotten used to being alone. It didn't bother me none.

Back at our farm, I was most often the first one up. There was lots of chores to do, but sometimes, shutting the door quietly, I would lean against the logs and look at the sky and take a few moments for myself. Inside, the cabin had the comfortable feel of people. Outside, it was empty and lonely and I had grown to like that too. I liked to look at the stars on the still and quiet mornings and listen for the howl of the coyotes.

I was still the oldest. So, with nobody saying it, I knew there was work to be done. The younger ones went to school, and that was my dream too: to go to school and learn to read. But I was sixteen now and that dream was fading. I could see where I was needed. Papa couldn't do it alone. Times hadn't been great, but now food and money were scarcer than before. Besides just working on the farm, I started outside jobs to help us get some money for the food that we couldn't grow.

The mill, a little ways down the valley, was up and running again. Papa took me down to get a job. They set me to hauling logs. Nowadays they move those logs with loaders and tractors. But not then. We would hook them up to a mule and pull the logs up to the saw. I would have to shift those logs to the right position and pull as hard as the mule did.

In those days, the pine forests was all over East Texas. Men would bring the logs in by wagon and lay them out in the yard. They were paid by the log. Those cutters told me that the pay wasn't great either, but their work was easier than mine. They worked in teams of two for it took one man on each end of the saw to get through those trees. They called those saws "misery whips" and I guess they had a reason for that.

Sometimes, there was a mountain of logs facing me. The foreman, a white man named Sam, said that I could take a rest when we had no logs to be moved. Day after day I would bring that pile down. And then it seemed just when I was near the bottom of the log pile, another load of logs would come. It always did happen just like that. Probably, I could have worked there forever and not get to the end of the logs, where I could sit and take a rest.

It was hot. The weather was hot and the steam machine that pulled the chain logs through the blade had a big furnace that was always being stoked. The heat would blast out at us and the sparks was always flying everywhere. Matter of fact, some years later, I think in the 1930s, the mill caught fire and burned down. It was always so hot and dry.

We didn't get paid by check. At the end of each week, they gave us a little silver disk about the size of a half dollar. My father would come each week, collect my disk, and exchange it for cash. I always did a good day's work, didn't cause no trouble, and there was always a disk waiting for him. So, I didn't really know what they paid, but Papa would set aside maybe a dollar each month that would be mine.

The work was awfully hard, and there was never a chance to make a decent wage for the men who worked there. It was only the owners and maybe some of the foremen that could ever make a decent living at the mill. Still, in those times, we were grateful for what we had.

Sometimes, if lumber prices was too low, the mill would shut down for a few weeks. I could always get hired back later, but it was nice to just be back on the farm. We had more acreage now and had our own livestock to take care of. With fourteen children, after slaughtering time, we didn't have much left to sell. We needed most of the meat and hides for ourselves. So, there was always fences to repair and animals to tend.

But we had a good time too. That dog that Papa got was a good duck-hunting dog. In the fall, I would take a shotgun and be out there with him in the reeds. I still remember how cold it would get, so cold that my fingers would hurt. But I liked it out there and it always made Mama smile when I brought some ducks into the kitchen. We even had wild turkeys back then, and I could bag some of those too.

Some folks saw bear, but I never got any. I'd seen tracks so I figure they'd seen me. There were plenty of deer and it was an awful nice feeling to have a deer hanging in the barn, knowing that we were going to eat well. That shotgun stayed with me a long time. I hadn't used it in years but just kept hold of it, until about ten or fifteen years ago, someone stole it from me. They stole that shotgun but didn't get any ammunition.

Sometimes, when we had ribbon syrup or some extra corn we went into town. We took the mule in with us, but in 1914, I saw something new.

I had never seen a car before and that Model T was beautiful. It was polished black with a shiny brass radiator cap. The top could come down, of course, and it was something to see. Over time, we started seeing a few more of them. They worked in town but weren't too practical. We didn't get a lot of rain, but when the rain came it was most often a downpour. Our roads turned to mud, and the autos just couldn't make it. After a good rain, I saw those same cars being towed by a mule or a team of horses. Most people agreed as to how they was close to useless, but I still liked them anyway.

Cars might of been of no use back then, but a couple of years later I got to appreciating that they didn't own the stubbornness of a mule. Now I admit, our mule, Blue, was a good mule, a strong mule. He could do anything that we needed on the farm. At plowing time, I always followed him and, Lord, did he and I crush a lot of cane together. He worked at his pace and I just followed. All those years, he gave me no problem.

He didn't always like to do things at the pace he was asked, but if a person gave him a bit of time to get moving he was dependable.

Still, he had a mind of his own. And I guess that's what caused us a problem, for when I got to be sixteen I had in my mind how I wanted to do things too. Around about that time, I got to feeling pretty full of myself and just figured that the mule could do things my way.

When Papa said to hitch up the mule, we was going to town, just the two of us, I was ready. The mule was off grazing by the barn and with a halter in my hand I went to get him. It would of helped if I had a lump of sugar or even a carrot in my hand. But I wanted to get moving and I didn't bother. I just called out to him.

Now, we had been working from sunrise till noon dragging fence posts. He probably thought that I had more of the same in my mind. So, he wouldn't come. Right there, 'cause I wanted to be going, that made me mad. I kept on calling, but he just looked at me from twenty or thirty feet away like he didn't understand. It was easy to see through that and I walked over to get him.

Trouble was, when I got within ten feet or so, he would just move away and graze on another patch of grass. I could of gone back to the house for a carrot, but I just didn't want to. I put a hand behind my back and pretended to look like I had a carrot as I walked toward him. He looked at me with interest and I grinned at the way I had it over on that old mule. Except that he looked me over some more and backed off again.

My pride got in the way—I didn't like having a mule get the best of me. I started shouting at him and said, "Get over here, you stupid mule." I don't know if he understood the words or he didn't like the tone, but that got me nowhere. I would move five paces toward him and he would step back and go to grazing. Pretty soon we was just working our way around the barn but getting nowhere. He was happy enough, but I was getting pretty steamed. I picked up a dried piece of manure to throw it at him and drive him into the barn. I missed, didn't even come close. It was a bad throw, and I could swear he was laughing at me, and that really got me mad. I picked up a rock to hit him on the flank. This time, I figured he had it coming. My throw was hard, but it went high and a little off to the side. It hit that old mule in the head, smack in his eye.

He started braying in pain. I ran over to help, but then he really wouldn't let me near him. He wasn't playing a game now. He just didn't trust me anymore and I felt bad. He looked over and I saw the juices was flowing out of his eye. I couldn't get near him, but I stayed till his eye started to crust over.

I felt bad, but I felt really bad about telling Papa. He was in the cabin waiting for me. I tried to figure out what to say, but there was no good way to say it. I just flat out told him the truth and didn't even try to polish it. I knew I had done wrong and I waited for the worst.

Papa said, "Let's go see."

We walked out to the mule. He still backed off when he saw me, but he let Papa put the halter on him. Papa looked at his eye. I didn't want to see it, but I looked too.

The juice had stopped flowing, but the eye was starting to turn a milky-white color. Papa said, "He's going to be blind in that eye."

I know we couldn't afford a vet and I didn't even ask. Papa hadn't said anything yet, and waiting for him to speak was as bad as looking at the eye.

"I'm sorry," I said. "I didn't mean to hurt Blue."

My father nodded. "My eyes are fine. You don't need to apologize to me."

We started walking back to the cabin. I knew I deserved a whupping or at least a talking to. I had let him down. If Papa had chewed me out right then, I could have taken it and then started to feel better. That would of been easier.

But it wasn't over and I asked, "How am I going to talk to Blue now? Is he going to listen to me?"

Papa shrugged. "I don't know. A lot of people can't forgive. You'll have to see about a mule."

We were in the cabin by then and Papa dipped a cloth in the bucket. As I was walking out, he said, "Why don't you take a carrot with you this time."

I felt shame that I didn't remember for myself, but I picked up a couple from a bunch on the counter. It was cooler in the barn, but even in the shade the eye looked bad. This time he didn't run, but looked at me with his good eye. I don't know if he blamed me, but it felt that way. I thought as to how that mule had been there since I was born and that I had hurt it bad.

I handed him a carrot and rubbed his head in the way he liked for me to do. I cleaned his eye as best I could, but I could see that Papa was right. He would lose the sight in that eye.

We was to have that mule for many more years. Every time he looked at me, I hurt inside. To this day, I still feel bad about it. I promised myself that I would never hit an animal again. And, though it's been more than eighty years, I never have.

CHAPTER 8

In 1947 life in America—at least my America, and Jackie's—was segregation. It was two worlds that were afraid of each other....

Jackie Robinson had to be bigger than life. He had to be bigger than the Brooklyn teammates who got up a petition to keep him off the ball club, bigger than the pitchers who threw at him or the base runners who dug their spikes into his shin, bigger than the bench jockeys who hollered for him to carry their bags and shine their shoes, bigger than the so-called fans who mocked him with mops on their heads and wrote him death threats....

Before Jackie Robinson broke the color line, I wasn't permitted even to think about being a professional baseball player.... All that changed when Jackie put on No. 42 and started stealing bases in a Brooklyn uniform.... With Jackie in the infield, the Dodgers won six National League pennants.

I believe every black person had a piece of those pennants. There's never been another ballplayer who touched people as Jackie did.

—"The Trailblazer," by Hank Aaron, from "Time, 100 Heroes and Icons," *Time,* June 14, 1999

When Richard handed me an article and asked me did I remember Jackie Robinson, I had to shake my head. I guess he doesn't know that there ain't no black man in America that was alive then would ever forget Jackie Robinson. That's okay. I am a busy man now with school and all. But if I have to educate Richard some, I can do that too.

I had let go of my dream of reading about when I was sixteen and took on responsibilities to help feed all the little ones that came to our family. Reading and school would of been nice, but I had people that needed me. That's how it was and I didn't mind. Besides, though I was glad the little ones went, I could see that, by sixteen, my time for school had passed.

I can't say it wasn't disappointing, but I accepted that was how things was meant to be. My life was good and I couldn't ask for more. It wasn't till thirty years later that I really missed knowing how to read. Yeah, when Jackie Robinson started with the Dodgers, it was as if life had changed, at least for the colored.

It didn't matter if they lived in Chicago, St. Louis, or Philadelphia. When Jackie came to the plate, colored folk everywhere were rooting for him to get a hit. He was up at the plate for all of us and we wanted him to make it in the majors. Folks followed every game. People read the box scores every day just to see how Jackie did.

I told Richard, "It was something to see. Everywhere I went, people wanted to know how Jackie's game was."

I didn't let on to folks that I couldn't read. Everyone talked about Jackie, so it wasn't hard for me to follow him. But I thought, yeah, it would be nice to read for myself the morning box score like most people did. Still, I was happy that Jackie did so well. I thought it was great when Jackie won the Rookie of the Year award.

I said, "Richard, it's not just because you're white that you don't know. Young black folk today don't understand what Jackie meant to us then either."

Back in the twenties I was a pretty good ballplayer myself, though nothing like Jackie. But in my time, I saw and played with some good ballplayers. My brother Johnny and I played on the same team, the Hornets. Johnny was pitcher and I was a catcher.

I was short and stocky and was always the catcher wherever we played. Though we were brothers, Johnny was tall and lanky. He took after our mother. He just looked like a pitcher. I called the signs and when Johnny was pitching, they were easy to call. His fastball would come down and in on the inside corner. Today, they might even call it a slider. Back then, in our league, it was simple. Throw the heat. Challenge the hitter and make him hit your best pitch.

I would call two or three fastballs. I would put my mitt on the inside corner for a target. And Johnny could hit the target. A couple of inside fastballs would most often push the hitter off the plate. Then I would call for a curve on the outside; that would surprise them. Some people don't know it, but the catcher has to do a lot of thinking.

When the ball hit my catcher's mitt, you could hear the pop throughout the stands. It would sting. I put a little sponge inside the mitt, but it would still have a sting to it. This be like 1919 or 1920 and catchers' mitts weren't as thick as today. For that matter, fielders' gloves were smaller too. A shortstop or even an out-fielder's glove just covered your hand. It wasn't no basket like you see today. Back then, a fielder had to judge it right or you would look mighty foolish.

Our team was pretty good, but for home games we didn't have a stadium. There were some stands alongside a pasture. Most of the time we had to keep it cut down ourselves. So, sometimes, especially when there were good spring rains, before practice we would be out there cutting the tall grass with a scythe. The star players, the bench players, even the manager pitched in.

It was usually our manager that collected ticket money. We did well to get enough for uniforms, bats, and balls. On a good day, there would be some money left over for the players too. But our families came and all the fans brought food. After the game, tables were set up and there was good food to share with both teams.

Sometimes, we took a road trip. We knew we could play baseball with anyone, but getting somewhere was never easy. If it was too far for the mules or horses to pull a wagon, we would go in some trucks, a bunch of us riding in the back of each one. When times got a little better, we traveled by bus. It wasn't like the buses you see today, though.

Our roads were rough and every time we hit a pothole it would bounce you around in your seat. The springs were worn out and the bus was old anyway. In the heat of the day or going up a hill, the bus was likely to overheat. We always carried extra water. While we waited for the radiator to cool, some players sat in the bus and slept, some of us went out and played catch on the highway. That's what I did. I always went out and helped the pitchers to loosen up their arms.

Whatever town we was playing in, we had to be ready to play when we got there. If it was a long ways and a day game, we rode all night. The seats were uncomfortable and it was hard to sleep. We didn't have much money for a hotel. Even if we had money it wouldn't make any difference. The hotels were whites only. After a night's ride, we would be pretty tired out.

After a game, we might have some money. On that bus, it was hot and dusty, and we sometimes stopped at a restaurant. We would choose one of us to go in, usually a rookie. He had to ask, "We got a team on the bus. We're hungry and we have money to pay. Can we eat in your restaurant?"

Now the answer was always no. But there were different ways of saying no. If the words and the tone wasn't mean—"Sorry, son, but we can't serve colored"—we would ask the next question.

"Can you make us up some sandwiches in the kitchen to take out to the bus?" Now most often, they said yes to that. We paid good money, the same prices, but we just couldn't eat inside.

But sometimes, and you could almost tell when you walked in the door, the answer was different. I remember once when it was my turn to go in. "What's the matter, you can't read the sign, *Whites Only*?" Those signs were everywhere and they was the only words I knew by heart. Fact was, I knew what those signs meant, but I really couldn't read. Course, I knew that I would get a beating for talking back if I said that.

In a loud voice, so everyone at the counter could hear, he said, "We don't serve niggers here." I just nodded and said, "Thank you."

Even with money in our pockets, we could be hungry on the long ride home to Marshall. Most folks were nicer than that, but the thing was, we never knew. I just hated when I was the one that had to ask.

Our first baseman, Hank Richards, loved to drive. I think he even had a license. By the 1920s they started charging for a license. I believe it cost two bits, but you had to pay that each year. Back then, a lot of folks couldn't or wouldn't pay and just never had a license.

Hank did most of the driving. But we all helped, especially on an all-night ride. Sometimes, when the weather was hot, one of those all-day rides could be rough too. Sammy wasn't a regular starter, but he could play anywhere in the infield. He worked in a garage, so when the bus broke, he pulled out his box of tools. Cars and buses were simpler then. Bailing wire or electrician's tape could fix a lot. If that didn't work, we could usually get the parts we needed at a gas station. Some of the game money we took in had to go to buy gas. In those days, gas cost less than twenty cents a gallon, but that was a lot then.

Those rides were tough and we was happy to roll out of the bus. There would be drinking fountains, colored and white. There could be the whole team, eighteen of us, waiting for some water at the colored fountain, and the white fountain next to it be empty. Now those fountains were the same; only the colored fountain, they never cleaned and kept up.

The rest rooms was kind of like that too. There would be a colored and white bathroom. It was easy to see that the manager had his help keep the white one to looking nice and pleasant. The colored rest rooms, they didn't bother with them, seemed like they hardly ever cleaned them for us. But some stations only had one rest room. Then you had to walk out to the woods behind the station.

That's right, we were grown men, but they would shame us like that. Even then, we knew that wasn't right. I remember our center-fielder, Johnny, same name as my brother. He never heard of civil rights, but we all had our pride. I heard him ask the attendant, "Where the colored rest room at?"

That man pushed up his baseball cap like he was thinking. "Gee, I guess we don't have one."

He pointed toward the gas pumps where the bus was. "Boy, it looks like you'll just have to get back on that bus and try your luck down the highway."

That gas station man was grinning and turned toward the soda pop machine. He was showing off for the half a dozen white men sipping Dr Peppers or Nehis. I could see the veins on Johnny's neck bulge, but he just nodded. Then, instead of heading to the bus, he began walking to the rest room.

I wasn't the only one to see that. I guess, 'cause of that man's tone and loud voice, everybody was watching. In a way, I suppose that put Johnny's pride on the line. A couple of players and the manager ran over toward Johnny.

The gas station man shouted, "Break the law here at my station, I'll call the sheriff. You just see if I will."

You could tell it was just what he had been waiting for too. Our manager was talking to Johnny, trying to cool him down. But Johnny wasn't going to have none of it and pushed his hand from his shoulder. There were three players in front of him now. Johnny was a big man. An easygoing type, he was angry now and pushed his teammates aside.

The gas station man yelled, "I mean it. The sheriff gonna throw you in jail, all of you."

The rest of the players started piling off the bus. Half the team had grabbed on to Johnny and was pushing him back toward the bus. There wasn't no one who didn't understand how he felt. But we knew if Johnny broke the law, the sheriff and his men were gonna make us all pay. He'd haul us to jail and maybe even have a beating in store for us.

Our manager had already paid for gas and I thanked God that this was one of those times the bus started right up with just a couple of cranks. We were a ways down the highway before we rested easy. Even so, in a few miles, we turned off and took an older, slower road that would loop back into the highway before Marshall. We didn't break the law but no telling if the sheriff would come out to bring us in or something. Or worse yet, some of those good old boys that was sipping Dr Peppers might follow us in trucks and see what they could do.

Still, every one of us loved to play baseball and didn't let the rest of it get in the way. We played some good teams. The crowds were good, often bigger than what you might expect for semipro. There weren't no TVs then and even movies weren't so common. Baseball was the game and the thing to come and see.

The game was simple then. There weren't no designated hitters or relief pitchers. The pitcher just did his best and knew he had to last nine innings. Nothing fancy to it either. The pitcher was going to go with his best stuff and challenge the hitter. For most of them, that was a fastball. That's what the fans wanted to see: the pitcher taking his best shot against a hitter who didn't back down either.

Companies had their own teams. So it might be a mill or a feed store that sponsored a team. You would see the name on the back of the uniform. That's how we got our uniforms. Along with the cigarettes, those same companies had their names on the ballpark billboards too.

We mostly played other colored teams, but we were good enough that we drew some white fans who just liked to watch good baseball. Sometimes, in the small towns, we might play against a white team. It was still the same game and that didn't change things. But sometimes it felt just a little different. It was more a feeling, something in the air. I could sense it from the fans.

Back then, those white boys didn't want to lose to a colored team. I guess it was fair to say that we wouldn't mind beating a white team either. Of course, we knew that if we were a better team, we weren't to make a show about that. It wouldn't be smart to rub it in. We always played to win, but just stuck to baseball.

I remember one game, the town wasn't even on the map, it was that small. But they had some stands at the fairgrounds, and they had a pretty decent crowd. Seems they had a boy with a strong arm. Even among those big farm kids, he sort of stood out. He worked with his daddy, who was a blacksmith, and he had big arms and powerful shoulders.

That town didn't have much going for it. But they saw Major League written all over him and they took pride in that. We heard the talk. When we watched him warming up, we saw a good fastball. I had been catching long enough to judge a fastball just by the sound. That ball had a real pop to it when it hit the leather.

Still, I knew that Major League pitching needed more than just speed; control and a good curveball had to be there too. Walter

Johnson, maybe with the best fastball in the game, could drive a nail in a fence post from sixty feet. Anyways, that's what people said. And I just didn't see that control in that kid. Matter of fact, he was wild sometimes. The catcher would have to jump out of his crouch and leap for a high one.

I mentioned that to Artis, our second baseman, who was standing next to me. He was our leadoff hitter and liked to study the pitchers as much as I did. He noticed it too. "Do you think that's for show, 'cause some of those pitches could put a dent in your head?"

In those days, we didn't wear baseball helmets. It wasn't hard to figure that a 95 mph fastball that was up too high would leave a permanent headache if you even got up from the dirt. Still, it could of been for show. If he made us think he was wild, the batter might step back from the plate and not have the right concentration either.

I said, "No, he don't look that smart. He's just wild."

Artis laughed. "Probably, but I don't know what's worse to face: a wild pitcher or a smart one."

We both laughed. "With that fastball, I don't know either."

Johnny was pitching for us. I guess he sensed the feelings of the crowd and it threw him off. At the start of the first inning, Johnny had his fastball too, but he hit the first batter and walked the second. I walked out to the mound. "What's the matter?"

Johnny shrugged.

"Well, pretend like we are just playing out in the pasture at Marshall."

Johnny looked out toward the stands. "That don't look like our pasture in Marshall to me."

"Yeah, you got a point there. But, hey, there's no pressure on you. No matter what, that scout ain't coming to look at you. He's out here to look at Red."

Johnny said, "Yeah, I guess that has to be so."

"You know it is," I said.

Word was that the man sitting by first base was a scout for St. Louis, out to scout a pitcher. Back then, if that pitcher had a good day, he might get a contract offer with a hundred-dollar bonus. But even more than that, he would get a ticket out of Texas and maybe make it to a big team like St. Louis.

"Heck, I could hit four home runs and you could pitch a no-hitter today. If he *is* a scout, he would sure notice, but you know it can't make any difference."

Johnny nodded. "Yeah, the big leagues is the white leagues."

"You got that right. Just relax now. Slow it down, get it over the plate, and let the fielders give you a hand."

I guess Johnny got my message. The next pitch was a deep fly to center field. It was a sacrifice fly and moved the runners to second and third with only one out. A ground ball scored a run, but now it was two outs with a runner on third. Johnny got his first strikeout

114

to end the inning and I could see he would do okay.

In the bottom of the first, their pitcher had his stuff, all right. The speed was there, but he also kept it down. Artis tried to lay down a bunt, but they nailed him at first. In between hitters the crowd was shouting for "Red." When you saw his red hair, it wasn't hard to figure his name.

We did get a hit that inning, but it was followed by two strike-outs. Up through the middle innings, both Johnny and their man, Red, had their stuff. It was a pitchers' battle with the score still at 1–0. That's maybe not so exciting for the fans, but it's good baseball.

Since the first inning, we had been laying back off Red's first pitches, making him throw a lot of fastballs and taking him deep in the count. We got some hits but couldn't string them together. Remember, they didn't have relief pitchers then and our plan was to be patient. Sure enough, by the fifth inning, his pitches were up. We had already seen his best stuff. He kept looking over toward that scout but he was getting tired.

We led off the fifth with a single. I took him to full count. That last pitch was a ball. Good pitch; it was close, but it was low and outside. I trotted to first. You should of heard the boos. I don't even want to repeat the words they was saying to that umpire, but they was cussing him good.

Our first base coach said, "Way to go. Good eye, George."

I nodded toward the stands. "They don't think so."

It was getting pretty ugly. Coach said, "Yeah, it's a home crowd, all right. They just trying to send that umpire a message."

Well, my walk didn't matter since I got nailed at second base in a double play. But I guess the crowd was loosened up that inning. With a hot day and lots of beer, they let the umpire hear it.

Red was definitely tiring, though. We led off the sixth with a hit. It's never good to walk a team's number-nine hitter, but they did. Some of the pitches were in the dirt. When the runners were moving up, the fans let the umpire have it for that. The boos were even louder, but now they were throwing apples and garbage and such things at the ump and out on the field.

I wasn't sure if "Kill the umpire" was maybe something that was meant half serious when they shouted it. I was in the dugout and heard our manager say, "I wonder if that umpire lives here in this town?"

I figure he must have. After play started again, anything that didn't actually roll in the dirt was called a strike. We got one more hit, an RBI double, but there were two more outs on called strikes. There was a force-out at first to end the inning. I've got to admit that that one was close enough to call either way. We didn't get the call, but at least we were tied 1–1 at the end of the inning.

After the sixth inning, the scout left the

stands. I guess he had seen enough. But the crowd, which had been hoping to have a Major Leaguer from their town, was angry. They wouldn't let up on the umpire. So, in the seventh and eighth innings, Johnny couldn't throw a strike, at least according to the umpire. He walked some players each inning. I threw a runner out trying to steal second base and we had a double play in both the sixth and the seventh. So nobody scored and we were still at 1–1 going into the ninth.

That scout didn't return and they were mad. When we took the field in the ninth, we heard the *N* word. Now, fans were sometimes tough in those days, but even so, we didn't take kindly to that. We dared not say anything, but we were getting mad too.

Pitches right over the knees were called balls and Johnny led off the ninth with two walks. He started throwing down the middle so they had to swing. We got some outs on a fly ball and two line drives but not before they had scored two more runs.

We knew any pitch against us was a strike so we went up ready to swing. We got two singles sandwiched around a strikeout and the crowd got ugly. Our third baseman moved up but a runner was forced out at first. We got another single from our left fielder, Mattie, and the score was 3–2 with a runner on first and second.

I came out ready to swing. First pitch was a fastball and I sent it to right field. I was safe at first and the score was tied. The crowd was getting uglier. I tried to block it from my ears but couldn't. Johnny, our center fielder, was at the plate. He heard everything too. I saw his neck muscles tense up and he connected with a big cut. It went deep to center.

I started running. From second base I looked to the third-base coach for the sign. I expected to be waved on. The runners in front had scored, which meant we had won the game. He pointed to the stands and then toward the bus. I got it. Our bench had already cleared and was boarding the bus. I was the only one from our team left on the field. I skipped third and ran straight past home plate as those fans started down on the field.

I was the last one on the bus. As we were leaving, we heard a few rocks hit the side of the bus. But no problem. It wasn't so much win or lose but our pride. And we still had that. I did get a lot of ribbing for skipping third base and heading straight to home, though.

I remember that game, but most folks were good people and they were nice to us. Some of the parks had lights. By June we had hot nights, and outside at the ballpark was the place to be. The lights weren't great then and it was harder to follow the ball at night. But to me that was baseball: a warm night, the smell of popcorn, and the sound of the ball hitting the bat.

At the plate, I was always patient. A player could learn a lot just by watching the pitcher. A lot of pitchers had patterns. So if I was wanting a fastball, I would watch and see how often he threw a fastball or if it always followed a curveball, things like that. I was a line-drive hitter. I wasn't the fastest runner, but I could usually put it into play.

When I was catching, I made sure to mix up the pitches a lot. Like I said, a catcher has to do a lot of thinking. I always had to know what that hitter could do. I had a good arm, but we played against a lot of teams that could do the hit-and-run and steal a lot of bases. I couldn't get them out every time, but if they was gonna steal on me, they had to earn it.

Today, it seems that players play baseball to make money. Back around the end of the World War and in the 1920s, players would quit baseball to make more money. Almost any job would pay better than what a ballplayer earned then. I guess in the big leagues you could do somewhat better. But, of course, that wasn't open to the colored.

The pay wasn't nothing like the same, but we had some good players in the Negro Leagues. I never had to hit against Satchel Paige, but I hear that he was one of the best. He was old when he made it to the majors. A lot of players, some mighty good ones, never got the chance at all.

I played ball as much as I could, but there was always work to do and that came first. I still worked at the mill, whenever the demand was up. It was steady pay. With baseball you just never knew. When I wasn't at the mill, I knew that I was needed on our farm. I just helped as much as I could, and hoped that maybe someday I could join more than a semipro team.

I was a good worker and seemed like if the mill needed anybody, they kept me on. I started at the mill in 1914. In 1917, a lot of workers were heading off to war. The war was far away. I did meet some soldiers that was heading off to chase Pancho Villa, though. They went with a soldier named General Pershing. I know that because we had to mill some boards for the floor of that general's open tent. The foot soldiers could sleep in the mud. They went to Mexico, right close by. Never heard if they found him, though.

I was about nineteen years old. I didn't know much about the war. But from the way people talked, I thought I might be going too. The mill owner changed my birthday on a piece of paper. I wondered about that. But my boss said, "Put your X here, George. You're a good worker and I can't afford to lose you."

Even then, I knew that you don't argue with your boss. I put my X on that paper he had. That kept me at his mill and out of the army. I guess the paper that he had would of made me seem younger, too young for the World War.

CHAPTER 9

New York, Sept. 10—This is Pershing Day, and with General Pershing at the head of the crowd…the first division of regulars marched down Fifth Avenue today, the crowning military spectacle of the World War for New York. Full panoplied for battle, 25,000 soldiers paraded the flower of the American army overseas. Behind the stalwart doughboys rumbled field artillery of every type, followed by divisional trains…. Never in the city's history has such a multitude turned out for any pageant. It seemed that New York was there with half of the nation besides.

—*The Marshall Morning News*,
September 11, 1919

From the mountain of papers, Richard handed me another article. He seems to like all this history stuff. So, I wasn't surprised to see it was another article about the war. He asked me if I'd ever seen the posters then that said, "Put the Kaibosh on the Kaiser."

I said, "Son, you forgot that I couldn't read then."

But the fact is, I was on the outside of things. There were all kinds of posters in those days; they covered the telephone and telegraph poles. I just never could read them.

I remember the parade in Marshall for the

soldiers. They did look fine in their uniforms as they marched through town. Some were marching, some were on horseback. There were some bands. It was a fine parade.

I remember soldiers coming home and then there wasn't no more talk about the World War. Seemed like it just come and gone, at least in Texas.

I did know one man that came back from the war. He was a colored man, name of Moses. He was a bit older than me, but I had talked to him a few times at the cotton mill, before he left for the army. I saw him there again when he got back.

Before it was always, "Hi. How you doing, George?" And that would be that. He was a quiet one but a nice man. Somehow he seemed different now.

It was right after the parade and I said, "Did you see the parade yesterday?"

"No. I didn't and I didn't march in it neither."

Now, all the soldiers that were marching were white and it never occurred to me that he would have been in the parade.

I nodded. I could see he expected something more and I said, "Well, it was a nice parade, good music too."

I didn't mean to, but I could see that somehow I had made him mad.

"I have the same uniform too, but I can't march in Texas. I marched in some parades in France, though."

"Well, that's good," I said. "I guess here we

didn't have enough colored soldiers for a parade."

"No," Moses said. "You got it wrong. We didn't have a colored parade there. We marched in the same parades, colored and white, side by side."

"Yeah, they do parades that way there?"

"Oh, it ain't just parades," Moses said.

"That right, what else is different over there?"

Moses said, "Everything is different. In Paris, that's a big city—"

"Bigger than Marshall?"

"Oh, yeah, way bigger. I could walk anywhere, eat in any restaurant I wanted to, and the people would treat me nice."

"That's good that they have a colored section in every restaurant," I said.

"No, no," Moses said to me. "They don't have no colored sections. I could go to any restaurant and sit wherever I wanted!

"They had drinking fountains all through the city. No white fountains, no colored fountains. All the water fountains were for everybody."

"That's nice," I said. "And the bathrooms too?"

"You got that right," Moses said.

"I guess this ain't Paris then."

Moses laughed, but in an angry kind of way.

I said, "I got to be checking at the mill and collecting for my cotton. Been nice seeing you. Welcome back."

I could see that he was going to have a hard time in Marshall now. I didn't shake hands with him since I wasn't sure how. His right arm was cut off at the elbow and the sleeve pinned to his shirt. I didn't know if it was okay to shake his left hand instead. Neither of us mentioned it, though I had noticed it first thing.

That was 1919. I was twenty-one that year. On my birthday, my father talked to me. Eighty years later, I remember every word he said to me.

We were out walking the orchard, checking how the trees were doing through the winter. The apple trees we had planted years earlier were bigger now. We stood beneath one of the trees that I remembered the two of us planting together. It was just a little sapling then. Now it was three or four weeks away from first blossom, but with heavy, solid branches. The ground was soft and there was an early thaw. My birthday is January 19, but I remember it was an especially nice day.

We were at the high point of the orchard and looked out across the farm. My father said, "George, when we planted these trees, we only had forty acres and most of it rock."

He pointed out past the barn. "We've got three hundred and twenty acres and you been working here all your life to help us make it produce something. Every paycheck you earned went to me. I am your father, and that was your due. But today you are twenty-one. From now on, what you do is for yourself."

It was nice to hear, but it made me feel awkward. I smiled a little bit and kicked at a clod of dirt.

"Son, you ready to be on your own now?"

"Yeah, Papa, I expect so."

"Good." Papa got a serious look and said, "Always remember, a man is born to die. A man is born to die."

He looked at me, but I didn't know what to say. He went on, "You just don't know when that moment will come so just always be doing the right thing. Don't do no wrong and you will make your father proud."

"I will, Papa. I'll remember."

"That's good," he said. "Today you're twenty-one. You're on your own now."

It wasn't like there was somewhere special or even anywhere I wanted to go. So, I stayed on and kept working at the mill. Only difference, once I was twenty-one, I went and got my own silver disk each week. Cashed it in for myself too. I never had any real money like that before. I had been there for a while and, with some raises, it was more than $1.50 a week, sometimes closer to $2. It all depended on how much overtime; anything over twelve hours a day was a little extra. It worked for me and I just let them figure out the numbers.

That winter of 1919 was the year so many people died. There was a terrible flu going around and the pneumonia took a lot of folks, especially older ones. Everybody in our family stayed healthy, though. Seemed to hit worse in town than out on the farms. A worker at the mill lost both his mother and father. I kept working and did extra time to help out there.

With some of my wages, I would bring home a dress pattern for my mother. Sometimes, I just gave her some money to get something. She said, "I don't like to take something from my son."

I said, "Mama, it's a gift. You can't deny me doing that."

When I was in town, I might get some penny candies for the little ones. There wasn't anything I needed, but I never had any money before and I enjoyed buying some gifts. Still, I had watched how my father always managed with what he earned. So, I saved some money too.

When spring weather came, there was good hunting and fishing to be had. Nothing better to me than being out on the lake at first light, watching the ripples from the fish feeding on the bug hatch. There had been a good rain and a lot of game that year. I knew the woods and every canyon by then. But that spring, I got to feeling restless for the first time.

I had never been anywhere much past Marshall; no need to. I didn't leave the farm much except to go to work and play baseball. There were few cars then and we didn't have many visitors either. We could grow almost everything that we needed right on our farm. There was money in my pocket and nothing holding me. I talked to Papa and he said, "There is nothing wrong with life in East Texas, but if you need to see the world, that's fine too."

On Sundays, after church, the preacher always had supper with one of the families. Papa always said, "The preacher comes here most often because he likes your mother's cooking the best."

I would say that was so. And when the preacher came out, Mama always cooked extra. He did have an appetite and the younger ones watched closely. They didn't take any food till he was clearly finished. Not meaning to be disrespectful, but some folks said, "The preacher tries to eat enough on Sunday to carry him to midweek. Then that leaves him a few days to start building up his appetite for the next Sunday."

He was a nice man, though. Matter of fact, he was out a few days after I talked with Papa. He had his usual blessing and then added, "Lord, protect young George on his travels. Help him to do well and to help others. Keep him from temptation and lead him to do the right thing. When the time is right, return him safely to his family and to those that love him."

The next morning, Papa shook hands with me, man to man. Mama gave me a hug and said, "You be good."

It wasn't much past first light, but my friend L.D. was over in a wagon that his brother was driving into Marshall for some seed. L.D. had got wind of my going and decided he would come too. Now, I had planned on going by myself and didn't know if his coming was such a good idea. But there wasn't no real reason to say no either; it was just a feeling that I had.

Having worked in the mill for a while, I had saved some money. I kept just a little bit in my pocket and the rest I kept down in my boot. The "boot money" was my way of planning for the days ahead. I had left enough in my pocket for a train ticket, but before we got to Marshall, I found out that L.D. didn't have nothing. That changed things right off and like plenty of folks then, I could see that I was going to be riding the rails.

Neither one of us had ever done it before but that didn't cause us no concern. Both of us were of a mind that we figured we could do just about anything. What with timber and cattle, Marshall had gotten to be a pretty fair-sized place by then and it had a decent-sized rail yard. L.D.'s brother dropped us off just before the yard. If we had thought as to what we were doing, it would have been on the other side of the station past town.

But no matter, it wasn't long before a train was coming and I couldn't have been more excited. It was all just perfect. The train was slowing down. We came out from the bushes and started running along beside it. From nowhere it seemed, a few other men were doing exactly the same thing. We picked out an open boxcar and made our move. We grabbed on to a bar on the car and sort of pulled up and jumped at the same time.

What makes it all so exciting is the way the train wheels keep rolling just beneath, ready to slice a body up if you don't have a strong grip or make the smallest of a mistake in your jump. And don't let anybody tell you that didn't happen sometimes. It did. But we did fine. Nothing was going to stop us.

Sitting in the boxcar, rolling into the station like that, I felt like a king. It had a lot more style than walking or being in a wagon pulled by a mule. I saw one of the rail yard bulls and scooted back a bit from the door. Not L.D., though. He laughed and, sitting on the edge, he waved his legs off the side. I said, "L.D., get yourself back from the door; that bull has a gun. Don't be making fun of him."

Just about then a shot rang out. "See." L.D. laughed. "That's all for show. They aim high just to scare us. Besides, he couldn't hit nothing anyway."

"Maybe so, but get yourself in here."

Two more shots rang out. L.D. fell off the car and started tumbling down an embankment. Not even thinking, I jumped out after him. As soon as I hit the ground, I started rolling and kept low to the ground. I caught up with L.D. and looked across the yard. The bull was already holstering his gun and walking away. He had proved his point, I guess.

A bullet had smashed L.D.'s knee. He was rolling on the ground and screaming. Some hobos had seen it all and jumped off their cars too. It wasn't all that long before someone found a wagon. We got L.D. to a hospital. It was the wrong one, though, and they sent us over to another one that served colored. He lost a leg at the knee.

I visited L.D. at the hospital a few times. At the end of the week, I told him I was heading out again. I said, "I ain't gonna wait for you. I'm leaving and gonna travel on my own from now on."

After that, I think my mama was hoping that I wasn't going to travel no more. But if so, she kept that thought to herself. But when she told me to be careful, I knew what she was thinking. I promised I would and left quick before she got to crying. I had a bedroll, some flour, some potatoes, and some biscuits already made up. Except for two bits that I had in my pocket, I put some paper money and a few silver dollars in my boot. I started walking. It felt good to just walk and I kept on going. I had never even been out of Harrison County before and I had the feeling that the whole world was before me. When darkness came, I found a dry spot off from the road and unwrapped the biscuits my mother had made for me.

I could hear the crickets and some frogs, but nothing else. I felt alone and for some reason thought back to the Littles'; how lonely I felt at first when no one was around. Now it didn't matter. When there were people, I enjoyed it. When I was by myself, I liked that too. I had learned some good lessons in those four years at the Littles'.

I thought about a fire but let it go. A colored man alone on the road didn't want to draw a lot of attention to himself. I knew enough to stay out of trouble. By the afternoon of the next day, I had gone farther than I had ever been from home. I had walked by the last farms that I recognized. Knowing it was all new from there made me just want to see the rest of the world.

Toward day's end, I came to an encampment by the railroad tracks. I was just a couple of miles shy of the next station. Back then, there were hobos that rode the rails and lived along the tracks in between times. I didn't plan to stay, but when some of them waved I stopped by the fire. They weren't bad folk, but I know my mother and father raised me to work hard and have more pride in myself. Besides that it was nicer and cleaner out in the bush than in the encampments they made.

Funny thing was, though, poor as they were, they were always generous. If one of them had any food, no one went hungry. They offered me a bit of rabbit that was cooking on the fire. To be polite, I sat down and joined them. They were talking about the vagrancy laws.

Back in those days, they arrested someone that just hung around and didn't work. Some towns was pretty strong with those laws and made life pretty unfriendly for a man without a job. I don't know if that was good or bad, but I knew I wasn't going to be arrested. I always worked. Seemed like I always had a job. The pay wasn't always great, but in that case I could work two jobs. There wasn't no work that I wouldn't do, nothing that I was afraid of.

Some of the men were white and some were colored. Texas wasn't such a well-off place in those days. I never met anybody that was rich. But as bad as things were, down by the tracks was at the bottom of things. But they were together and got along. I guess poor white and poor colored had enough in common with just being poor.

When there was some money, then it was the same old story. It was rich and poor, white and colored, us and them. So, in a way it had a nice feeling down there without all that. Still, I felt sorry for those men. It couldn't feel good knowing that a whole town didn't want you, that they would throw you in jail for being there, or put you on a chain gang because you were without a job. So, they moved around to stay ahead of trouble. Some of them were never settled, I expect. But they had been to places that I had never seen. When they were talking, I listened closely.

It was just turning dusk and I could make out the man talking across the fire. Think he was the one who introduced himself as Billy. He was a white man, with a face that spoke of hard times. But he was clearly the oldest and people listened to him. In those days, no matter where you were, age carried some respect.

Billy had all his hair but it had turned white. His face was lined and toughened in the sun. I expect he had worked outside a lot or maybe he had just lived outdoors like he was doing now. He was one of those fellows that talked with his hands as much as his voice. As he moved his arms, the shadows were big and jumped around behind him. While I gnawed on my rabbit, I watched as much as I listened.

"Down by Galveston, you set up camp on the beach. The fish, they were this big."

I grinned as he stretched his arms wide. Another man, I think named Ralph, said, "Right, Billy. How come I've never seen such big fish?"

It was easy to see that he was just trying to get Billy riled up. And he did.

"You don't believe me, huh?"

"Well, I have to admit, it makes me wonder."

Billy said, "Well, it was actually bigger than that, it's just that my arms won't stretch any farther."

Ralph was clearly enjoying himself and said, "How about that."

Billy said, "That's not all. If the fish weren't biting you could just go down by where the boats unloaded and pick up some shrimp that fell onto the dock. Haven't been there for a couple of years, but it's that easy."

Another man, I don't remember his name, asked, "Are they rough on the vagrancy law down there?"

Billy nodded. "You out and about without work and they'll haul you in. Seems that there's never much work there either, unless, of course, you own a fishing boat."

To that group, he may as well have been talking about owning the king's yacht. Everything they had was right with them in that camp. A colored man spoke up and we looked toward him. "There ain't no fish, but I just been to where there's work to be had."

I listened close and so did the others. "It's hard work and low pay, though, but there's plenty of work," he said. At that, I could see most of them losing interest right quick. Not me.

"What is it?" I asked.

"Building levees."

"How does that go?"

"It goes likes this: hard work, in the hot sun, all day."

"Harder than picking cotton?" I asked.

"Oh, yeah, you be moving dirt all day. That's heavier than cotton."

"And there's jobs," I asked.

"Always. People come and go but don't last long. The work is hard."

"Where this be?" I asked.

"Along the Mississippi, a little south of Memphis. That's in Tennessee."

Standing up, I threw my rabbit bones in the fire and wiped the grease off on my pant legs.

"Now, where you be going off to?" the man that had just been talking asked.

"Memphis."

"Memphis! Ain't you been listening to what I just said?"

"Sure." I grinned. "Heard every word of it too."

They all just looked at me and I said, "Gotta

go. Want to walk to the station before it's pitch dark."

Billy said, "Why don't you wait till morning? The *City of New Orleans* rolls through here in the early morning. I'm not even sure there's anything to Memphis tonight and, besides, that's the best train for jumping."

"Well, I..."

"He's right," said the fellow from Memphis. "They got the best boxcars on the line," he added with a laugh.

"That be fine. If there's no Memphis train tonight, I can just get going in the right direction."

I had never been just free like that with no one else to take care of.

"Thanks for the dinner," I said and started off toward the station.

"When's the next train for Memphis?" I asked the ticket master.

"Not till morning," he said. "But I'll tell you right now the yardmaster don't cotton to riding the rails. A fellow got killed last week and we shut down for the morning. You picked the wrong station, boy."

He had a nasty tone to back him up, but I was feeling too good to let it bother me.

"Well, anything going in that direction?" I said.

"Boy, didn't you just hear what I said about riding the rails at this station?"

"Yes, sir."

Reaching down into my boot, I pulled up some money. I enjoyed his surprise in seeing

135

a colored man with money, but I was smart enough not to let it show.

"Texarkana," he said in a nicer tone now. He pointed to the train on the siding. Looking at his watch, he said, "That will be leaving in about forty-five minutes from now."

"That on the way to Memphis?"

"Yeah, it's about halfway there. From there, you can catch another train on Tuesday to Memphis."

"How much?"

"That will be $2.35 third class."

Though I wasn't great with my numbers, I handed him a bill like I was sure of things so that he wouldn't think to try to cheat me on the change.

He waved me toward the benches. "You wait there. It boards in twenty minutes. The colored car is at the back."

I acted like I knew what I was about. Matter of fact, I was feeling pretty fine. I was too excited to just sit like the man said, so I picked up my bedroll and walked around.

It was a small station, though I didn't know that at the time. The ticket master's office was the only building. The benches were under a covered roof, but it was a warm night with no wind to it and it wasn't even needed. I wandered over to a big map that was posted between some poles. Maps I had seen back home were not this type.

Over by the cotton mill, I would see men drawing a map in the street with a stick to show where they had bought some new land for cotton. Or they might be showing someone how to get to a farm where a fellow had a mule for sale or some such thing. But they didn't write in names. They marked in rivers, maybe a crossroads or made a picture of a general store. It was all in the dust, but there were some good mapmakers in Marshall that could do it that way.

I studied this one for a while. It was a good-looking map. I figured the black lines with the little marks through them were for the railroad tracks. There was a big red arrow that I figured might of meant the station, but I couldn't be sure. I tried to figure if Texarkana were on that map. Maybe Memphis was on it too. That would be something. But right then, I figured that just about anything was possible.

Some white folks came over to look at the map and I went back to my seat. They were pointing, probably to where they were headed, and the man and the woman walked off toward the front of the train. We weren't boarding yet, but the man had pulled out his watch and he seemed to think it would be leaving soon.

I didn't own a watch, but I could tell that was so. The train was building up steam. It wasn't long before the porters started to open the doors. The conductor stepped down to the lower steps and shouted, "All aboard, for Woodlawn, Jefferson, Lassiter, Hughes Springs, Linden, Red Hill, Maud, Wake Village, and Texarkana."

He was good too. He had it all come in one breath. At the end he stretched Texarkana out long like he was holding on to a note. The conductor probably just did that for style and not because Texarkana was both in Arkansas and Texas. But either way, by daylight I would be leaving Texas for the first time in my life.

I climbed up the steps. The porter looked me over right quick but didn't bother to take my bedroll for me. He was real nice, though. He said, "Welcome aboard the Texas and Southern Railroad," as if he owned it himself.

I liked that and handed him my ticket. I was proud to have a paying ticket and not be riding the rails. Always paid for my ticket when I could. That was the honest thing to do, from the way I see it anyway.

He punched my ticket and said, "All the way to Texarkana, huh?"

I nodded. "Well, that's good. Take a seat and there will be someone coming through selling sandwiches and cakes in a little while."

There were some passengers from earlier stops, but there was plenty of space and I found an empty seat for myself. I looked around. Mostly there were families, some men on their own, and a few soldiers too. In 1920, two years after the World War, the soldiers was still traveling about. Actually, some of the colored just stayed in the service: A few of the colored units were kept going and it was a paying job. Everyone was colored and I knew I was in the right car.

Some people was pulling out pillows and blankets. The porter actually was passing out pillows to rent. I shrugged, but watched him at his work. I wondered if the porters slept on the night trains. Back then and for many years, all the porters were colored. Being a porter was one of the best jobs that colored folk could hope to get. The pay was better than most jobs that they would find. Those jobs were hard to find, though.

I wasn't going to pay money for a pillow, but I wasn't planning to sleep anyway. My first time on a train and no way was I going to miss it. I held tight waiting for the lurch, but it wasn't as bad as I expected. The rolling motion and the clacking sound on the track made me feel I was really going somewhere. In Woodlawn and Jefferson, more folks got on. The stations looked pretty much the same and they were quiet at night. We waited for a while at each stop and then the conductor came through to punch tickets.

I just liked it, the idea of everybody going somewhere. I was a part of that now and watched closely. I saw everything that was out the window and didn't even notice a man till he nudged me on the shoulder as we were pulling out of Hughes Springs. He pointed to the empty spot on my bench and I nodded at him. In a quiet voice, for folks were sleeping, I said, "Sure, help yourself. Ain't nobody sitting there."

He put a suitcase up on the rack above us. "Name is Charles," he said as he gave me his hand.

"George."

"Where you heading to?"

"I'm going to Texarkana tonight and then on to Memphis."

"Yeah, I'm just going as far as Texarkana myself."

I had never been this far from home. As excited as I was on top, I was a little scared underneath. I looked at Charles with interest. He looked to be about my age, maybe a little older, but he seemed to know what he was about. He dressed nice, clean clothes, store-bought too. He had his own suitcase for more stuff.

I asked him, "You been to Texarkana before?"

"Sure, been there lots of times."

"Nice place?"

"Oh, yeah, I've always liked Texarkana."

I nodded at him. I knew I would like it too, as if I had been riding trains all my life. "You work in Texarkana?"

"No, but I got connections and it's always worth my while to stop there."

I didn't have a clue, but I nodded as if I knew what he was talking about.

"Stick with me, George, I'll take good care of you and show you around some before you catch your train to Memphis."

He took his jacket off for a pillow, set his seat back a bit, and said, "It's a long ride to Texarkana; I'm going to catch some sleep."

Not me. I was going somewhere and I didn't want to miss a thing.

CHAPTER 10

PRESIDENT IS PLEASED WITH TRIP RESULTS
MAKES SPEECHES FROM REAR PLATFORM
AS HE CROSSES DAKOTA PLAINS

Aboard President Wilson's Train, Sept. 10—President Wilson made several rear platform speeches to cheering crowds today while his train was enroute westward across the North Dakota plains. His only set speech for the treaty was at Bismarck. The next scheduled stop is Billings, Montana, tomorrow. The President told crowds today that his week of travel convinced him that the nation stands together for an international guarantee of peace.

—*The Marshall Morning News,*
September 11, 1919

I liked to hear the porter call them out, but Linden and Red Hill looked pretty much like Lassiter and Hughes Springs before them. Hard to tell at night, but if anything those towns looked to be getting even smaller. They was big enough for a station, but not much bigger than what we called a whistle-stop. A whistle-stop was just a little platform by the track where people would stand and wave the train down. The train wouldn't even stop if there was no one there.

That's why the train was so slow. Even at night, that train made whistle-stops in places

141

where there was nothing but farms or a small mill. People would hold up a lantern to signal the engineer. Course, most folks couldn't afford a car, and besides there weren't no highways then. Electricity wasn't so common and the night was dark out there.

I had it in mind to see everything, but I fell asleep too. To this day, I never have seen Linden or Red Hill or Maud neither. If I had known I wouldn't be back in the next eighty years, I probably wouldn't of let myself sleep right through. Fact is, I didn't wake up till it was full light and we were a couple of hours before Wake Village.

Even then, it wasn't the light that woke me. The train came to a sudden stop. Now, all those stops during the night, I felt those, even noticed people getting on and off, but each time I fell back to sleep. This was different. I crashed into the seat in front of me. People that were on the aisles, some of them fell to the floor. The engineer had hit the brakes that hard.

It was a good thing too. Some dirt had sloughed off an embankment and some track had moved itself a bit. There was someone waiting ahead on the track and waved us to a stop. It looked like a flash flood had come through and just taken out too much soil. Some men were already out working with shovels and getting things patched up.

I got down to look around. There was nothing to be seen at either end of the tracks. In a couple hours, they started moving the rail back to its place. Those rails are heavy. Some passengers pitched in to help move it. I did.

We were rolling again before the sun was even warm. Charles looked at his watch. "The Memphis connection is leaving in an hour. We won't make that. You gonna have to take the midnight train."

"Suits me fine," I said. "If I travel at night, it just saves me having to find a place to sleep for the night."

"We'll still be in this morning. I know Texarkana. I'll show you around."

When we hit town, I stayed close by. "Texarkana, the town big enough to be in two states," he read from a big billboard that he pointed at on the station wall.

"Two states. What do you think about that?"

I said, "That's mighty fine. I've never been out of Texas before."

"Good. I know a cafe a few blocks down. We'll go have some lunch in Arkansas." He grinned.

Like in most cities, the black section of town was along the railroad tracks, so we didn't have too far to go. Everybody at Papa Joe's seemed to know Charles. He was good about that and told everyone, "This is George, a friend of mine."

We didn't have cafes this nice in Marshall. I wished I could of read the menu, but it wasn't a problem. I just said, "Sounds good. I'll have same as Charles but no coffee." Never did drink coffee. Never had the taste for it.

143

Texarkana was a big city, but the cooking was just as good as home. I ate while I listened to a friend of Charles that sat down. Now Charles, he introduced everybody else to me, but not this man, so I don't know his name. I just listened.

"All on the Arkansas side still?" Charles asked.

"Oh, yeah. There's a cockfight this afternoon at Ronnie's."

Charles nodded when the man said, "Oh, and there's a game at the usual place tonight, starts by dusk."

"See you there," Charles said and the man got up and left.

Papa Joe said we could leave our stuff, Charles's suitcase and my bedroll, at the cafe. We just put it behind the counter. If I was ever going back, I would check to see if they still had the pecan pie at Papa Joe's. It was the best. And then we walked that pie off. We went down past the farmers' market that most towns had back then. People were selling off the back of their wagons and a few of them off the back of their trucks. Still weren't a lot of those yet, but there were more and more trucks all the time. Made it a little easier to walk the streets since it cut down on horse manure.

From the market, we worked our way down some alleys that ran every which way. We was back to dirt road and it was all old wood-frame warehouses. Charles knocked at one. The door opened. The man didn't say anything but let us in. The floor was dirt and there was straw bales along the walls. When my eyes got used to the dark, I looked over toward a group of men gathered on the other side. I walked with Charles, who was already headed toward them.

We stopped at the edge of the circle. People was laying down money for a cockfight that was about to start. Charles nudged me. "Here's a tip. That one's smaller, but he's a fighter. I'm putting my money there."

He pulled some money off a roll of bills and laid it down. My money, I left in my boot. I didn't gamble. I thought about heading to the station, but my train wasn't till midnight and I wasn't sure of the way back anyway. Besides, I didn't know this town and a colored man just hanging about all day at the station could end up in trouble. So, I just figured the best thing was to stay put.

If you've never been to a cockfight, it's not a pretty show. Those roosters are bred for killing and I think they enjoy it too. They come in looking all fine and pretty. Each of them is carried under the arm of its owner. They are quiet and peaceful till the owner sets them in a circle. I don't know what it is, but after that all hell breaks loose. They are at each other from the get-go. Those birds seem to know why they is there. Their claws have been filed and sharpened and they use them for scratching and cutting.

It's not just the roosters that change either. The men that have been hanging about and joshing each other form themselves in a circle.

From then on, you couldn't find a more excited bunch. Every time the roosters drew blood, there was cheers and groans, so much so that you might of thought it was those men themselves that was getting all cut up.

The fight would start with those birds all in a panic, and the first blood seemed to get them going even more. But soon they get worn out and slow down. Then you can see a change in their eyes. They almost seem to know that one of them is going to die and soon it ain't so hard to see which one will be left standing. When that happens, the men seem to sense it too. Depending on where they put their bets, it brings on cheers or curses.

Since I had no money riding, I was in the back of the circle, just watching. With different birds, they had round after round. On most of the fights, I figured it right. To me it wasn't so much the size of the bird but its attitude and the speed that it looked to have. At least that's how I seen it, and if I had been betting, I would of been a winner more than not.

That wasn't true for everybody there, though. Some men won and then stayed long enough to lose their winnings. Seems to me that if they had been satisfied, they could have left happy. Some just lost straight off from the beginning. So, the crowd got smaller and the fighting just seemed to fade out. Seemed like there were a few winners, though. Charles came up to me smiling and laughing.

"Hey, you must bring good luck, George. You can come with me to these fights anytime."

Now, if you was asking me, one day was okay, but I don't think I would ever need to see it again. But Charles was nice about it and I just grinned.

"No, no, I mean it," he said. "Come on, let's get some dinner and I'm buying."

I recognized everything on the way back and it wasn't so hard as I had thought it might be. The market was shutting down; just a few trucks and wagons left. Papa Joe's was busy now, but Papa Joe came over and got us a table. Charles said that they made good ribs and he was right. I've had some just as good but nothing better. During our meal, Papa Joe sat down with us.

"Did you do better today?" Papa Joe asked.

"Oh, yeah," Charles said. "I did great. George here is good luck."

"Yeah, you gonna show me?" Papa Joe asked.

"Hey, don't you worry. I got something for you."

Charles pulled out a roll of bills that was bigger than when I saw it before. Peeling off some of it, he pushed a pile of money across the table to Papa Joe. "Here's to settle things," Charles said.

Papa Joe nodded, picked up the money, and tucked it behind his cooking apron.

Handing him a smaller pile of bills, Charles said, "And this is to say thank you."

Papa Joe grinned and the two of them shook hands. As he got up, he put that money in the apron too. "Looks like you'll be set for tonight."

"That's right. I'm in good shape."

"Good. Well, you can always check back with me, if you need to."

My bedroll was still behind the counter. This time I took it with me as I still had it in mind to catch the Memphis train that night. Papa Joe shook my hand and said, "Next time you in Texarkana, stop by at Papa Joe's. There'll be a slice of pie with your name on it."

I promised I would. When we stepped out, I could feel that the day's heat had let go. Dusk was just approaching and I saw a few bats in the air as we walked. We were going in another direction from the afternoon. But this time it was more of a straight line without the twists of the alleys. We got to where there were still storefronts, but things, except for the bars, was mostly shuttered down.

The streetlights had come on, but the streets were fairly empty. It stayed that way till we turned one corner. The small crowd that was there didn't seem to surprise Charles at all. There was maybe a dozen men and it took me a minute to figure out what was going on. At that corner, there was a sidewalk of cement. They were rolling dice so they would bounce up against the building.

After the way the afternoon went, I guess that I shouldn't have been surprised. I thought about going right then, but I knew that with dusk just settling, there was plenty of time for the midnight train. Besides, in that minute, it was easier to stay than to just go and have to explain myself. I could feel my money in my boot and I just left it there. No one seemed to be bothered by my being there, so I just watched.

There be a lot more action at a cockfight than there is with rolling dice. Still, there was just as much money, maybe even more, floating around. I imagine that's what kept those men moving like there was no tomorrow.

They'd be shaking the dice and I'd hear them saying, "Make it a seven, make it a seven."

They would be going on and on. Some of them was still and cool. Others rolled their bodies like they wanted the dice to move in the right direction for them. It was something to watch. So even though my money stayed in my boot, it was a great show for a boy from Marshall. I had some worries about what my mother would of thought, but I figured it wasn't no harm in just the being there.

Funny thing was, I was thinking just those thoughts when the dice stopped rolling. It stopped just like that when some man yelled, "Hey, you been cheating me!"

Now even I knew those wasn't words that was spoken lightly. I wanted to back out of the way, but I stood still. I dared not move. Looking around, I saw that everyone else had froze.

"Aw, now why you be saying something like that, Robert?"

Now I don't know if that accused man was innocent-like or just putting on a show. But I could see that man named Robert was having none of it.

"I say it because you be cheating me, Lester."

Without any room for that man's pride, I could see that things were leading to no good.

"You better drop that talk, Robert."

"No, not till I see your dice."

"You saying you want to see my dice?"

"You heard what I said."

"Stay back, Robert. I'm warning you."

"No, I think you been shaving those dice. I want to see them."

At that, I looked around. When a man talks like that he might as well be accusing someone of carrying aces up their sleeve. The way it works with dice, if you shave just a bit off one side, you supposed to be able to roll more sevens and elevens.

Robert was a tall man and as he advanced he cast an even bigger shadow. Lester said, "I'll show you something."

But it wasn't dice. He pulled out a pistol. It happened so fast, but it felt like slow motion. There was a shot. Robert stopped and two more shots followed. The man next to me was screaming. Blood was dripping from his arm. Another shot followed and hit Robert in the chest for the second time.

Spinning around toward the rest of us, he carried a surprised look. But he didn't say nothing. Instead, a little blood came up out of his mouth. Seemed like he stood there forever before he crashed to his knees and fell over. He settled right near my feet. I looked down at him and then at the man next to me holding his arm.

Someone rushed over. "Damn, he's dead."

I heard the gun land on the street and saw Lester running hard. The man next to me with the hurt arm said, "The police be here soon to arrest somebody."

Another man spoke up, "Yeah, and to them any colored man would do just fine."

All at the same time, I started backing up and looking for Charles. I could see he was already off and running. I did the same but went in the other direction. My mother had been sending a message to me that I needed to get myself out of trouble. I figured the opposite direction from that man was the right way for me to go.

My heart was pounding when I got to the station. I knew I had done nothing wrong, but I didn't feel so good about being close to trouble. Besides that, my mind kept seeing it again and again even though I would as soon let it go. The mind can be funny that way. When it's trying to tell you something, it just won't let up no way.

As my breath slowed down, my mind did too. I thought about what Papa said: "Always do the right thing, and you will make your father proud."

It seemed like a long wait, but I didn't talk to no one. While I waited for the train, I did some thinking. I hadn't done anything wrong, but I almost walked right into trouble anyway just by being where I was. From then on, I decided, when I saw trouble I would just walk to the other side of the street. I wouldn't change direction, but I would just let trouble alone. It's worked that way for me ever since then. When I boarded the train, a long day in Texarkana was over. It's been eighty years, but I haven't been back there since then.

Being the night train and all, it wasn't too crowded. The porter rented pillows on this run too, but I slept just fine without one. I always could just sleep anywhere. I didn't try to stay up. Having already been on a train, I chose sleep this time. It was first light and we was already along the Mississippi before I woke.

I asked the porter if he knew about jobs on the levee.

"Sure do," he said. "There's work there for colored if that's what you're after."

I nodded. "That's what I want. I hear it's up by Memphis."

"Well, it's that direction, but still a ways south. It's actually between Chatfield and Bruins."

I got a few breakfast cakes from the lady selling them in the aisles. Trains was pretty relaxed in those days and the porter sat down next to me and pulled one out of his pocket too. See, back then it wasn't just the porters and the conductors and such that worked on the trains. There were people that must have cooked all night, because they would get on the morning trains and have food to sell to the passengers. There were a lot of us that never could afford to eat in the dining car, and the peddlers would board the trains every day. The dining car was closed to coloreds anyway, except, of course, for the waiters and the cooks back in the kitchen.

"Those towns be coming up pretty soon?" I asked.

"Yeah, not too long now, but that's not exactly where you want to go. See, they working on the levee between those towns, probably a good six- or eight-mile walk from either place."

He kinda cocked his head and looked at me. "Besides, I don't know if either of those towns is the safest place for you right now. There was an incident up that way not much more than a month ago."

It wasn't easy for a colored person to be traveling back then. Matter of fact, it could be dangerous. Sometimes, other coloreds would step in and warn a traveler. I knew right away what he meant.

The Klan was growing and running strong then. Most likely, the "incident" was a lynching or the Klan torching a house or neighborhood. The burning crosses and shots in the night were common enough then that the porter wouldn't have bothered to mention it if it was just that. Sometimes, after an "incident," people seemed to be pretty worked up and things got even worse than before. In that case, stepping off in a strange town where the sheriff didn't know me, and then walking down the road all day, was just asking for trouble.

A lot of soldiers had been returning from the World War with some new ideas that didn't set too well with some white folks. But if some folks were worked up, they wouldn't bother to be asking me either. They weren't much for talking. I wasn't scared or I wouldn't have been out there traveling in those days. But I wasn't no fool either.

"What do you think?" I said. "Could I get off in one of those towns, stay off the roads, and just walk through the woods?"

The porter laughed. "Son, I can see that you ain't from Tennessee."

"What do you mean?"

"Well, it's like this. You could be keeping your eyes peeled for the Klan, come down in a hollow, and walk right into somebody's still. Their hounds would be out before you know it. You couldn't be any worse off if the Klan came to your house for dinner."

I wasn't happy to hear that, but I said, "I'll have to take my chances. What else am I supposed to do?"

He grinned. "I thought you would say that. But you just listen to me, I got a plan. When the train stops, that will be halfway between those towns. As soon as it slows, jump off on this side," he said, pointing. "You got that?"

"Yeah, I hear you. But why is the train gonna be stopping right there?"

"Leave that to me," he said with a smile. "Maybe I might see a cow on the track and there'll be an emergency."

I nodded. Even with a cowcatcher on the front, the trains often stopped for a cow on the track. They hit enough of them, but stopped when they could.

"How you able to predict cows like that?" I laughed.

"Don't you worry about that, young man. But when the train stops, head south for just about half a mile. You'll come to a road. That one is safe. Just follow it downhill. You'll see the levee crew in no time."

The porter got up to make his rounds. I didn't see him no more, but when the train lurched to a stop, I was already by the door. From the other end of the car, I heard the porter shout and I looked up to see him yanking the emergency cord that run along the baggage rail.

"Nobody panic," he shouted. "I just saw a cow on the tracks. This will be a short stop. Remain on board."

There was a wide curve in the tracks and when I looked out the window, I could see a ways ahead of us. But I didn't see no cow. Before I opened the door to the stairs, I caught the porter's eye. I waved.

He grinned at me and shouted, "Everything be just fine folks. We'll have the cow moved off the tracks in a minute. There's no need to worry about a thing."

I held the door so it shut quietly. I took a couple of stairs real quick and braced myself on the last one. I tossed my bedroll and then took a good jump to clear the railroad ties, but when I hit the ground there was a good slope to it. I lost my footing and rolled a few times before I landed on my stomach. I grabbed at some clumps of grass, but didn't really stop sliding till I hit the bottom of the hill. No matter, I was in Tennessee, another new state, and things was looking good.

C H A P T E R 11

...from Pittsburgh down the Ohio and Mississippi they ship their structural steel and other products. Much iron pipe for the Oklahoma and Texas oil fields is brought out this way and hauled from New Orleans on sea barges to the railroads at Houston and Beaumont.

—*National Geographic,* November 1927

"They talk about what they'll do with this river.... Let me tell you something. This river is the god and master of all this country. It's been here 10,000 years, and it'll be here a lot longer. They're fooling themselves if they think they'll do anything without its say-so."—Lifetime worker on the Mississippi

—*National Geographic,* August 1983

Handing me some magazines, Richard said, "Since you worked on the levees, I thought you might want to see these."

156

There were two *National Geographics*, old ones. Each magazine had a bookmark at an article about the Mississippi River. Ships like I remember were in the pictures. Men like me were working on the shore. It brought me back all right.

"Yeah, son, this looks pretty close to how it was," I said.

"You remember the levees?"

"Sure, I remember, Richard. I remember from the first moment I got off in Tennessee. I can tell you about it if you want."

The train had started and I waited for it to pass before I scrambled back up to get my bedroll, which got stuck in some bushes about halfway down. It wasn't that long of a hill, but it was steep. When I caught up to my bedroll, I sat down to catch my breath. There had been a steady noise of the engine and the rolling on the track that I hadn't even noticed. But now that the train was gone, there was a powerful silence that settled along the tracks in the moments before the songbirds picked up. I was high enough to get some view. It looked mighty nice to a boy from Texas.

Being springtime, the leaves were out and the woods stretched as far as I could see. I was just high enough to look over them and see the Mississippi. From where I sat, it looked flat. At that point, it was big and wide, but it was a wandering every which way. Small fingers of it would run off course and only stopped when they hit some higher ground. Even from there, I could see that in a rainy spring, that

157

old river would really choose its own direction. There was nothing to stop it.

It was a beautiful river just in the way it was. God had done a wonderful job when he built the Mississippi and there could be no way to improve on what nature had done. As human beings, we are just too small. That's what I know eighty years later. But being twenty-one and free and just full of myself, I thought, it's a good thing I'm here. Holding back that river is gonna be some job. They will be needing my help to build that levee.

I could see that job was made for me. I scrambled back down the slope and walked through the tall grasses till I got to the edge of the trees. I stopped to look at the sun to get my bearings. Then I stepped into the woods, heading off in what I thought to be south and trying to keep a straight line. The woods were dense and that wasn't so easy as it sounds. But when I saw more light and some blue sky through the trees, I changed my direction a bit. Sure enough, there was a road ahead just like the porter said.

Funny thing, now that I think about it. I didn't even know that porter's name. But he did help me, maybe even kept me away from enough danger that he might have saved my life. Who knows? No telling what I could of run into in those days without someone like him stepping in to help.

The road was just like he said, sloping downhill. People say I walk pretty good now, but in those days I could set a real good pace.

And being downhill and all, I was eating up the ground. I heard a wagon coming before I saw it and dropped down into the ditch.

I stayed down and out of sight. The wagon was riding low. It was full of dirt. I grinned when I saw that the driver was a colored man. I figured he must work on the levee and I jumped out of the ditch.

"Whoa," the driver yelled and pulled back hard. He gave me a look that made me wonder if I had stepped out too quickly. He was looking me over, so I stood still and waited.

"What is you doing there, young fella?"

Now the driver wasn't that old, but I figured he might have been around my father's age.

"Is the levee down below here?"

"Yeah, it be at the bottom of this road. Why does that matter to you?"

"I hear there might be work."

"Yeah, there might be, but it's hard work."

"Oh, that doesn't scare me. I been picking cotton since I been four years old."

"Well, this ain't cotton, son."

"Yes, sir. I am still hoping to find work, though."

He nodded but wasn't making it easy. "I can tell you ain't from here. Where you from?"

I could tell then, that was the problem. Folks didn't travel much then, and anyone from somewhere else sometimes had to prove himself. People weren't mean or nothing. It's just the way it was.

"I'm from Texas."

"I thought so, because you talk funny."

I thought the same about him but had the smarts not to mention it.

"Son, if you come all the way from Texas to work on this levee, might as well hop on up in the wagon here. We only ten minutes away but I'll give you a ride. Besides, you'll do better coming in with me."

On the way down, I gathered his name was Henry, he'd worked for more than a year on the levee, and that there was plenty of work for those that wanted it. When we got to camp, it was close to noon and we headed over to find the foreman.

We stopped in front of some empty wagons. "Hey, boss. There's a boy here that wants a job."

The foreman stepped out from around a mountain of dirt. I was sitting right next to Henry but he acted like he didn't see me. "He a good worker?"

"He says he is, boss."

Henry's tone and attitude had changed when he was talking to the foreman. I knew how to talk to a white man too and did the same when he waved our wagon over closer.

The wagon was right beside him now. When Henry gave me a nudge, I jumped down. I just waited but didn't say nothing. I could feel him looking at me and I looked down. He said, "Wait here, Henry."

Then turning to me he said, "You ever worked on a levee before?"

"No, sir."

"Know how to drive a mule?"

"Yes, sir."

"Know how to shovel dirt?"

"Yes, sir."

"Got your own mule?"

"No, sir."

He frowned and said, "You get three meals and fifty cents a day. It would be twice that if you had your own mule."

"That be fine, sir," I said.

"Henry, find him a bunk."

"We still got space in my cabin, sir."

"Fine then. Empty your dirt and then set him up with a mule and a wagon," he said before he turned and headed to his shed.

"Stick with me. I'll show you what this is about and I'll help you to get set up."

The whole area was clear of trees and brush with roads going every which way. There was men coming and going but they all stepped around us as Henry drove the wagon over toward the river. We started climbing. The mule pulled the wagon so that we was on top of a wide wall of rocks and dirt. We went a little farther and stopped behind another wagon.

Henry said, "See this lever here?"

I nodded.

"Okay," he said and then pulled. There was a big clatter as the bottom of the wagon opened. I looked back as the dirt went crashing.

"See. It's gotta fill in between those rocks or, when there is flooding, water gonna seep through. Think you can do that?"

"Sure. Looks easy enough."

Henry grinned. "I thought you would say

that. Oh, you got to fill the wagon up each time. I'll show you about that too."

We went a little farther ahead, following the other wagon. But pretty soon, we went off in the direction of a large shed that was on the far side of the clearing. He set the brake and we climbed down. The shed was open on that side and I could see that some mules were stabled there. Most of them were out, but there was still six or eight left.

"Take your pick, but you stick with the one you choose."

It was midday and I figured the better ones were already gone. They sure enough weren't the best-looking critters, but I didn't worry none either. I knew mules enough to know that temperament is more important than size or strength. You want one with spunk but at the same time ain't too stubborn. Most people don't know that and wouldn't even take it into account.

In the heat of the day, they were all pretty quiet. But I wandered through and looked at each one. The mule I settled on wasn't the biggest, but it paid me some notice when I walked by. I figured that would maybe count for something.

"He's named Joe," Henry told me. "He'll be all right."

We put a halter on him and hitched him to the back of the wagon. Some harnesses for the wagons were hanging along the wall. They were a little different than the ones we used in Texas, but Henry helped me get what I needed.

We threw those in the back of the wagon and then went up a ways past the foreman's shed. The wagons were in a line side-by-side, and we just pulled up along the end of the row.

I untied Joe and walked him over to a wagon. Henry stood by with a harness and we had the mule hitched up to my wagon in a short time. I say "my wagon," because when I clucked at Joe to follow along behind Henry's wagon I was as excited about "my wagon" and "my mule" as if I was just a kid and not a man of twenty-one years of age.

I may have been grinning like a kid, but I felt like a man, all right. I admit it. With my own mule and wagon, I was mighty proud of myself. I had never really owned anything of my own, except for Pete's baseball. And I knew that wagon and mule were mine, at least for as long as I was working there. As the wagon worked its way up the hill, I figured I was a man now and maybe about the luckiest one alive to be able to build a levee on the great Mississippi River. Of course, there was hundreds and hundreds of men working along the river too. But right then, if you had asked me to build the levee all by myself, I wouldn't have seen it as a problem. I felt that good.

Wagons loaded with dirt were coming by in the other direction, and I nodded to each driver since these were men that I was going to be working with. I acted like I was in charge, but, the fact is, Joe seemed to know where he was heading and I just needed to let him have his way. After crossing the railroad tracks, we followed right behind Henry when he turned off on another road. In a short whiles we came to a clearing. We made a wide turn and pulled in behind the other wagons that was up against the slope of a hillside. Men were shoveling out dirt and carving up that hillside good.

When I hopped out, Henry waved his arm toward the hillside and shouted, "Help yourself."

Men were loading up their wagons. I took the shovel that was tied up in the corner of the wagon and did the same. Now I've always known how to work, but I admit, it took a little while for my excitement to pass so that I could work at a proper pace. The wagon wasn't even half full before I was getting worn out. After that, I paid more attention to what I was doing and worked at a pace to last all day.

My pride was such that I wasn't going to let nothing stop me, but I was muttering to myself, "That man was right, this is a lot harder than cotton." Still, I looked around; if there were other men could do this job and stick it out, then I could too. That thought kept me going the first couple of days while my body got used to the work.

Henry's cabin had an empty bunk for me. All the cabins had four bunks. Besides Henry, Eben and Thomas had the other two. That first night, I sure did sleep. I sat down to take off my boots. I was so tired that, with one boot off, I fell back with one leg still hanging off the bed. I didn't wake up till morning, with one boot still on.

After the first few days, the work did get easier, though, and in a week or two I felt just fine. Still, even with steady wages and three meals a day, there were a lot of men that left within two or three days. The work was just too hard. So, after a couple of weeks, I felt like I had earned my place and felt right at home.

Each day was pretty much the same. After I loaded up, I would fall in line with the other wagons. That was the easy part, riding down to dump my dirt on the levee. I suppose it didn't really matter, but I always looked for the spot that looked like it had the most empty space between the rocks. That's where I figured my dirt was most needed. See, I was taught that on any job, I was to do my best. So, besides my muscles working with the shovel, my mind worked too.

Fill the wagon, head down to drop my dirt, turn around and head back up to fill the wagon again! It went like that all day long. From early morning, there would be a steady line of wagons on each side of the road, going up and down the hill. From the beginning, I looked around and figured what I was supposed to do. I never slowed things down or caused a problem so that the foreman had to say anything to me. All the workers were colored and the foreman for each crew was white. They were okay, never caused me no bother, but they never really talked to us unless there was a problem.

At noon, there was a whistle, and we headed to the cookhouse. There would be stew with some biscuits and maybe some meat and potatoes for dinner. Of course, there was always some complaining about the food, but it was all right. To me the best part about the meals was there was always enough food. I was thankful for that. Beyond that, I wasn't going to be picky. That wouldn't be right.

There were a lot of cabins. After the evening meal, men would be wandering about some and usually collect by a fire. If it was one of the warm summer evenings, there would still be groups congregating, just without the fire. There was a lot of talking, and then usually some instruments came out. Almost always there was some music being made. I liked that.

When picking a mule, a man takes his chances. But I would say that I made a pretty good choice with Joe. Even so, with any mule you treat it right and he'll be okay. Back at home, I had learned that the hard way. You got to be patient with a mule, get him to work *with* you instead of just working *for* you. I always took good care of him—rubbed him down and got him a treat, a carrot or an apple if I could, before I stopped to sit down. At the end of the day, I would want to just stop and sit, but I never did till I took care of Joe first.

Fridays was payday. Like I said, there were a fair number of men a coming and going. But one thing you could count on, even if a man had a plan to leave, most stayed till payday.

I stood in line to get my check. Most weeks I had some extra hours in there, but I just had to trust they figured it right for me since I couldn't read for myself. Back then, there were some others that signed their checks with an *X* too. No one said anything about it. That's just how it was. But did I always get my full check? I'll never know, but I doubt it.

Still, it was enough for me and I had no complaints. As a matter of fact, I didn't have anything to buy and I always saved most of my check. That turned out to be good, for it gave me the chance to better myself. A couple of months after I been there, Henry came running up to me one night. "George," he said. "You know a man named Jeremiah?"

"No, I don't think so. Why you asking me?" I said.

"He got a mule to sell."

"Yeah. Why is that?" I asked.

"He took sick is what I hear."

"I'm not gonna buy that mule then," I said.

"Why not?"

"Well, it wouldn't be right to buy a mule from a man that was sick."

"Hey, the mule is fine."

"I know that. It just don't feel right."

"You mean like taking advantage of a man and such?"

"Yeah, that's it. It don't feel right."

"Well, this man Jeremiah, he sick. He gonna have to sell the mule to somebody."

"That be fine. He can sell it to somebody else," I said.

"George, sometimes you can be a stubborn one."

"That's right. Sometimes I am that way."

"Well, you listen to me," Henry said. "Jeremiah took sick. He gonna sell that mule to somebody no matter what. Who gonna give that man a fair deal, you or just anybody in camp?"

"I see what you mean. Let's go see this man."

Jeremiah was toward the other end of camp. The mule was tethered in front of the cabin. I looked him over before we went in. It was a nice, warm night, but we found Jeremiah inside his cabin a laying in bed. I hadn't remembered him by name, but I recognized him and had even talked with him some. He was on a different crew, worked a different section of river so I hadn't seen him much.

One of his bunkmates said, "Jeremiah, there's some men here to see you. One of them wants to buy your mule."

We stepped in and Jeremiah nodded at us. His bunkmate propped him up with some pillows and said to us, "His talking isn't so great anymore, but if you listen good you can understand him."

We stepped close. Jeremiah nodded, and in a weak voice said, "I need to sell my mule. Be obliged if you buy it. You interested?"

I said, "Yeah, I think I might be."

He waved toward the door. "Go take a look."

Along with his bunkmate, we walked back outside. I had already seen the mule and asked his bunkmate what his problem was.

"Jeremiah took sick a few months ago. He kept working, but about two weeks ago when he was loading his wagon he just fell over. I guess he's been in some awful pain and this tumor on his leg keeps getting bigger."

"What's he gonna do?" Henry asked.

"He's got a brother in North Carolina, where he be from. He's worked here five years or more, but he sent money to his mama when she was alive and took in less pay these last few months when he was working sick and slow. Before that his wife took sick and died, but he had to pay the doctors. When he sells his mule, he'll have money for a train ticket and I'll take him to the station."

"What do you figure this mule is worth?" Henry asked.

"He's not a bad mule, but he's old. Probably twenty dollars."

Henry said, "Yeah, that sounds about right."

Taking my money out of my boot I counted it. I kept most of it and put two dollars back in. Papa said, "Be generous in your dealings, but always have something saved for rainy weather."

Back in the cabin I gave Jeremiah forty dollars. He nodded at me but didn't even count it. "Thank you, son."

Back outside, Henry whispered, "He said twenty dollars. Didn't you hear him?"

I said, "Yeah, I heard. Like you said, twenty was for the mule. The other twenty was to maybe be a little help for an old man."

"That's good. I'm with you there."

In those days, we figured a man was old at fifty. Jeremiah was maybe pushing sixty. He was old for this kind of work anyway. But folks worked for as long as they could. They had to. We didn't have any retirement to look at. When you were sick or too old to work, there wasn't no unemployment, Social Security, or nothing. We had nothing to fall back on. I expect he just wanted to get home before he died.

Joe went back to the stables. Samuel, the mule I bought, and me got along all right. He was a little slower than Joe, but, no matter, you don't run races with a mule. But even for a mule he was a little bit cranky. I always thought it could of been because he and Jeremiah had been together so long. He wasn't used to taking orders from anyone else. Some folks think that creatures like that don't have feelings, but I think he missed his master and I went easy on him. He would do what I asked, but in his own time. That was just him; I didn't let it bother me. Still and all, he was mine and I took good care of him.

But Samuel was old when I got him and I could see that he was slowing down. Every morning he moved like he was stiff and sore. I felt badly to have to get him moving. He would do what I wanted, but it felt like he was working in pain. I wondered what to do, but had no answer for it.

One morning, I guess you might say that the Lord answered my question. When I went out to the stables, I saw that Samuel had died in his sleep. I didn't call the rendering man. Instead, I took my first day off in over two years and buried him myself. When a mule dies, I don't know where he goes, but Samuel had a nice spot that looked out on the Mississippi and on the levee that he helped to build. Jeremiah would have been pleased to know that.

Joe was taken, but with a company mule I was back at work the next day. My pay was cut back, but I had saved a lot and it didn't matter to me. With a different mule, I did the same work as before, but somehow it was different. I guess death, even with a mule, can change things. For a long time, I had something that depended on me, something to take care of. All of a sudden, I only had to take care of myself.

I would of thought that would make life easier, but it only made me restless. Till then, I figured to be working on the river my whole life. I had been there more than two years and I hadn't missed a day's work. It felt good to be a part of something as big as taming the Mississippi. The work was steady. Men came and went, but if you had asked me, I liked it well enough that I had thought I could of stayed forever. Now, going along in the wagon on the same road, back and forth all day long, I wondered about the rest of the world that I hadn't seen and how little time there might be to see more of it.

Still, I stayed where I was. One day after work, I went to look at buying another mule. A man had saved some money and was gonna go back to his family. There was nothing wrong with the mule and it made a lot of sense for me to buy it. But when I got to it, I let it go. It just wasn't in me then. That restless feeling hadn't left me and I listened to that.

The next morning, I caught a ride with the delivery wagon into Memphis. There was some time before the train. I bought some food for my journey, some candies for the little ones, and a dress pattern and some cloth for my mother. This time I took a direct train that would stop at Marshall.

CHAPTER 12

TEXAS BUILDS MOST ROADS IN A YEAR

Austin, Jan. 22—Texas completed more highways during the year than any other state in the nation, according to the report [Bureau of Roads of the Department of Agriculture]. The Lone Star state is credited with completing 933 miles of highway during the year, which the average mileage completed by all states was slightly over 200.

USED CAR BARGAINS

2 Ford Tourings
(non-starter), each $100
1 Ford Touring with starter $250

1 Ford Coupe,
   like new; dressed up $450
1 Dodge Touring,
   in fine condition $375
1 Buick Touring,
   '17 model, in good shape $225
1 Buick Touring, '20 model,
   runs like new.....................$350
1 Hudson Super-Six,
   in A1 condition $400
1 Willys-Knight Touring,
   in fine condition $500
1 Special Six Studebaker Touring,
   a real car $650

The above cars are priced to move
and are guaranteed to be exactly as
representted

WE CAN ARRANGE LIBERAL TERMS

S. E. WOOD, JR.

STUDEBAKER DISTRIBUTOR

—The Marshall Morning News,
January 25, 1923

When Richard handed me another article,
I said, "You ain't gonna ask me again if I
remember, are you?"

Richard said to me, "Well..."

"Son," I said, "I would of thought by now
you would know I don't forget anything I've
seen. I don't know why that is, but that's so.
I remember the first car I ever saw, a Model
T Ford, all black and shiny. The tires, I

believe, was solid rubber. That was in Marshall in 1913."

When I came back to Marshall in 1923, things hadn't changed. My mother liked her dress pattern and the little ones their candies, but the next day I was out helping in the fields like I had never been gone. I didn't have regular chores anymore, so a few days after I was back I took some cotton into town.

It must have been lunchtime when I got there. I had it loaded up in the wagon and waited for the buyer to come back. Since my return, I seen there was more cars and even more paved roads. The mule seemed to have adjusted, though, and I didn't give it too much thought either. So it didn't surprise me that while I was sitting in our wagon, a man pulled up in a Model T.

He started talking to me and from the way he talked, I could tell he wasn't from Marshall. He was the type that didn't like waiting. Drumming his fingers on the wheel, he said, "You know when the manager's coming back?"

"No, sir. I expect he's gone to lunch."

Now I knew he didn't have cotton to sell, but he looked like one of those travelers that was selling something. Of course, I didn't ask and minded my own business.

"Know where I can get some water for the car?" he said.

"Yeah, I can help you with that." I filled up a bucket at the pump off the side of the mill and brought it back. He already had the hood open and we poured some water into the radiator.

"Thank you. It's going to be a warm day and I will be back on the road this afternoon."

He offered me some money. I didn't think it was that big of a deal and I said, "No bother, sir."

With most folks, I would figure that that is that. But he kept going on. He was a one for questions.

"Well, I appreciate it. You ever driven a car before?"

"No, sir. I can't say as I have."

"You want to try it?"

"You mean this car, drive your car?"

He laughed. "Well, I mean this car. But it's not really mine. I have it for work. It's a company car so I don't worry about it."

I wanted to but wasn't so sure.

"Well, if you don't want to or don't think you can... See, I sell cars and the more people that's out driving, the more cars I'm going to sell."

"I see, but I got to admit that I don't have money to buy one."

"No matter. The more people out driving, the more cars I sell. Someone sees you driving and someone else will buy it. That's just how it works."

That did it for me. "Yeah, that makes sense. Just show me how it works."

He was in the driver's seat and said, "Just pull the stick in the direction you want the car to go. The car will do the rest."

They didn't all have a steering wheel like they use today. Some of the cars, like this one, had a big steering stick that came up out of the floor. It sounded easy to me. I cranked the car up like I had seen people do and got in the driver's seat. He reached in and pulled the brake release.

I could feel the car start to roll back and when he shouted, "Put your foot down on the gas and pull on the stick," I did just that.

I could feel the wind in my face, but the car kept going around and around in circles. I didn't know what to do so I just pulled harder on the stick. It was the only thing there was to hold on to.

The man came out and then jumped back so as not to get hit. Most times, I would of worried about hitting somebody, especially a white man like that. But right then all I did was push my foot to the floor and hold on tight to the steering stick. As the circles went faster, he shouted, "Push the stick back to the middle and lift up your foot."

I did that all right, but when it straightened out I saw that the big cottonwood tree off by the side of the mill had popped in front of me. I didn't need to use the brakes since the tree did such a good job of stopping the car. The man came running over as I was climbing out. Seemed like it bent the spring underneath that the car bounces along on. The blacksmith could fix that and nothing else was hurt. Maybe because it was his idea, he didn't seem too mad.

I guess he got a good story to tell out of it and I got my first driving lesson. Being the first

Dawson to ever drive a car, I told everybody what I had done when I got home. Even Papa hadn't driven a car yet and everyone was rightfully impressed, especially the youngest ones. I didn't make too much mention of the tree, though.

There was work for me when I was back, but I could see that things had gotten along all right without me. I guess I felt good about that, but that restless feeling that I had along the river came back strong in a week or two. I helped to get some spring planting in, but it felt different. Somehow, I just knew that I wouldn't be around when the crops came up.

I hadn't said nothing, but one morning when I brought the water in Mama said, "It's good to see you again, George."

I smiled. She wasn't finished, though. "I can see that you won't be here too much longer."

It's kinda what I had already been thinking, but I said, "What do you mean?"

"Since you've been back, I've seen something different in you. You're grown up, but you still have to find your own way."

I wasn't sure exactly what I had been thinking, but she said it well. She gave me a big hug and said, "You can always come back to visit your mother and father, but I know that you've got your own life to live too."

Two days later, when Johnny was taking in some ribbon syrup, he had a passenger. "How the baseball team going?" I asked him.

"It's going good, George, but we've seen some good teams this year."

"That's good. How's your arm holding up?"

"Hey, I can still pitch nine strong innings and even extra innings if that's how the game goes."

He looked at me. "You know, our catcher is doing all right, but the team could really use you again."

I missed baseball, but I shook my head. "No, not right now." Then I said, "Johnny, you got an arm. Are you going to leave and try to go pro with a traveling team?"

Johnny smiled at me. I could tell that he was pleased that I had asked him.

"Yeah, I thought about it some. Too much work on the farm, though. I can work at the mill this summer too if I want. They pays good. There's a new league opening up in Dallas, I hear. I just don't think I could afford to play pro ball right now."

I laughed. "Know what you mean."

There were a lot of Negro leagues popping up for colored to play in. But it was only the majors and some of the white semipro leagues that paid anything decent. There were some good teams in the Negro leagues, but they just didn't have much money. Some of those players could play with anybody, but the white leagues were off-limits to us.

"What you be doing?" Johnny asked me.

It felt funny to hear myself say, "I don't know."

But I really didn't. I figured on heading south to start with, maybe off to Mexico, but beyond that... That felt all right, just hard to explain to anyone else. Johnny took me to the station before taking the syrup in. I could see Johnny didn't need my help anymore. That made it easier to leave, but made it harder too.

At the station, I grabbed my bedroll and jumped down. Johnny did too.

"Wherever you going, you be careful now, George," Johnny said.

"Oh, yeah, I will."

We felt awkward, just waiting there. I slapped him on the shoulder and said, "Now listen to me. Even when it's a three–two count, don't back down. Go with that fastball."

Johnny gave me a hug and said, "I will. Don't forget, I always need a catcher that can call a good game."

I knew that was an invitation to stay, but I said, "Maybe someday we'll do that again. Right now, I gonna be going."

With a couple of barrels in the back, the wagon went slow enough that I could of run and caught it. Part of me just wanted to do that and head back home. I didn't. Even though I wasn't sure where I was heading, there was a journey I needed to take.

The stationmaster didn't want to pay me no notice, but I made sure I showed him my money. Funny how, even if people don't like you, most cases they be happy to sell you something. There were some folks that didn't like to see the colored traveling about. I guess he was just one of those that wanted us to stay at home. He looked at me like he wouldn't give me the time of day. But he was willing to take my money.

"Where you going, boy?"

I was a man, but that didn't matter to him. Though I didn't read and had no use for a map, I knew my directions well from days of hunting and fishing. My last trip, to Tennessee, was to the east so I figured to skip that direction. I thought about going north. People, at least the white folks who had visited there, said that Yankees up north weren't friendly and didn't like you if you was from the South, though. Course, a lot of families were still busy fighting the war in their heads. "The war" will always mean the Civil War, not the World War that just ended. Still, I thought maybe north might not be so good either.

"I'll be heading south, sir."

"Down to Houston or beyond that toward Brownsville?"

Now, I had never even been to Houston. In the way he asked, he talked down to me like he thought I could barely go that far on my own. He didn't say it with words, but that was his tone.

That made me mad enough to say, "Yeah, Brownsville, down past Houston. That's where I want to go, sir."

Even though he made me mad, I didn't let it show and I talked respectful-like. But I could see that I had surprised him and I liked that. I decided it was worth it, even if it cost me more money.

"Train doesn't leave for three hours. You can come back or wait here."

I took a seat in the colored section. I didn't own a watch and didn't want to miss the train. Now I've noticed that most folks don't like waiting at the station. It doesn't bother me. I can look at the tracks and know they be going out to places I've never been to yet and I can just sit and get ready for what will be coming. See, I do like the trip, but I even like the wait at the station. Just knowing that I'll be somewhere new makes me feel good. I can pass an hour or two or it could be a day or two and I bet it would feel like the same thing.

Houston was a big city, all right. I could tell that just from the station. It was bigger than Marshall and a lot bigger than I needed. With a long stop there, people got off and I did too. It didn't even smell like Marshall. There was a smell of cars and diesel. After a piece of pie, I was glad to get back on the train.

Back in those days, there were cities and there was country. There weren't no suburbs in between like there is now. Once we left Houston, the countryside started to be what I knew again. Along the tracks, there was railroad towns. Those were little towns that wouldn't even be there if it weren't for the railroad running through. Once out of Houston, the roads weren't paved and didn't connect so well. Country people didn't travel so much, but when they did it was on the train.

We made a lot of stops, with just a few people getting on or off at each town. Those towns didn't have no electricity. Once darkness fell, there would be some lights from house lanterns. Out past the towns, every now and then, there would be some light from a farmhouse. But besides that, it got real dark. It was a quiet night like that all the way to Brownsville.

Brownsville was the end of the line and bigger than the railway towns. I had a good breakfast there. The cafe served refried beans with my eggs instead of grits like they did back in Marshall. Matter of fact, a lot of people spoke in Spanish. The cafe waiter and all the railroad workers spoke Spanish. It wasn't so common in Marshall, but I had picked it up from mill workers and farm workers that were Mexican. It didn't bother me none.

Fact was, when I started looking for work, I noticed that all the laboring jobs were held by Mexicans. Like in Marshall or back in Tennessee, whites were the owners or the foremen. Except that back home the laborers were colored, not Mexican.

I didn't fit in. I don't know if that's why I had a hard time finding work, or because things were slow. Brownsville was kind of a down-in-the-mouth town. Any way you looked, it didn't look too prosperous. The river running through the middle of town was slow and muddy. The bridge that crossed over it was busy, though, with people moving in both directions. Turns out, the other side of the river was in Mexico and that side of town had a different name. But it was really like one town.

If you asked me, it was like Texarkana, with one half in Texas and one half in Arkansas, except that here, one half was in America and one half was in Mexico. The bridge was wide enough for a wagon with a horse and a mule and even for a car. But there wasn't much pavement and not many cars. There were none that I saw on the bridge, probably 'cause the roads were even worse on the other side. Mostly people just walked across.

There were a lot of peddlers bringing their wares across and setting up on the Brownsville side. They only took what they could carry, but you could buy vegetables, bread, jewelry, blankets, clothes, lots of stuff. Some of them even set up food stands. I didn't need nothing, but I looked around a bit and at midday got some rice and beans.

The stand where I ate had a whole family that came over and worked every day. From them, I learned that the trains kept on going. Only thing was, you had to walk across the bridge and start over. So, since they had trains in Mexico too, I figured that I could keep going.

The bridge was still busy with foot passengers, but I just stepped into the crowd and started across. Toward the end of the bridge, I got a little worried, though. People went through a gate where a policeman with a rifle slung over his shoulder stood. All my life back in Marshall and during my travels,

I had done a good job of staying away from the police. Like all colored people, I had learned that from a young age.

But looking around, I could see that to get away I would have to fight against the crowd and make a scene, something else a colored man knew not to do. It wasn't good, but I let myself be carried along toward the policeman. I was in line as he talked to each person walking through. There didn't seem to be any problems, but that didn't mean nothing. I was used to problems and different rules for colored and white. Only thing was, I didn't know if I was breaking any different rules down there that I didn't even know about.

There wasn't much I could do, though. When I got to the gate, I nodded at him.

"Buenas tardes, señor," he said.

"Buenas tardes," I answered.

"No vive usted aquí?" (You don't live here?) he said to me.

I thought, Here's where it starts, but just said, *"No, señor, vivo en Texas."* (I live in Texas).

He smiled and said, *"Buena suerte y bien viajes en Mexico."* (Good luck and good travels in Mexico.)

No policeman ever wished me good luck before and I was barely able to say, *"Muchas gracias,"* before I had to move along for the people waiting behind me. I walked through the town square wondering about that. But before I could give it much thought I noticed that people were nodding at me or saying, *"Buenas tardes, señor."*

Till then, I always figured it was just as well if folks never took notice of me because as much as anything, that could mean trouble. But people were treating me decently and there was no trouble. I can't say that I minded it, but I didn't know what to make of it either. Even with my Spanish being so-so, I felt safe in asking a man coming out of a shop where the train station was.

Being that it was a small town, the station wasn't that far. He actually walked me there. The station wasn't much, but there was a train waiting. Pointing at the train, I asked the ticket master, *"Donde va?"*

"Va a Valle Hermosa, señor."

That meant nothing to me and I shrugged. He said, *"Esta en los montañas, señor. Esta muy bueno."*

I nodded. I had never been to the mountains before and I caught that word pretty clearly.

"Qué clase, señor? Más barato o más caro?"

I knew enough to say *baroto*, the cheapest fare, but I couldn't figure out how to ask for the colored car and he didn't say nothing either. The conductor would know and he was there to take my ticket so I wasn't too worried. He walked me over to one of the back cars.

When I got in, I could see that it was nothing fancy. Matter of fact, it was a worn-out-looking car. That didn't especially surprise me, but when passengers started loading, I began to get worried. Some Mexicans were dark skinned, Indian from the way they dressed, but some light-skinned Mexicans got on too. I didn't know what to make of it and wondered if I was on the white car by mistake. I didn't want no trouble, but nothing was said and I stayed put.

It was a pretty full train and I kind of forgot about it when I saw goats being handed up to the roof and people coming on with their chickens. The people didn't look like they was more well off than me, but they was friendly. I bought some tortillas from the tortilla lady and settled back for the trip. I had heard enough Spanish from Mexican workers that following the language wasn't so hard. It was easier to understand them than to say something. But they were all nice enough and it seemed that everyone wanted to talk to me.

People asked me where I came from and what I did. When I said I was a traveler they gave me a million ideas of where to go, though I don't think any of them had been far from those close-by valleys themselves. The little ones just looked at me. They didn't say nothing, but I could tell they were staring because of my dark skin. I could tell they were just curious. It didn't bother me at all.

Trains weren't built for speed, but, as old as this one was, it was probably the slowest train I've ever been on, especially after it started climbing. Those mountains were steep and I wouldn't have thought you could lay a track through some of the spots we went along. It was a long ways down and I had to hope we were going to be all right. The villages were getting smaller and smaller. I didn't see any roads connecting the villages and at the smallest patch of level ground, someone would flag the train down and get on carrying bundles of firewood, lemonade, or tamales for sale.

Jungle covered those mountains, except for a village clearing. Those towns were even poorer-looking than I had seen around Marshall. It stayed that way till the next morning, when we cleared a pass and came to a town that covered parts of both sides of the valley. I had slept all right, but it felt good to get off. I was unsure where to go. The people nearby that visited with me on the train were laughing and talking, but they didn't forget me.

They left together in a group and let me know that I should walk with them. The houses were small and of adobe. They were right on the edge of the street so that when I walked by, with their doors open, I felt I was in their living room or in their kitchen. No one seemed to mind, though. The people who lived in them looked up from making tortillas or eating breakfast and smiled at me. There were lots of children and the little ones would run to the doorway for a closer look.

Besides some shops and a cafe, the center of town had a pool with water running into it. It was still early morning and people were coming with buckets to fill and take home. Sometimes people just put a cup under the spout or even just opened their mouth and put their head under it. Being thirsty, I looked around for another spout. Though I looked around, I didn't see the water spout for the colored. It seemed like there was only one.

In a small Texas town, they often didn't have colored bathrooms or fountains either. In that case, we just had to move on and I was used to it. But down there I didn't even know which direction to start heading to find a fountain I could use. Right then, a man that I had sat next to on the train came over. He was named Jorge, same name as me except it was in Spanish. He tapped me on the shoulder.

"*Tienes sed?*" (Was I thirsty?)

Glad to know that he could send me over to the colored fountain, I nodded at him. Instead of directions, he handed me a cup that he pulled out of his pouch.

"*Gracias,*" I said. "*Pero a donde voy for la agua?*" (But where should I go for the water?)

"*Aquí. Esta buene agua.*" (Here. It's good water.)

Though tanned from the sun, Jorge wasn't Indian or mestizo, a mixed blood. He was white and I figured if he said use the fountain, it must be all right. But to share his cup? I just wasn't sure about that and I handed it back to him.

"*Lo siento. Hay solo este una taza.*" (I'm sorry. There is only this one cup.)

I laughed. What strange country was I in where a white man offers to share and even apologizes to me for using the same cup that I would? I didn't know what to think. No one in Marshall would believe I was telling the truth even if I told them.

Jorge frowned when he saw me laughing. "*Senor, lo siento, pero...*"

I could see that I had offended him when I questioned his offer. *"Sí, yo tengo sed,"* I quickly said. *"Si permitte, su taza esta bien, gracias. "* (Yes, I am thirsty. With your permission, your cup will be fine, thank you.)

A smile replaced his frown as I took his cup. I got in line behind the others that were waiting, some with old gourds and others with buckets. Waiting in lines never bothered me, but a woman motioned me to follow her. She brought me up to the front of the line. *"Señor, para usted el frente de la linea. Estoy seguro, que tiene usted mucho sed de su viajes!"* (For you, the front of the line. I am sure that you are thirsty after your travels.)

Knowing my place and all, I had never been in the front of any line before in my life. It felt funny, but I could see that I would only offend someone again if I didn't do it. The people in line nodded toward me; they weren't put off as I would have figured them to be. After all these years, straight out of the mountain, that's still the best glass of water that I've ever had. Maybe I just enjoyed that cup of water a little extra too, because I wasn't in the back of the line. Could be part of it; I don't know.

When Jorge took his cup back, he said, *"Ahora, tiene hambre usted? "* (Are you hungry now?)

"Sí, seguro. " (Yes, sure.)

"Entonces, venga. " (Then come.)

This time I knew enough to agree. We walked over to a little restaurant that spilled out onto the street. There were a few tables

189

in front and more inside. Jorge walked in, but I stood at the door and watched carefully. I didn't know if they be serving colored here and was just trying to figure that out. There was no way to tell and when Jorge turned around and said, *"Venga,"* I just followed him inside.

I sat down at a table with him and relaxed when a woman came over and Jorge said, *"Dos platos of huevos and frijoles."* When she looked at both of us and smiled, I figured it must be okay for me to be there. While we waited, I looked through the back door. A clay stove was out back with a fire in it. A large pot with beans was hanging by the edge of the fire. She set a frying pan over the flames and broke some eggs into it. Just watching made me realize how hungry I was, and I figured if no one else was worried about colored or white, I wouldn't either.

Course I was no fool and I'm not saying that I wasn't going to pay attention to things. I didn't ask no questions 'cause I didn't know how to say "Jim Crow laws" in Spanish. But I was beginning to see that things was different down there than they was in Texas.

Pretty soon, even though we was white and colored, we got to talking like we was just people. Jorge worked the fields and did laboring jobs just like I did. He said, for those willing, there was always work on the coffee haciendas. The pay was poor, but I was used to that too. That would start up soon. Till then, he and his family lived in the next village

190

over and worked their own farm, tending crops and livestock. They had their own corn harvest coming. It looked to be a good harvest this year, though in the way of sharecroppers, they had to pay off the landowner first.

I didn't have any plans and so when our meal was done, I walked with Jorge toward his village. The roads out of town were steep and rutted. I saw some wagons, but unless you had a heavy load it was no slower to walk. I don't think we went so many miles, but it was slow walking. He brought out some tortillas and we stopped by a stream at midday. The road narrowed to more of a path before I began to see some houses.

The houses were adobe and clustered together and like Jorge said, the village was small. It was much poorer too. It had its center and fountain, but there were fewer stores and it was quiet enough that the dogs could sleep on the street and not be bothered. Still, just like that morning, I could go and drink from the same fountain. Everyone knew Jorge, and I met his brother, Emilio. He had a smaller farm for he was a maker of blankets.

Jorge wasn't much older than me, but he already had three children. Their home was crowded and though I agreed to help for a few days with the corn harvest in exchange for meals and a place to sleep, I stayed with his brother and his wife, who had no children but an extra room. Early morning, I was out with them in the cornfields. Their corn was a little different. Ours was cattle corn. Theirs looked almost the same, but it was a little sweeter.

Some other workers from his village came in the mornings, white or mestizo, it didn't matter. When Jorge's corn was done, it would be his turn to help his neighbor. Same as in Marshall, children, unless they were very young, worked too. It was the children who seemed to take notice of my skin. Most were shy. They stared at me, probably couldn't help themselves for that if they had tried. But there was also children that asked me, "Why is your skin so dark?"

As to an answer, I could only shrug. "It's just the way it is."

No one had ever asked me before. It didn't bother me to be asked. Back in Marshall, no one said anything about my color, but life was different because of it. I could tell that there were folks that didn't like me for the color of my skin. It was still my habit to be careful: to wait for everyone else, touch no food unless I was asked, and to serve myself last. But though I was a worker, everyone treated me like a guest.

Just like in Marshall, we broke for a meal right in the fields. Difference was that people took notice of me. It was my habit to keep working past everyone else, but someone would say to me, *"Jorge, basta alto!"* (George, enough already, stop!) Then, they would serve me first. It was only rice and beans with corn tortillas, but it made me feel like a king. The work was the same, but I wasn't just somebody's field hand. That made all the difference.

The village had always been poor. They told me that Pancho Villa had ridden through about five years earlier, after raiding some towns in Texas. The U.S. Army was after him and the village gave him food and slaughtered a goat for his men. He had promised change and justice, and some of the men even left with him. The Mexican *federales* followed and just took the food and livestock that they wanted and things were worse than ever. But General Pershing never caught him. It was the Mexican government that betrayed and killed Pancho Villa earlier that year of 1923. Of course, after he died, every village in Mexico claims that Pancho Villa came through and that they gave him food and shelter. I figured if all the stories were true, he would have to have lived to be older than me just to eat and sleep in so many villages. Of course, I never said that while I was down there.

The work only lasted a week. I was welcome to stay and gave it some thought. Part of me could picture settling down, even having my own wife and children and spending my whole life right there. I had never had feelings like that before, but I guess that's what can happen when people treat you so decent-like. Still, I knew there wasn't so much food and, besides, I could never do it.

No matter what, I knew I would always go back to Texas. Sometimes, I didn't feel welcome there by some folks, but that was home.

In the morning chill, I put a bundle of corn on my back and walked down with Jorge and some other villagers to sell it in town. They had their village to go back to. I took the train down to see the ocean. It was something else.

Fishing the surf is a whole different thing than doing catfish, but it's fun. There was lots of fish, but except for the mackerel, I don't remember the names. It was warm enough to sleep on the beach at night. There couldn't be anything nicer and everything I would ever need was right there. I took good care of my money, keeping train fare in a different boot and being slow by nature to touch the rest anyway.

There were a couple of cafes that I stopped in, not so much 'cause I was hungry but because they would serve me. I knew I was in another country when I could walk through the front door and where I sat could be my own choice. I liked that. Life was good, but I was too used to working, and after a week I caught the train back to Texas.

CHAPTER 13

Scene I: Calvin Coolidge—Pushing off in fishing boat with his dog.

To reporters: "The country is doing well and there are good times ahead for all. My job is to make sure that the government does nothing to hurt this prosperity. The less the government, the better off America will be. So, you see, gentlemen, I do my job best when I work as little as possible."

Scene 2: In a back alley, barrels are being rolled out of a truck toward an aproned, beckoning barkeeper and through the back door of a brick building. The scene shifts to the front of the building along Main Street. Customers are streaming in to enjoy themselves at a busy club.

Narrator: "Whether the idea had merit or not, Prohibition doesn't work. It is only creating a society where it is normal to break the laws and encouraging the growth of our criminal element, who prosper the most. The longer Prohibition lasts, the less regard the citizens of this country will have for our nation's laws."

—From a newsreel, 1923

Calvin Coolidge, I remember him. But he doesn't stick out in my mind. The prosperity in America then, I sure don't remember that.

Prohibition? That's another thing. I hardly ever drank anything myself, but I bet most people drank more during those "dry" times than they ever did, before or since. I don't know why, but that's the truth.

Once I was back from Mexico, I wasn't fool enough to just walk into a restaurant or drink at any fountain, but I missed that. Texas was home, but I didn't feel so welcome there when I got back. I stayed long enough to mend some fences, help plant some crops, but that was it. As big as it was, Texas felt too small. I wasn't ready to sit still yet. I hadn't said much, but there wasn't no one surprised to see me go this time.

Same ticket master was at the station and I expected him to recognize me. But then I realized he never really even took notice of me. He just took my money. That kind of put me off, but on the other hand, I didn't want no trouble.

"Boy, you got money for a ticket?"

It was kinda strange. He didn't know me, but I remembered him, even knew the questions that would be coming. But I couldn't let on and show him up neither.

"Yes, sir."

"Well, then, where you going to?"

Out of Texas: That's what I wanted to say.

"Chicago. Ticket to Chicago, please."

Now I knew nothing about Chicago except that's where people headed when they went north. I knew he would get mad at me if I said, "Going north, anywheres out of Texas do just fine."

"Nothing going to Chicago today, boy. Closest is a train to St. Louis; that's on the way to Cleveland."

I nodded. It really didn't matter and I could be happy with that.

He scowled. I understood that he would have

liked me to have been saddened some by what he had told me. That even made me wonder if there might actually be a train leaving to Chicago that he wouldn't tell me about. Didn't matter; it wasn't going to ruin my life. I smiled as if he had made my day.

"Cleveland is just fine, sir."

"One way or round trip?" He snapped at me.

"Round trip will be fine, sir."

Kinda surprised myself to be saying that for I didn't know what my plans were. I could tell that he sure didn't care if I came back or not. As much as I was ready to leave, and no matter what some folks thought of me, I knew my roots were in Texas. Besides that, as bad as the colored were treated, some folks got real mad when a colored left and moved up north. And there were a whole lot doing just that. Someone might just get angry enough to cause me some real trouble if they thought I was leaving the South to move up north. No reason to push it too far by asking, but in spite of the way he talked, I bet he hadn't been as far away as Cleveland, probably hadn't even been to St. Louis. So, I just grinned at him and said, "Thank you kindly."

I put the return ticket in my boot. This wasn't my first train trip anymore, but I still got a feeling in my stomach that only came from being in the station. I waited in the colored section, but it wouldn't matter if I was allowed to sit on the white benches. Not knowing what I was gonna see or who I was gonna meet or what I was gonna learn left everything out in front of me. Only the Lord would know what was gonna happen, though I expect he had bigger things to check on and probably just let the trains run by themselves.

I never had any complaints, but after Mexico I would say the train looked mighty fine even in the colored car that I rode in. The porter told me that when the cars get old and worn out, they sell them to the lines in Mexico. I guess it's the last stop before the train junkyard, if there is such a thing.

The train headed north and it wasn't long before we left the pine forests. The porter called out that we was in Oklahoma. Outside of a few lakes, there was only hardscrabble ground and the soil wasn't so deep for growing crops. The whitewash was faded off the houses and some looked close to falling over. The barns were kept up better than the houses.

The trains ran slow and made lots of whistlestops. It was early summer but already hot. Folks were outside. We went slow enough that, for a moment, we was a part of their lives. Some little children stopped their hoeing to wave and watch the train. I waved back. Their father, standing behind, stopped and looked at the train too. He didn't wave. He looked old and worn out, without hope.

Three times a week, the train passed through their lives, but it didn't change nothing. Nothing was going to change there. They was white but didn't have much chance in life either. Farther out, I nodded to a colored man driving his wagon on a dirt road alongside the track. We came up beside an automobile.

There was no roof or windshield and the driver wore goggles. His hands were tight on the wheel and he looked to be racing our train; doing all right too! On the uphill, he pulled ahead. Downhill, the train went faster and he couldn't keep up. It was a mighty fine-looking car but was no match for a train.

It would take him longer to get to Tulsa by car. Least, that's what I figured when the porter came through shouting, "Tulsa, Tulsa, Oklahoma."

He stretched out the word "Oklahoma" like it went on forever. Then he said, "This be a two-hour stop. You can leave your luggage, but be back in two hours. This train don't wait for nobody."

Usually the track runs right through the colored section of a town, but I couldn't be sure. I just wanted a bite to eat without causing no trouble. I saw a couple of cafes down from the station, but I couldn't tell. A man that I had seen toward the front of my car seemed to be looking for something too.

I put out my hand and said, "George Dawson." I think it's traveling that makes a person think you can just walk up and talk to someone like that. Growing up in Marshall, I never would of done that whether it was a colored or a white man. But I wasn't in Marshall anymore.

"Artis, Artis Smith," he said. Artis didn't

wear homespuns like me; as a matter of fact he was dressed pretty nice, even had polished shoes. But as two colored men on the road, we had enough in common to be talking with each other.

"You know somewhere to get a bite to eat?"

There were a couple of cafes down the way, but any colored man understood that question to be "a restaurant that will serve to colored?"

Artis shrugged. "Yeah, I know of some, but it's been a little while since I been through Tulsa. Come on, we can check a couple out."

We walked over toward the cafe. Artis read the sign on the door. "No Indians. Whites only."

Now, that was a new one and I looked at him. "Well, they got a lot of Indians around here. And they ain't white either. No problem, follow me," he said.

As we passed the other cafe, he didn't read the sign out loud. I figure it must of said the same thing since we kept on going. In about four blocks we found the cafe Artis was looking for.

I let Artis order first. He ordered spareribs that came with cornbread and potatoes. I set my menu down like I had read it for myself and said, "That sounds good. I'll have the same, except no coffee. A cup of hot chocolate do me fine."

Used to be that a cup of hot chocolate would taste a little different each time. Some chocolate had the bitters and you added sugar. Some blocks of chocolate was sweet. There were some people might scrape a little chocolate off each type of block and blend them together. Even the milk could be different. Hot chocolate with fresh, sweet milk tasted different than a cup where the cream had been taken out of the milk first.

It was a nice change from the sandwiches that you get on the train. The porters said that they had a good cook, but the dining car was whites only. For a long trip, the colored often bring a hamper with food. After that runs out, they hoped that at some stations there would be food for colored. Peddlers boarded the train to sell sandwiches and such, but a long trip still wasn't easy.

Artis had a watch and we got back to the train on time. After Tulsa, the towns got smaller. In the moonlight, the farms didn't look so broken and worn out. I had a whole bench to myself to stretch out on. During the night, I felt the train stop in small towns. But I never really woke up till dawn.

Joplin was nice, mostly wood-frame buildings, but they was clean and covered with paint or whitewash. I stayed at the station to watch for when the train blasted out steam since I didn't carry no clock. While I waited, I went to the food counter and bought some rolls and some apples.

I waited till the porter's call and then boarded just as the train was about to leave. That made me feel like a traveler that knew his way around, all right. When I stepped in the aisle, I was blocked from other people standing in front of where my seat was. I didn't mean to be eavesdropping or nothing, but I couldn't move ahead any farther toward my seat and it was getting to be too late to step back off the train.

"Mama, Daddy, you better go now. I'll be just fine."

Another woman's voice said, "There's all the food you need to get you to St. Louis right in the basket."

The younger woman's voice said, "Thank you, Mama. I'll bet there's enough if it took a whole week."

The man's face was to the side and I could see him smile at that. "Now your mama just takes good care of you, of all of us." He handed her a letter and said, "Give this to my sister. And you be good when you're up there and study hard."

"I will, Daddy. Good luck with your sermon on Sunday."

They talked so educated and all, but him being a minister explained it. My bench was still empty and I sat down. I tried not to look, but I noticed that she was dressed in real nice clothes. She would have been pretty in homespuns too. I had been sleeping in and wearing my clothes for days. In my bedroll, there was a fresh shirt, but there was nowhere to bathe or change. I hoped she wouldn't even notice me. She had pulled out a book and commenced reading even before the train left. That left me nothing to say.

I made a show of looking out my window.

Like in a mirror or in a flat pond of water, I found that I could see her reflection if I leaned back and twisted my head. It sort of startled me but I heard her book fall when she opened her basket. I scrambled out of my seat to hand her the book. "Why, thank you, that's very kind of you."

"No problem." I wanted to say something intelligent-like, but that's all I could do. She waited as if for me to say something else. A lot of folks around Marshall will tell you that usually I can tell a good story along with the best of them. But right then my tongue was stuck and my brain was frozen. Nothing came out.

Finally she spoke up. She held her book toward me to show me the cover and asked, "Have you read this?"

After picking it up, I made a show of looking at it. "No," I said. "I haven't. Is it good?"

I felt country enough in my wrinkled home-spuns and I didn't want to be saying that I couldn't read. I liked listening to her tell me about the book. People that in real life wouldn't even be speaking to each other can talk on a train. At least I got my tongue back enough to introduce myself. I could see that besides being pretty, she had a quick mind. Matter of fact, she was going to teach school and stay with an aunt in Springfield, Missouri. I wanted my trip to sound like a worthwhile journey, but suddenly my travels felt aimless. I could never do what she was doing.

I thought of asking her permission to stop

and visit while I was on my trip. But I under-stood that not being able to read made us too different. When she got off in Spring-field, I helped her with her bags. But I never saw her again.

We got to St. Louis that same afternoon, but there were no more trains leaving that day. The station was right downtown and I had never seen anything quite like it. There were lots of brick buildings and some tall ones too. All the roads was paved and they was full of autos.

When I got something to eat at one of the street-corner groceries, I noticed that it cost more money than it would have in Marshall. I had already spent money for the train, but I figured I could always go a couple of days without eating, if I had to. It had never taken me long to find a job before so I wasn't wor-ried. The station wasn't all that far of a walk from the waterfront. It was the Mississippi, the same river that I had worked on down south of Memphis. It had been dredged out and it was a busy harbor.

I sat down next to some pilings, dropped my bedroll, and pulled out my lunch: a small loaf of bread, a couple of apples, and some meat that was kind of spicy but I couldn't put a name to. A barge was unloading right in front of me. Wooden crates were being hauled down the walkways, two men to a crate. The foreman stood by the plank and checked them off before they went to a truck. Over by the truck another white man kept looking at his watch.

He finally left the truck. He passed close

enough that I could of reached out and touched him, but I don't think he even saw me. He shouted to the foreman, "It's moving too slow. We're falling behind. These trucks need to be loaded and out of here."

The foreman said, "Hey, fine with me. But I got a man didn't show today. That means we run one team short since they work in twos."

The man from the truck said, "Glad to hear it, but they aren't paying us for excuses. They gave you enough cash to pay good money, so go find somebody!"

He turned and walked away. I was close enough to hear the man on deck cursing and swearing. "First I get a lazy-assed bastard that don't show up for work, and then I got to listen to that son of a bitch tell me what to do."

I grinned. It wasn't my fault he was shouting loud enough for me to hear.

"Hey, Louis." He shouted at a worker that was about to grab on to a crate. He had been lining up the crates for the other men to carry off deck. "Find me another worker for this crew."

"Sure, boss. Where do I do that?"

"How the hell do I know? I can't do everything around here. There's a job waiting so go down on the docks and find somebody!"

Louis had to be sorry he'd asked. I saw him muttering to himself but heard him say, "Right, boss."

That was enough for me. Grabbing my bedroll, I stuffed some food in my pockets and jumped up. I started walking away from the barge at an angle to cut Louis off. He noticed more than those white men did and spotted me from the corner of his eye.

"Hey, there," he shouted and waved me over. "You want a—"

I grinned at him and said, "A job!"

He laughed. "You heard him, I guess, hard not to. So, you know what the foreman's like, but if—"

"It's fine. It'll be fine," I said.

He shrugged. "Okay, then. You want to know what it pays?"

I nodded.

"Dollar a day and there's a cook that will make some lunch and a dinner meal too if the work goes real late. This job will probably last about two more days."

"I got no problem with that," I told him.

"Good. I see you got a bedroll. If you need a place to stay, you stretch out on the barge. That's what I'm doing."

"Sounds good to me," I told him.

As we walked back to the barge, I looked over at Louis. He looked to be about my age. He was taller than me, but not by that much. He didn't carry a Texas accent.

"Where you from?" I asked.

"I'm from Malden. That's down by the Arkansas border."

"You been in St. Louis long?"

"Naw, just a couple of weeks. Not much work in Malden."

At that time, a lot of colored were leaving

the farms and moving to cities in the North. They were all doing it for the same reason: to better themselves. I didn't know if it was gonna help, though.

"There good jobs in St. Louis?"

"Sure, there is. This is a big city."

I nodded but didn't ask why he was working on a two-day job unloading barges, then. Funny how if you don't ask a question, someone answers even faster for you.

"I could be back in Malden right now," he said. "This is September. Harvesttime would be wrapping up soon and then there would be nothing till next spring. Most of the crop goes to the owner anyway."

A whole lot of folks weren't as fortunate as us Dawsons, who owned our land. Share-croppers could only keep a portion of their harvest and the rest went to the landowner. It was common, but there was no way to get ahead.

Louis went on. "I got a chance here."

That's all any of us wanted then, a chance.

The barge was a pretty good size, a lot bigger than it looked. The plank came in about the middle of it, but the foreman was on the other side and up front. Louis shouted, "Boss, I got somebody."

"What, already? You been gone all of three minutes!"

Louis wasn't disrespectful and point out that he did something faster than his boss. I could tell that he enjoyed getting one on him, 'cause it was his boss or 'cause he was a white man,

I didn't know. I just stood off to the side and waited till he said, "This is George."

The foreman looked me over and said, "Boy, you a good worker?"

"Yes, sir."

"You got a problem with hard work?"

"No, sir." With a boss, especially a new one, I always kept it short. I knew I could think as well as him, but I also knew he didn't expect much from me anyway.

"What the hell. Louis, he'll need to work with you. Show him what to do."

It wasn't hard to figure. I just took the other end of the crate. The barge was stacked deep with crates from front to back, with only the middle open. Two crews worked their way up front. Louis and I worked our way toward the back.

The crates wasn't too big, but they was heavy. They had writing and labels on them.

"Louis, what are we lifting here?"

He said, "I don't know."

"What's that mean, 'you don't know'?" I asked.

We didn't stop but he looked around. In a low voice, he said, "Nobody tells me nothing, but I figure it's spirits."

That made sense, but all I could say was "That's a whole lot of it then."

Louis said, "I hear tell that since Prohibition, there's a lot of money to be made in selling spirits."

I didn't say nothing. Louis must have caught

what I was thinking and said, "I'm just paid to move these boxes!"

At that point, questions would only have gotten me in some real trouble.

The other crews must have lived in town. They left at night and came back in the morning. I liked sleeping on the barge. It felt like fall: warm days and cool nights, a bit cooler than Texas, but it wasn't too bad or nothing. As they had said, we finished in a couple of days.

It felt good when the foreman paid us off and I had a couple of dollars to put in my pocket. Then I didn't have to touch my boot money, the money I was saving for rough times. The foreman said, "This barge is moving out on Monday. Today being Friday, if you can spend the weekend on the barge just to keep an eye on things, I'll pay you each four bits plus you can eat from the larder of the wheel-house."

I guess he didn't want to stay around himself, but I just took it as good luck. Next morning Louis said, "Why don't we go over to the stadium. The Cardinals are playing today."

Knowing I would be on the road again, I wasn't too keen to throw two bits down just like that. Louis must have figured what I was thinking. He said, "It won't cost nothing. We get there at the right time, we'll get some work inside and they'll even pay us to be there. Jimmy from this barge did that last weekend."

"I'm ready."

"Good. It's less than an hour walk and we won't need to use the streetcar if we go soon."

That stadium was brick that was mostly covered in ivy. There was only one door open then. It was too early for the fans to be there and only workers was going in. Right by the front of the door, Louis shouted, "Hey, Jimmy!"

Jimmy had been with us on the barge and he came over. "Jimmy, think they can fit us in for some work?"

"Yeah, I'm almost sure. Wait here."

He came running back. "Boss says to go out and help with lemonade. It's gonna be a hot day. And then after the game, stick around and you can move to the cleanup crew in the bleachers. It's four bits, a free ballgame, and in the bleachers, what you find is what you get!"

Before the game started, I never chopped so many lemons in my life and that's when I wasn't carrying big sacks of sugar. I didn't do the mixing, but trust me when I say there was a lot of lemonade. The ice would melt down quick, but there was enough to keep it cold. They made it in big earthenware crocks and then took those out to some counters. There was actually a good view of the field from there.

My job was to keep the supplies moving but once things got settled I could just stand and watch the game. Good game too. The Chicago Cubs was in town. That was the time when the Cardinals had the old Gas House Gang. And there it was late September and a close pennant race.

I had only been in St. Louis a few days, and I had never been to Chicago, so I rooted for St. Louis. I watched closely. They had decent pitching, but they looked a bit tired, probably worn out from a long season. Now don't get me wrong. They was good, but I couldn't help but wonder that my brother Johnny, if he wasn't colored, could be a big help on the mound. Johnny would never have talked like he was that good, but I think he could have held his own. It's not just because he was my brother that I am saying that. After all, I caught more of his games than anyone and I should know. Thing is, I would have liked to have caught Johnny and called that game myself.

Those two teams played smart baseball, the way I liked to see it. The Cardinals were fast on the base paths and they weren't afraid to try to pull off a hit-and-run. They were good line-drive hitters, and while I don't claim to be the greatest, that's my style too.

The stands was full and we sold the last of the lemonade at the seventh-inning stretch. I don't even remember who won. It was just good baseball. It must of taken as many hours to clean up the bleachers as it did to watch the game itself. We filled sacks and sacks of garbage. Besides the garbage, I found some car keys that Jimmy said were from a DeSoto, a couple of teddy bears, some watches, a couple of wallets, and a few jackets. I took a big pile up to the office. The wallets had some names, but they told me to pick a jacket if I could find one that fit. Since I heard it could be cold up north, I took a nice blue one with a blanket lining.

Back on the barge that night, Louis said, "There's gonna be more work on the river. And if you stick around a long time, a job will turn up."

"That's something to think about, all right," I told him. "But I paid for a ticket that goes all the way to Cleveland."

"What's up there?"

"I don't know, but I wanted to see some snow. I never saw that in Texas."

Louis said, "Yeah, I don't expect you'll see it in St. Louis either. I saw snow once when I was on a hunting trip in the hills outside of Malden."

"Did you like it?" I asked.

"Yeah, it was nice."

"I heard they have snow in Ohio," I said.

"I heard that too." Louis nodded.

I picked up my bedroll and my new jacket. We shook hands. "Maybe I'll see you on my way back through St. Louis."

"Check the barges down along the river. At least one of us got sense to stay with a good thing." He laughed.

CHAPTER 14

O'Keeffe's desire for remoteness and for
closeness to nature led her to settle for four
years into teaching jobs near Amarillo
in the vast, dry, seemingly boundless
region of the Texas Panhandle.... Her
paintings of desert skulls, the quality of
fantasy arises from a contradiction: the
strength of the image and the hard-edge
precision of its rendering are at odds
with the ideas we normally associate with
a skull.

—*The Story of American Painting,* by
Abraham A. Davidson

Nowadays, I work hard at school. On Sunday
morning, I get up and go to church. Saturday
is the day that I catch up with things or maybe
now that spring is coming, I'll just go fishing.
Last week I puttered around in my yard, had
some visitors over during the day. Decided I
would go to bed early that night for a change.

It was dark when I heard a pounding on the
door. "Who's there? What do you want?" I
shouted.

I used a voice like I meant business. You just
don't know about people these days, and
while most people are good, a person can't trust
everybody. I figured that I probably run him
off. But there was more knocking. "It's me,

Richard. I came over to visit. Is that still okay?"

I opened the door. It sure was him, all right. "You is late, so I figured you wasn't coming tonight like your letter said."

"Well, my plane got in a little late and then there was a delay with the baggage."

"Well, good," I said and opened the screen door. "Come on in. You're lucky I don't own a shotgun no more."

Unless he brings fishing gear or something, Richard usually travels light, though not as light as I used to with just a bedroll. This time he had bags across the porch. He carried in a suitcase and I picked up a rucksack. It was a big one and weighted down too; must have weighed twenty-five pounds.

I carried it across the living room and dropped it on the couch. "What you carrying, some lead fishing weights?"

"No, it's full of books," he told me.

"Son, if you wanted something to read, I've got books in my house now." I admit, it felt good to be able to say that.

"Thanks, that will be nice. But I brought these books because I wanted to share them with you," Richard said.

"I've always shared everything I had, but never was able to share any books before. That will be mighty fine."

I pulled some out of the rucksack. "These books are big, all right."

"They're called coffee table books."

"Why is that?" I asked.

"I think they're supposed to look good sitting on your coffee table."

"These big ones must be expensive to just sit on your table."

"Probably. I got these from the library."

I know they were heavy to carry down and all, but I had to wonder if they was worth the bother. I held one of them open. Richard had carried a heavy book a long way and I was feeling kind of bad for him, but then we finally found something. "Now this one, I can tell this picture. That's a cow's skull. Who did that?"

"That's by Georgia O'Keeffe," Richard said. "It's called 'Cow's Skull—Red White and Blue.' "

"Yeah, it looks just liked a bleached skull that been out there after a long, hot drought.

"I like this one too," I said.

"That's by Edward Hopper, around 1930. It's called 'Early Sunday Morning.' "

"Most of those pictures don't look the way I saw things in the South then. But that one looks like Marshall did about the time I left for traveling in the 1920s. It has the same barber pole and everything."

Richard asked me if that was on the same trip when I had gone to St. Louis. Truth was that I had plans to go farther north than that, but I almost didn't make it any farther. My ticket had been safe in my boot and I took it out when I got to the St. Louis station. I asked the ticket master, "How long it be till the Cleveland train?"

"Leaves at three o'clock. Do you want to buy a ticket, boy?"

"No, sir. I got off in St. Louis, but I already bought a ticket that goes to Cleveland." I slid it across the counter and under the grate to him.

He looked at it and frowned. "No way, boy!"

I knew there was trouble. To question him might invite more, but I had to know. I had maybe given up finding a good job in St. Louis so that I could continue my journey.

"Sir?" I said in a tone that asked but didn't challenge.

"This ticket says round trip, Marshall, Texas, to St. Louis, Missouri. Don't you try to put one over on me."

"No, sir. But I paid all the way to Cleveland."

"That's the case, then why did you get off here in St. Louis?"

" 'Cause the man said I had to change trains in St. Louis."

"No, boy, your ticket ends in St. Louis."

"Well, I paid the man for a ticket all the way to Cleveland."

"Boy, I don't know what you paid." He shoved it back at me and said, "Read it for yourself. It says St. Louis. Doesn't say Cleveland."

I looked at the ticket but didn't say that I couldn't read it. "Except, sir, that I paid—"

"Boy, are you accusing the ticket master in Marshall of cheating you?"

Right then I knew I had been cheated, but I said, "No, sir."

"That's good. Now get out of this station, boy, or do I need to call the police?"

I turned and left. I had been had good and I knew it too. I walked along the track and hoped to one day see that ticket master in Marshall again. It was him, all right. But then I knew that even when I saw him, I couldn't accuse a white man of cheating.

There were some trains in the yard and I looked around. No one was in sight and I started walking alongside a freight train. Up and down the yard, I saw other men doing the same thing. When I came to a car with an open door, I took a quick look for the bull and pulled myself in. It was dark and full of chicken manure, but it wasn't bad. The manure was old and dry and didn't carry too much smell.

More and more men was doing the same thing and I figured the train to be leaving soon. In case the bull came by, I moved down out of sight of the door and waited. About the time I heard the engine building up steam, a couple of more men hopped in. They was white but there wasn't no problem. They nodded at me and then moved down toward my end to get away from the door and out of sight.

One of them put out his hand and said, "Jerry." The other nodded at me and said, "Alex." The one named Jerry said, "Going all the way to New Orleans?"

"I don't know where I is headed," I said. Both of them laughed but nodded.

The one named Alex said, "Well, we hope this is going to New Orleans."

Jerry said, "If by nightfall we've left Missouri and we make a stop at Cairo, then we're on the train to New Orleans."

Jerry picked up for Alex. "If by nightfall we hit Kansas City, then we're on the way to Nebraska."

Alex raised his hand in the air. "Nebraska is pretty rough on hobos. Here's hoping that we're on the *Spirit of New Orleans*."

When Alex smiled there were a couple of teeth missing up front and some fresh bruises still on his face. I didn't say nothing, but he saw the question in my eyes. He pointed to his face and said, "The bull in Omaha carries a big stick. I took it in the face before he threw me off the train. That was less than two weeks ago and not where I want to go back to, all right."

Jerry said, "That's right, we're going first class on the *Spirit of New Orleans*. You'll see."

I smiled and said, "I hope you're right."

Once we were out of the yard, the train picked up speed. The sun was strong enough that the wind whipping in just felt good. Even then, St. Louis was a big city, but before too long the buildings were lower, mostly the back sides of factories and then lots of slum-like apartments. I could see children on the fire escapes or hanging out the windows. Sitting in the doorway, I made sure to wave to all of them.

On the edge of town, there was some squatter camps just off the tracks. More hobos were running along the train and coming on. The train had to slow and they must of known. Of

218

course, if you're not paying attention you can still lose your legs or even get killed on a slow-moving train.

By the time we got to Cairo, we had a pretty full car. In a way, we had become friends and I stayed at the end of the car with Jerry and Alex, but everybody got along. I listened in. There was people on the move from all over the country. There was some people that had been riding the rails for years. A person could learn a lot just by listening.

Those that had food passed some around. It was an odd mix, but there was some sausage, some bread, and some apples. Someone had raided a cornfield and that helped out too. There wasn't a whole lot, but it was enough to get through the night. Mostly, I just listened to the talk about New Orleans.

On the rails, Chicago was the big city, but it was New Orleans that would get people to talking. Even the food was different. According to what I heard, New Orleans was about music, gambling, and women. Coming from Marshall, I didn't have much to add since I didn't know much of that. But I could listen since it wasn't like I couldn't learn more.

Sleeping on a freight train is like nothing else. The wind keeps flowing through the door and it got in my dreams. If I woke, I could just lay there and look at the stars. Knowing that in the first light I would be looking at a new part of the world made it special.

The yard in New Orleans is a big one, all right. All in all, they say that the bulls aren't too bad there. But there's always a few that enjoy their job too much, that like using their sticks to crack heads, so you got to be careful. As the train started slowing people were falling out of the cars like potato bugs on a spring plant.

It was something to see. Not wanting to get to the central yard and meet one of the bulls, I joined them. Falling out of a freight train looks easier than it is. If you don't hit the ground running, it's hard to keep your feet. I know that, because it happened. I tumbled and rolled. Good thing was that I headed alongside the train and not back toward the rails. Jerry gave me a hand up and we was running between two trains. We passed the caboose of the one we rode in on. From there, I could see out across the yard.

Before making a dash across the yard, Jerry and Alex paused at the corner of the caboose.

"Where to?" I said.

Jerry said, "Either direction works. We're just trying to figure."

"I've got a little money. Wouldn't mind going to a boardinghouse and taking a bath," Alex said.

"Whatsa matter? Chicken shit got to you?"

"Yeah, kinda." Alex shrugged.

"Hey, the hobo camp will be there tomorrow. I wouldn't mind a bath neither."

Alex and then Jerry turned and looked at me. They didn't say nothing. But I could figure.

I asked anyway. "I got money. Will that work?"

They both shook their heads. "Sorry," Jerry said.

"Don't worry," I said.

I knew it wasn't a boardinghouse that would take colored. "I understand. Just tell me which way to go."

Alex pointed in the other direction. "Follow them. They're off to the hobo camp."

I could see a group of colored and white running across the yard. I nodded.

They each put out their hand to me. On the rails, we was all one, but outside the yards, it was a world of white and colored. Even friends couldn't cross those lines.

There was maybe a half-dozen of them on the run. I caught up to the pack of them. We stopped when we got to the last siding. There was a train on it and we crouched behind it to check for any bulls. Then, as one, we broke from the rail.

Just then, a bull stepped out from around a train. He fired a shot in the air. It wasn't leveled at us but sure did get us moving. Once we was past the train, we were down below the grade and then we run along the track. Pretty soon we slowed to a trot when it was clear no one was following.

Had to be that someone knew where we was going so I stayed alongside. When we slowed to a walk, people started talking and laughing.

"Did you see that bull?"

"Yeah, he couldn't hit the side of a barn," another one said.

221

"I don't know. You was running fast enough after he fired that shot."

"Well..."

They went on and on like that till we got to a camp. Most of them seemed to know each other, but I felt right at home. The camp was a way out and bigger than I thought it would be. It was down in a gully, but not as far from the tracks as it seemed. It had been used enough that there was a path that turned off from the tracks that I could have followed if I had been alone.

Except for its distance from the tracks, it looked like most camps I had already seen in my travels. People had settled themselves around and out from a fire pit. A few had made shelters from the sides of old packing crates. Most had just smoothed down a spot for a bedroll. Someone was going to try to collect some food, and I put in a little change that was in my pockets. I didn't touch my boot money for there was no way of knowing how far that might have to carry me.

It didn't really get cold, but by dusk a fire was going and some stew was cooking. Someone must have known of a store or connected with a farm. There were good smells. There was even chunks of meat in the stew.

Like most places on the Mississippi, I heard that if there was any work, a person could find it along the river. Next morning, I didn't waste any time. I was off before daybreak with a colored man named Larry. He'd lived in New Orleans on and off for years so I knew we would do all right and stay out of trouble.

In cities up the river, it was mostly barges that you see tied up. Now, New Orleans, it had its ships and big ones too. Larry seemed to know some people on the docks. The word out was that the *New London* had just tied up last night and would be unloading.

We worked our way down to the docks. The sun was almost up when we got to the *New London*. There was a crowd already hoping for work too. Larry grinned and said, "Stick with me."

He wove his way toward the front and I stayed right with him. Good thing too. From the water's edge, he shouted up, "Red, is that you?"

A big white man with red hair smiled. "Hey, Larry, long time no see."

"I just got back in. Got some work for us?"

"Sure thing," he said. "In a short while, I gonna be sending a man down to the docks to round up a crew." Pointing at me, he said, "He a friend of yours, Larry? He want work too?"

Larry said, "Yeah."

He dropped a rope ladder over the side. Larry scrambled right up. I had never been on one, but found that it wasn't so hard.

Red waved toward the crowd that was getting bigger. "It'll be almost an hour before he pulls a crew out of that mess. Cook will get you some breakfast."

Wasn't long before we was working on a mess of eggs, grits, and biscuits. Turns out that Larry had shipped on one of Red's crews all the way to South America and back. I wasn't quite sure where that was, but I got the idea that there wasn't anywhere in the world that New Orleans didn't send its ships to.

Coconuts is what we unloaded. They was in big bins. We loaded them into smaller crates and then moved them off the ship. They weren't so heavy, but even by mid-morning, the heat was just something powerful.

The heat don't really bother me, though, never has. That might be because my great-great-grandmother came from India as a slave. I hear tell that's even hotter than New Orleans or a Texas drought that's doing its worst. Good thing about that New Orleans heat was that work stopped early, about middle of the afternoon.

"That's awfully nice of them to take those concerns for our comfort."

Larry laughed. "Oh, yeah, awfully nice. And besides that, they would like this crew not to die this afternoon so as we can come to work for them tomorrow morning."

Because Larry knew Red, we was able to get a little draw on our pay. I've always liked that nice, tired feeling that comes from a good day's work, and to leave the ship and wander into New Orleans with a little money in my pockets—well, I figured to be at the top of the world.

New Orleans was like nothing I had seen before. It was big and busy, but so was St. Louis.

224

It was more than that. It was just different. We walked the streets and the people, some of them, wasn't even speaking English. Larry knew, or at least acted like he knew, what they was saying.

He said, "Around here, some folks speak French, some speak in Creole, and they is some that speak Spanish."

"Don't they know to speak English?" I asked.

"Well, the Cajun is part English and part French. And some can speak English anyway, but just don't bother. People here, they do things as they want."

I could see that was right. The streets were crowded with people. And the houses was right up to the sidewalks. The doors were open and every house had those porches where the people were.

I wasn't all that hungry, but the smells from the restaurants we passed would fill the streets. It smelled good, though it was like nothing that I knew. New Orleans was a night town, but in late afternoon, the restaurant patios had people out drinking. We didn't stop, though.

Larry had something in mind and I stayed with him till he stopped. "Here we are," he said.

We was in front of one of them buildings like the others we had passed for block after block. It had a whitewashed side, though truth is, it could have used another coat. Like the other buildings, it had its porches with the iron rails.

The door was open and Larry called out, "Gloria, you home?"

In no time, an older colored lady came out and looking none too happy either.

"Now who that be shouting out my name, when I got a nice buzzer in the door for a civilized person to use?"

Larry grinned. "Well, since the door was wide open..."

"Is that you, Larry? Why, let me look. It sure is."

She came down off the porch and Larry got a big hug, all right. "I should be plain angry the way you be gone long enough."

"Aw, you know how it is."

"Don't you hand me that. I know how men is, all right. That's what I know. Always running off and leaving some nice girl behind."

"Good thing I've known you since you was a little boy. That's why I know you've got your good side too."

She looked at us and laughed. "You don't want to hear that, do you?"

Without waiting for an answer, she asked, "Who's your friend?"

"His name is George. He's all right."

"I expect you both want a room?"

"Yeah, work looks good and we're gonna be here for a while," Larry said.

"You always say you're gonna be here for a while," Gloria snapped. "Is that what you told Alice?"

"Well, when I said it, I thought I was. Say, where is Alice? You seen her lately?" Larry asked.

"Now you just forget that girl and leave her alone. She done got over you."

"You didn't answer me. Is she still around?"

Gloria crossed her arms and told Larry, "No, she isn't. She found her a good man that would stick around just like she deserved. They done got married and they be up in Alabama, where he got a job."

She looked closely at him, but Larry just said, "That's good. I was only wondering."

"Hmph. I'll bet you were."

"Hey, come on, Gloria. I just got into town—be nice to us. How about some rooms for us, a couple of lodgers with good jobs?"

I never had a room like that all to myself before. It was right on the first floor. There was a window that opened out on the back garden. It was a low window and I could enter through that or walk through the house to where my room was in the back. Larry got a room down the hall. We dumped our stuff and headed out to eat.

Over a big plate of jambalaya, Larry told me that the best thing about Gloria's house was we were so close to Bourbon Street. That's where all the music was. The street was just lined with clubs. It wasn't like Marshall. Every night there was music in New Orleans. Folks was up to all hours at those clubs. And there was lots of beautiful women too.

Growing up in Marshall, I did like everybody else: worked all day and slept all night. And like everybody else in Marshall, I heard music in church on Sunday, not in clubs. I had been happy there and didn't know that there was anything different. For a few years I had been on my own and could do as I pleased, but that didn't mean much until I came to New Orleans. I soon found out that New Orleans was just like the preacher warned against. It was great. I had never seen anything like it.

I had always worked hard and done without. And the next day I would do pretty much the same. Never thought nothing about it neither. That's how folks in Marshall lived. It wasn't like I forgot about the preacher or my mother or father. It was just that New Orleans felt like a long way from home and I could put some things they might say in the back of my mind. I came to New Orleans at the right time of my life and it was far away from Marshall. I was meeting new people and they were having fun!

From New Orleans, you would sure never know that the country was in Prohibition. I was never much of a drinker, maybe had a drink every now and then. But I went to the clubs because I found that I liked the music and the dancing. The whole way I lived started to change. Matter of fact, I became what you would call a regular roustabout, a "ladies' man." Fact is, after we finished unloading the *New London,* I didn't work so often. I was out too much at night to want to go to work!

In those days, New Orleans could do that to a person. I still took pride in being a good worker, but it was almost like I could do that anywhere else. Good thing for me that I had saved my money. The music was as good as it could get. Besides that, I found that I met a lot of women in those clubs. And there was a lot of pretty women in New Orleans. It wasn't the way I had been brought up, but I found that I liked the big city, all right. There wasn't people watching over you all the time like there had been in Marshall.

In those days, people in New Orleans also liked to gamble, roll the dice. A person couldn't be in New Orleans and not try it; at least, I did. Sometimes I even made some money, but it wasn't hard to lose some either. I never got too carried away like some did. Some nights there could be a lot of money on the table and I would just watch. That was part of the excitement, but at times, a big gaming night could bring in a different crowd. There might be a few that hung on the edges, not the regulars, that might choose to cause trouble.

Of course, sometimes trouble just popped up when there wasn't even much money out there. When trouble came, it happened fast. I remember one night down at Crawdaddy's. You could listen to the music, dance, get a plate with a mountain of shrimp, and do some gambling in the back. It had been less than a month since I got to New Orleans and I was having fun.

I had gone in with Larry, but he was busy talking up some woman and I had wandered off on my own. I was sharing a plate of shrimp with a young lady and wasn't paying attention to much else. When the first shot was fired, we dove toward the floor, but the man a little ways down the bar wasn't so lucky. He took it in the arm. Real quick-like, two or three more shots followed. And then it was over.

Later, I asked Larry about it since he was closer to it all. He shrugged. "It was one of those misunderstandings."

"Shots been fired, a man was hit. What does that mean, a misunderstanding?" I asked.

"In New Orleans, it happens all the time."

"Why?" I asked.

"Oh, it's always over a woman or gambling, sometimes both. You're new to New Orleans. You got to watch yourself, George."

"Hey, I don't cheat at gambling and I don't mess with another man's woman. I can stay out of trouble."

"Sounds good," Larry said. "Too bad it ain't as simple as that."

"What do you mean?"

"Well, you can be minding your own business and still find that you need to protect yourself."

"So..."

"So, here's what you do," Larry said as he pulled a small pistol out of his jacket.

"Let me see that," I said.

Larry set the gun down on the table right between us. I picked it up and turned it over in my hand. I was used to some good-sized hunting weapons and this was pretty puny-looking. "I suppose this be big enough to hit a squirrel or even a raccoon. I don't think it would do a lot for a deer unless you hit it just right."

"That's not what this gun is about, George. A gun like this isn't for killing nothing. It's to protect yourself. A man sees you have a gun like this, he leaves you alone. That's how it protects you."

"I guess I can see that," I said.

The next afternoon we had a drink on the restaurant patio with a man that showed us two pistols. I know it wouldn't shoot any better for it, but I bought the one with the pearl handle even though it cost fifteen dollars. I wore it on my belt every day. And it was just like Larry said. No one ever bothered me and I never had to use it.

That's how New Orleans was. I noticed a lot of pretty women, but I also had a girlfriend named Nora. We would go out to the clubs, listen to the music, dance, and do some gambling. Many a night I came into my room through the garden window. I did that when it was late and I didn't want to bother no one by walking through the house. That happened a lot. But I didn't have to get up to feed the chickens at dawn like I did in Marshall.

In the 1920s, New Orleans was a hopping place, at least for a boy from Marshall. I did work some, maybe on a ship for a few days or weeks. For the first time in my life, I didn't work every day, just now and then when I needed to. One of those times, I worked on a ship unloading Brazilian nuts and coconuts. It took just a few days, but I must of impressed the captain because he asked if I wanted to ship out when the ship left.

Now I liked New Orleans, but this here boat was going to India, where my great-great-grandmother came from. I knew it was far away, but I always wanted to see India. The ship wasn't leaving for a week and I figured to have a good time before it left. I told Nora about my chance to go to India. I thought it was a great idea. But she got so angry about my leaving that she said, "Forget it, George. I'm leaving you."

And we had an argument that went on from there. But she left, all right. She stormed right out of the club we was in. Now that wasn't my doing, but I figured if I had only a week left in New Orleans, I might as well enjoy myself and I did.

On the day I was leaving, I had checked out of my rooming house and left all my gear on the boat. But it was a late-day sailing and I didn't see no sense in missing any excitement on shore. As a matter of fact, I was having a fine time on the dock trying to impress a couple of good-looking ladies with telling them about the journey I was to be taking. I guess I got a little carried away with myself. The boat left without me. To this day, I never have been to India.

All of a sudden, I had no ship, I had no rooming house, and I had no girlfriend. I could read the signs. It was time to hit the rails again.

CHAPTER 15

By 1925 anti-evolution feelings ran so hot that Tennessee made it a crime to teach anything but the biblical story of creation in public schools. High-school teacher John Scopes defied the law and was arrested, setting the stage for a trial that became a symbol of the clash between traditional religion and science.

— *Events That Shaped the Century: Our American Century,* by the editors of Time-Life Books

The picture and the article that Richard showed me were from that book that covers the whole twentieth century. I guess he likes to check that book out with me because I been alive for every year of this century, and even a few years from the century before that.

I've seen that book a lot but right on the table next to it there was a big fat book. I asked him about that. He told me that it's a fifth-grade social studies book.

"Big book all right. And they all read it?" I asked him.

"Well, that's the idea. But for some of them the reading level is too hard. They don't all read at grade level."

"We have that in Dallas too," I said. "Mr. Henry calls it social promotion. About half of them in my reading class got their high school diploma, but they never learned to read. They just showed up at school and got moved up grade to grade. Now they are back with me to learn to read."

"Well, I don't think it's that bad at my school, but there are some kids that can't read it very well. There are a lot more that just don't care about history. They weren't there for these events and they don't want to know about them," Richard said.

"Do you remember the Scopes trial?" he asked. "It was in 1925 and they called it the 'trial of the century.' "

"No, I don't remember that," I said.

"It was in Tennessee, but it was in all the papers."

"I didn't read the papers then, son."

"Right," Richard said. "But I thought that your friends might have talked about it."

"Was the teacher a colored man?"

"No," Richard said. "The teacher on trial was white."

"Well, then," I said. "Back in the 1920s that would have been white news. It had nothing to do with the colored."

"But it's a part of American history," Richard said.

I laughed. "That's good, son. But it wasn't part of the America I knew. If it was, I would remember. There were a lot of trials then, but the only ones that colored folks noticed were when a colored man went on trial for raping a white woman. Those trials were made-up things, but the hangings to follow was all too real. No offense, son, but I don't think we was too worried about what a white man was allowed to teach. A lot of us never had the chance to go to school anyway. At that time, I was heading out to see the country for myself. Didn't hear a thing about it."

The same rail yard I came in on is where I headed next. I hadn't been there since coming to New Orleans more than a year ago. This time, I knew what I was doing or at least thought I did. Except for the pistol I carried on my belt, all my gear was on the way to India! This time, instead of a bedroll, I stopped at a peddler's stand. He had a pair of overalls that fit me.

I wore those over my good suit. When I got somewhere after riding the rails, I could take them off and have some clean clothes to wear. Being in New Orleans had made me spruce up my dressing a bit. And I didn't want to just look like any old hobo when I got off the train.

At the rail yard, I felt like an old hand. I didn't need to ask the ticket master for directions. I stayed at the far end of the yard with a group of hobos waiting for a train. No one seemed to agree on exactly where it was going except that it was heading north. That was close enough for me.

By the time we was running alongside the freight cars, everyone had thinned out. I didn't pay much attention to no one else, just kept my eyes on the car and the handle I was getting ready to grab on to. I didn't want to go and lose my legs under the wheels.

That moment when I was off the ground, one foot against the side of the moving train, one hand holding on to the train or maybe an outstretched hand, that moment would last forever. There'd be an instant when I wasn't in the train and not on the ground. I can still feel it right now. There's nothing else like it.

The wind and the motion of the train want to pull you down and under the wheels. It takes everything you got to overcome all that and heave yourself into the car. Maybe somebody will be there to help and maybe not. Either way, it was a mighty good feeling after I would get in, roll over, and then sit up. It was something special, all right.

It was an early morning train and the wind coming in the car was a little cold. I didn't mind. It felt so good to know we was moving and to look out at the rail yard disappearing and not know what lay ahead. I stayed by the door just to watch. Our freight car had enough fellows on it to keep the conversation moving. There were some big lies being traded, let me tell you. There weren't many stops. Someone said that was because we was on an express.

They had that right. We went through all of Mississippi with just some short whistlestops. I got out in Birmingham and got something to eat. But even that wasn't a long stop. Somewhere during the night we went through Tennessee. In the morning light, someone recognized that we were in Kentucky. Not that it looked so different, but that tells how fast we was going in just a couple days' travel.

When we crossed the Ohio River and got to Cincinnati, the train stopped. That was the end of the line. It would change tracks and head south again. To go any farther, we had to find another train. That was okay by me. I had slept well enough in the boxcar, but I was ready to stretch out after a couple days in a freight car.

Ohio was a new state and I figured to look around. I took my coveralls off and stashed them in the bushes just down from the station. I figured that way I didn't look like some hobo that was riding the rails. In a nice suit, I felt pretty good about myself and headed out past the station toward downtown. Cincinnati is one big place with some mighty fine stores. I looked in at one hat shop. They don't make hats to order these days like they was doing then.

In New Orleans, I could of used a nice hat like they made in that shop, but it didn't make sense for riding the rails. But I looked through the window and watched the man make those fedoras. I noticed that there was both white and colored coming out of some of the same shops and even from the same restaurants. Some of the men in my car said it would be like that in Ohio: Colored and white could go to the same restaurant. But those same men could tell whopping lies, so I watched closely.

One diner had a big window across the front. There was white and colored, all right. I looked more closely and, at the counter, saw a white and a colored man sitting next to each other. Seeing it with my own eyes, I believed it, but I didn't push my luck. Now, fact is, it would have been easier for me to walk into a colored diner. That's just how I was raised. Still, I figured if that's how everybody did things in Ohio, it must be all right for me too.

I was hungry, but just to be sure I walked past a few more and picked a diner that looked comfortable. It wasn't crowded. There was a colored man at the counter and a couple of white men at a table. As I walked over to the counter, the colored fellow got up to pay his bill. I just nodded and sat down.

I looked around. The two white men were still at a table behind me. There was a big hole cut into the wall to serve from the kitchen. The cook was white, but he was busy frying something and he didn't care about me. Even so, my being there just didn't seem right.

A waiter walked over with a rag to wipe off the counter. He was white too. I waited for something to happen, but he only said, "Cup of coffee?"

"No thanks."

He set a menu in front of me. I left it there and looked around. I was looking to see what they was serving in that restaurant. But from where I sat, I couldn't see the plates in front of the two white men. They had just cleared off the plate from the man who had been at the counter.

I can eat almost anything and I had money in my pocket, but I didn't know what they served. In a cafe, usually I just pointed to a plate of something that was already out and ordered the same. But that couldn't work.

"You know what you want?"

His writing pad was up and he was waiting.

"Jambalaya, a plate of jambalaya?"

"Sorry, boy, this ain't New Orleans."

I felt kind of stupid. "Okay, I'll have some pork chops with hominy and grits."

"Hey, like the menu says, 'We serve pork chops on Wednesday.' And hominy and grits, you aren't gonna see that up north. Let's make it easy and order off the menu, huh?"

I nodded and would have given anything to be able to read the menu. But I said, "I guess I'm not really too hungry."

"Hey, sorry if the food ain't good enough for you!"

I felt really dumb and walked out. On the next corner, there was a small grocery. With a loaf of bread, some meat, and an apple, I did just fine. From then on, that's how I usually ate. Those cafes up north would serve a colored man but not one who couldn't read.

After getting some food, I figured I had seen enough of Cincinnati and started back toward the station. I got my coveralls from the bushes. But this time I went over to the ticket master. I had to do that for my pride. I had been shamed enough in that cafe that, while I liked riding the rails, right then I wasn't going no second class. While I liked to save my money for hard times ahead, I would use some for a paying ticket.

Without touching my boot money, I took out two silver dollars and some change in my pocket. I asked the ticket master, "How far north can I go on this much?"

"You can go to the end of the line. This train don't go into Canada, so it stops at Toledo on Lake Erie. It leaves in forty-two minutes, but you can board anytime."

He pointed to the train. The steam was up. I walked down to the last car. I started to sit down and then saw a white man already there. I looked farther down the car and saw a white couple already seated. When I saw the white woman, I froze. I backed up and when I got to the door, I started down the steps.

I was happy to get out of there without no trouble. Just as I was about to hit the pavement, a colored man started to head for the steps. I grabbed him by the shoulder and said, "Wrong car. You almost went in the wrong car there."

"What do you mean? This train going to Toledo?" he asked.

"Yeah, but this isn't the colored car, it's a white car."

"Let me go. What are you talking about?"

I could see he was mad, but I was only trying to help. "Suit yourself. I was only trying to warn you, save you some trouble."

Suddenly he grinned and asked, "Where you from?"

"Texas."

"Lived there all your life?"

"No." I wasn't meaning to brag or nothing,

but I said, "I been in Tennessee and New Orleans too."

"That's good. Well, you're in Ohio now. There's no colored and there's no white train. There's just a train. Come on with me. Where you going?"

"Toledo."

"Good. Well, then, turn around and climb aboard. I'll go with you."

Toledo wasn't as big as Cincinnati, but it was big enough. It was afternoon and I still hoped to catch a boat to Canada. I found a man selling apples that knew the harbor.

"Go three blocks north and turn right. Then walk half a mile to the Red Apple Diner. You got that?"

"Yeah."

"A block past that, you'll see a sign that says 'Stadium.' Follow that for eight blocks. You'll come to a sign that says 'Harbor.' It'll work best if I write it down for you. It's a long walk, take about an hour maybe."

I headed north for three blocks and then I walked for what I figured to be about half a mile, but didn't find no Red Apple Diner. Still hoping to find it, I tried walking in different directions.

No luck. I could have looked at his directions forever and it would never be of any help. When I finally got to the Red Apple, I wasn't sure where to go from there. I didn't want to go into no diner with foods that I didn't know. I waited outside and got more directions from someone that was leaving the diner.

By the time I reached the harbor, I felt like I must have walked over half of Toledo. It was nightfall and I had missed the last boat. I looked for a grocery but couldn't find one. Though I was hungry, I wasn't going to step into another diner. I found a spot on the pier behind a pile of ropes and settled down for the night and hoped there would be a ship in the morning.

A ship did leave in the morning and I could see why they called Lake Erie one of the Great Lakes. We don't have any lakes that big in Texas. It was foggy and cold to start with, but even when it cleared, the shore in Canada was too far off to be seen. I got some breakfast on deck and it wasn't a bad trip. At the dock, we all had to go through a line and talk to some men in uniforms.

"Where are you from?"

"Texas."

"And the reason for your visit?"

"I want to see some snow."

He laughed and said, "You came to the right place, but June is the wrong time of year! Well, have a nice visit, sir."

I didn't know much about Canada, but I liked the way he called me sir. I had been called a lot worse in Texas! The tracks were nearby and I hopped a freight train. Listening to the talk, I heard that we was going to Toronto and then heading west.

When we got to Toronto, some of us pooled our money. We got some fried fish and what they called chips, fried potatoes. They was all covered in vinegar and then wrapped up in newsprint. It didn't taste bad, but it ain't like no Texas barbecue either.

It was a long run to Sudbury. I stayed there a bit and did some serious fishing. I brought some fish, mostly good-sized walleye, back to camp. I was the only one to bring in any fish, but they spun it differently. "Tastes good, but not as big as the one I caught over by North Bay last fall," one of them said.

At those hobo camps, they would sit around and lie their heads off all day. I liked to listen. There were some rough characters in those camps and I wouldn't bother to argue. The women were just as rough as the men, and I think they was the ones with the foulest language. That's the honest truth. I had a good time in those camps, though. I could drop in anywhere. I shared what I had and could help myself to what I needed. They was poor folk but with a generous nature.

There was a lot of wide-open spaces in Canada. The people weren't mean up there, but some had a kind of standoffish nature. The prairie was flatter than anything I had ever seen. There was good soil and the wheat was good, but I missed the rolling hills of Texas. I didn't see many colored folk either. I had been gone a long time and about then I would have liked to have just been home. I didn't know of anyone from Texas that had traveled as far as I had. Right then, if I would have had enough money for a ticket to Marshall, I would have bought one.

In some small prairie towns people looked at me like they never seen a colored man before. There was no laws that said I couldn't work, but no one hired me either. People wasn't unfriendly, but I got the feeling they wasn't used to strangers.

I did like Calgary, though. It sits on the prairie but on the edge of the mountains. They had one fine rodeo there. I didn't have my own horse or I might of thought about entering something myself. After the rodeo, I hopped on a night train out of Calgary. With a full moon, the shadows of all those mountain peaks was something to see. Before I went to sleep, I lay on my back and just watched one mountain after another. It was summer, but it was the coldest night I had ever felt.

When we pulled into the town of Banff at dawn, I found out how cold it can be in the mountains. Even the floor of the freight car felt cold. The sun wouldn't light on nothing till it was high enough to clear the first peak. So I had to walk to the other side of the rail yard to reach those first rays.

Back in Texas, it seemed that we always looked to get out of the sun so as not to get cooked. But it was different there. The pain from the cold had gone into my bones. Finding just the right spot on a giant rock, I stretched out like a lizard till the sun warmed me through. Once I started walking again, I got to where I took my coveralls off and stashed them behind some rocks.

Just walking through town, the air felt different. I wouldn't of thought that air could feel any different from one place to the next, but it did. I felt so good that I walked into a cafe instead of looking for a grocery. It was small, but there was a breakfast crowd of working men. With lots of food on the tables and at the counter, there was plenty of choices to pick from without using a menu.

I had some hot chocolate and then ordered some eggs and potatoes. There wasn't no grits on anybody's plate and I didn't even ask. They didn't have biscuits neither but they had these big rolls with white frosting on top. They were kinda sweet for breakfast, but they was good. They filled those plates high with food.

With customers like that, you would have to. They was mostly loggers. All of them had the heavy leather cork boots. Over their long underwear, they had work shirts with stripes and a zipper, while a few of them had blue work shirts. All of them had the sleeves cut off above the elbow so that they wouldn't have any buttons around that might snag and pull an arm into some choke chain, where it would be crushed by a log.

"Where you from?" the man next to me at the counter asked.

"I'm from Texas."

"Where's that?"

These were the kind of folks that never went anywhere in their lives, so somebody different, they wanted to know about. There were no coloreds that I had seen and I didn't

245

have logger clothes on neither. Still, to be sitting at the same counter with a white man and just doing everyday talk was different for me too.

"Texas is in the South."

The man on the other side of me said, "What brings you up here?"

By then, some other folks had turned and was listening in. Back home I tried not to have any notice taken of me for that could lead to trouble. But this felt different and it didn't cause me no bother. I just said, "I came to Canada to see the snow."

For some reason, that got that breakfast crowd going, all right.

"Came to the right place, aye."

Another man said, "Yeah, and please take some of it with you."

The man next to me turned back to me and asked, "Well, have you seen enough snow to suit you?"

I shrugged. "No, I haven't seen any at all."

"What? We might not have much else, but snow we have no shortage of. How long you been here?"

"Oh, about a month or so."

Someone from back at a table called out, "It's summer, but we can still show him some snow, if that's what he wants."

The man next to me put out his hand and said, "Jack."

"George."

"Come on with us then, George. We be loading up the crummy in five minutes. You can snag a ride with us and the snowfields are on the way to our cutting site. We'll drop you off." He grinned. "We can't have you in Canada and not see some snow."

Someone else had paid my breakfast bill and said, "That's okay. Keep that funny-looking money for your travels."

Now they was the ones that had the money with all the different colors to it, but I thanked him anyway. I guess they called it a crummy because it was just that. It was about the most beat-up truck I ever seen. Inside, there was benches to sit on, but that was all. Their saws and axes bounced around on the floor and I'm sure that didn't help. The benches had no cushions, and it was muddy as anything inside.

It was a sturdy truck, rolling right through every kind of pothole that you could ever imagine. On the big potholes or in the deep mud, we would kind of sway side to side. Those fellas was used to it, though. They wouldn't stop talking and would even keep pouring some coffee from their Thermos. They peppered me with questions about Texas. Without quite saying it, I could tell they was wondering if there was other coloreds down there beside me.

I finally said, "You all should come down and visit sometime."

I knew that wouldn't happen, though. Back then, few people traveled as far as I did. About then, we stopped at an opening in the woods. Someone shouted, "There it is for you, George. That snowfield is there all year long, even in the summer. We're going farther up the road, but there's some trails you can follow."

I jumped out of the back of the truck. The trail kinda followed along a rushing creek. The water was cold and tasted good, but I didn't see no fish in it. The trail was good, though, and I made progress. About midday, there was a cold wind blowing across the snow. When I got closer, the high wall of snow looked more like fingers of snow stretching out on the ground.

Water was running out from underneath and the ground was soggy. I touched snow. It was cold and felt like shaved ice. The finger of snow by me was about knee high. Stepping up on it, I started scrambling to the top of the snow wall. I thought it would of been slippery, but my foot went in about ankle deep and I didn't slide none at all.

The snow sloped out all the way up the mountain, but it wasn't too steep where I was standing. I heard a curious thing. Up ahead, I found a canyon in the snow. There was a swift-moving stream running right through it. Inside that canyon, the snow had changed its color! Down in there, the snow was this light blue color. It was awful pretty, but I have never seen that color again in my life. I've never mentioned it before. Anyone in Texas would think I had gone crazy once I started talking about blue snow. But I know what I seen.

I was feeling pretty good about the way I

could handle myself on snow, but I was humbled real quick. Closer to the edge, the snow wasn't as soft and had crusted over with ice. When I fell, I went into a slide and felt myself picking up steam. The snow sloped down toward the canyon and I tried to stop.

I kept sliding. Finally, I flipped over on my stomach and dug in with my hands and the toes of my boots. Just above that ice canyon, I came to a stop. The skin on my fingers was all ripped up and my legs was shaking. It was a long ways down and the water was running faster and deeper than I had figured.

A person that fell in there couldn't get out without someone dropping a rope, but there wasn't no one else. My fingers hurt and was getting cold, but I dug in deeper. Staying as tight to the snow as I could, I dug my feet in, pushed off with them, and pulled with my hands. Every few feet I took a rest. But I did get myself away from the ledge and got up on my feet.

By then I was wet through and cold. I had to wonder why I came so far to see some snow. I would rather look a Texas rattlesnake in the eye. It was time to go home.

CHAPTER 16

In a boxcar doorway a Texas-bound hobo
called Slim waits out a delay caused by
brake trouble on a freight train in California. "Knights of the road" quickly
took to the rails behind the new iron
horse in the 19th century.

—Caption to a photograph of a man
sitting in the door of a freight train,
*Railroads, the Great American
Adventure,* by Charlton Ogburn

In 1928, I was on my way home. The snow
and the cold weather told me it was time to
head for Texas. I had a return ticket in my boot
for St. Louis to Marshall, but that wasn't
gonna do any good in Canada. So I hitched
a ride on a freight train that was heading
south.

It was late fall and cold in the mountains.
The train was cold, but when it crossed into
Montana, I heard we was heading all the way
to California. I just wanted to get to where it
was warmer. During the longer stops, I got out
to scavenge some food, but I stayed with it.
I just had this need to get home and figured
if I got to California, I would make it.

Once we was out of the mountains, it got
warmer and warmer. In a couple of days, we
was going through mile after mile of orange
groves. I couldn't quite do it, but I wanted to

reach out and pick an orange. During some long stops, though, I did get a chance to do just that. Juicy and sweet; I still remember those oranges today. For more than seventy years, I haven't had nothing like it.

Back then, it seemed like the orange groves went right to the edge of Los Angeles. It was a nice-looking city, but I just wanted to go home. When I got off at the edge of the Los Angeles yard, I heard tell that I wanted a train to Arizona to keep me in the right direction to Texas. Trouble was, there wasn't going to be a train that way for a few days. One of the bulls, the one in the yard that didn't have no mean streak, told someone that a bridge was down out that way.

At the hobo camp I had tacos and made plans to catch a work truck in the morning. It was heading out with day workers to Santa Monica, which was supposed to be on the ocean. Right then, the work didn't matter much one way or the other, but I went so as to see the ocean. And it was something too.

The water was warm, the fishing was good, and it weren't no problem to sleep under the boardwalk or even out on the beach. The weather was that nice. If I hadn't wanted to be home so badly, it would have been okay if the railroad bridge never did get fixed.

The next day someone lent me a pole and I was fishing in the surf. Just down from me, a family was set up. They had a blanket and even an umbrella for their baby. The rest of them was all fishing. As near as I could tell,

251

that dad hardly ever got to fish, though. He was untangling lines, baiting hooks, or helping them reel in a fish. His children needed him and it seemed like he hardly ever got his own pole in the water.

I caught more fish than he did, but I would have traded places. Don't get me wrong. I liked that freedom on the rails, but for the first time, it didn't feel right to have no roots, to have no family. Right then, I wanted to be with my family and I wanted a family of my own.

I had pulled in a mess of fish and brought some over to them. They were surprised but thankful. They were already cooking and I shared some fish they were grilling. I didn't even bother keeping any for later. I was going to fish some more, but instead, I hitched a ride into Los Angeles. The scuttlebutt was that the trains was running on regular routes in the morning. That night, I slept in a freight car. And, sure enough, at dawn we was rolling.

I had never in my life been too hot. But crossing the desert was something else. Someone said it was named the Mojave Desert. I don't know about that, but the heat in that boxcar was powerful. Some people got sick. I didn't feel so great myself, but got through it okay. I wanted to get off, but there wasn't a shade tree to be seen. After that it got better and I stayed on that same train all the way to Amarillo.

There was a familiar look to the rolling hills and cattle country. At Amarillo, I was able to go to a cafe and order foods that I knew, and I had my first Texas barbecue since forever. In Amarillo, I used the last of my money for a paying ticket to Marshall. It had been years since I had seen my mother and I was going to make it home in style!

Of course, I hadn't heard a word from my family in all that time. I didn't know how to write and, besides that, a letter wouldn't have done much good. Mama and Papa didn't know how to read either. By the time we passed Wichita Falls, it was hard to be sitting still in my seat. I didn't have any money left to buy a sandwich. I probably would have done better in a boxcar, where I could pace back and forth.

The conductor called out Ft. Worth, Dallas, and the little towns like Kaufman, Canton, and New Hope. At Longview, I checked in my burlap sack. The material and dress pattern I had bought in Los Angeles for my mother was in good shape. I knew she would like them.

There was still some daylight when the train got to Marshall. Even today, my walking isn't too shabby, but right then... I don't know that I hardly touched the ground. The sights and smells, even the air felt so familiar. Even before I got there, I knew what it felt like to be home. I wondered if Mama and Papa would be outside finishing up evening chores or if I would be able to walk in and surprise them in the cabin.

But I guess you could say the surprise was on me. When I cleared the hill, it was awful quiet. The stillness set me to wondering. I swung open the wide gate. Even though I didn't see any animals about, I shut it behind me. It wasn't just Mama and Papa that I expected to see. When I had left home, there were thirteen brothers and sisters. Walking down the road, I didn't see or hear nothing.

I caught a glimpse of a deer bolting across the field. That made me realize that I hadn't seen or heard the dog. As I walked, I heard some songbirds and an owl. They had always kept more to the back part of the farm, away from the cabin and the barn, where people were.

I could see the cabin but turned off to check on the barn first. It was shut down, which, for so early in the evening, was unusual. When the door swung open no sound and no fresh smells came at me. I waited for my eyes to get used to the darkness of the barn. It was empty, all right.

Habit made me shut the barn door. My step had slowed, but I still headed toward the cabin. The cabin was quiet, too quiet. Outside the door, I stood and listened. I kept waiting for Papa's voice, for Mama to say something. With all the little ones about, it was never quiet, but I heard nothing. That was not right, but not knowing what to do, I stood and waited.

It was my own house and I guess that I could have gone right in. Instead, though I'm not sure why, I knocked on the door. By then I expected no answer and there wasn't. Part of me thought I should just go in and another part said something was wrong and

I should just leave. I pulled on the latch and the door, as well greased as always, swung open.

There was some late evening light pouring in through a window, but most of the front room, the main part of the house, was in shadows. It was empty: no kitchen table, no chairs, no nothing. I felt better. There was nothing left so I figured that everybody had moved out. I didn't know why, but I felt that at least they were okay if they took everything with them.

I could of stayed, but with only the buildings and no people, I didn't want to. There was an aunt that lived on the other side of Marshall, and I headed over that way. I wanted to know what happened and to find some family. I had nowhere to be, and if it came to that I figured that I could walk through the night. Turns out that I didn't have to. A farmer from down the way was out and gave me a ride in his wagon.

By the time I got to my aunt's house, I found out that I had missed them all by only a couple of weeks. Prices were low and times were tough. The whole family had moved to Kaufman when Papa got some work there. It was dark when I got to my aunt's. Although no one had seen me in more than five years, she took me in. I had my first bath and real home cooking in a long time. She treated me well, but the next day I hopped a train and headed back to Kaufman.

Kaufman is closer to Dallas, but it ain't all that big, at least back then. It wasn't so hard to find them. Five years is a long time and the little ones weren't so little anymore, but it felt good to be back. I still had some material and a dress pattern for Ma. I think she liked it, but mostly everyone had given up on my ever returning. This time, I could tell them that I was here to stay.

Good thing for me that work was never hard for me to find. I did some odd jobs, some day-labor work, but before long I found out that the railroad was hiring and I got on.

I found a place near my family and I would be at work by dawn. After all those years of riding the rails, I guess it was my time to lay down track for other folks to use. Kaufman to Dallas was the section where we mostly worked. Sometimes we would rip up a section of track and fix it. Every now and then we would just build a brand-new spur. No matter what, most days I drove spikes with a heavy sledge-hammer.

It was hard work, but after a while a person got used to it, not that it ever became easy. We would ride back in a railroad car at the end of the day and it was always quiet. Everybody was too worn out to talk much. But in the morning I would be there with my crew. We worked from sunrise till dusk, five or maybe six days a week.

Seems like we would work and work and then one day, sometimes even in the middle of the day, they would say go home, come back in three or four days, whatever. Sometimes we was off even longer than that. I guess that if we was caught up and they didn't need us, they didn't want to be paying us either.

I never minded a few days off. On a day off I was not one to sit still. This would have been 1928, but even back then, Dallas was a fair-sized town. Still not too far out of Dallas, it was country. I used to like to go north, up on the Panhandle. From my traveling days, I had learned how to break horses, and that's what I would head off to do on my off days. I would catch a ride on the train and check in at a ranch, see if they needed a little help. I didn't get paid or nothing, but that's how I got a chance to ride since I never owned a horse of my own.

Most people don't know this, but I seen more than a few colored cowboys. So, people wouldn't be too surprised to see me show up looking to see if they had horses to break. Sometimes, I even came back to the same ranch where they already knew me. That's what I was doing on the Cartwright farm up on the Panhandle.

The Cartwright farm grew a lot of cotton: hundreds, maybe a thousand acres. It seemed like that anyway. Growing up, I had done my share of picking cotton. But it was a big place and they also raised horses and brought in some wild ones too from off the range.

I remember once there was a little Appaloosa that had come in from the range. No one had ridden it yet. With a horse like that, you can never know what you might get. Still, I was up for it and this horse wasn't so big and didn't seem too mean-spirited to me. He didn't even buck or cause a ruckus when they put a saddle on him for the first time. I actually thought his quiet ways meant that it would be a piece of cake to ride him.

But right away, I found out that he was just smarter than all of that. When I got on, he didn't take to bucking, which was something I was ready for. Still, he didn't want me riding him. He just ran straight for the fence and crashed us both into it. Being surprised and all, he almost threw me right then. He wasn't mean, just smart.

It hurt like anything, but I held on. He ran back out into the corral and did a few circles. This time I saw it coming and braced myself. That helped some, but it was a barbed-wire fence and so it kept ripping up my legs. He wanted me to jump off, and part of me, I admit, thought of doing just that.

Thing is, though, with a wild horse there is always a crowd watching. And after all, I had my pride. Besides, in that crowd there was a girl watching me. She was awful pretty and I hoped that she would notice me. So, I just stayed on and took a beating from that horse. By then, people were shouting, "Jump, jump!"

That made sense and I was getting worn out. But when I heard her say, "That man is a damn fool!" I felt great.

I still didn't know her name yet, but she had noticed me. I figured that it was worth staying on. Finally, the horse did tire and I was able to rein him in. Truth is, when I got off, I didn't look so good. But I guessed that maybe I had impressed her and I walked on over to the rail.

Taking off my hat, I said, "My name is George."

"I'm Elzenia," she said.

She wasn't making this easy, but I went on. "Do you like to watch them breaking horses?"

"Sometimes."

"Well, did you like it today?"

"Today? That was the stupidest thing I've ever seen."

"Huh." Here I'd gone and done everything to impress her and she went and said a thing like that.

"Look at you. You're bleeding and all torn up. For what?"

"To break a horse," I said. "And that's just what I did. You never seen that before? Where you from?"

"Sure, I've seen that before," she said. "I've lived here all my life if you've ever bothered to notice."

Turns out that she had been living there with her mother picking cotton. I guess they was sharecroppers on the farm. She was sixteen then, but the last time I was at the farm must have been years earlier. That explained why I hadn't paid any attention then, but I sure noticed her now. She had a nice smile and was as tall as me.

I tried again. "Would you care to take a walk?"

"No. I be out walking all day long," she said.

"You maybe want to go have a soda?"

"Thanks, I'm busy."

"Maybe this evening then?"

"Well, I'm—"

I got kinda mad. "What do I got to do anyway to get you to take notice?"

She stood up tall and said, "Oh, I noticed, but I just got to wonder about a man that hasn't enough brains to get hisself off a horse like that."

That did it. "You don't think I wanted to? I saw you there along the rail and stayed on since I hoped you was watching."

"Oh." She grinned at me. "I am busy right now. Afternoon break be over in a few minutes and I gotta join my mama in picking some cotton. A soda this evening sounds good, though. I'll meet you there by the store."

She turned around and left. I knew the store. Cartwright Farm had a store for its workers. It didn't have everything, but they sold Dr Peppers and Nehi, both the orange and the grape. There was a soda machine but no electricity, so they set a block of ice inside it and kept the sodas on that. I tried to ride a little more that day, but my legs was cut up pretty badly.

She did show up at the store. We talked and talked. I was settled in my mind. I had been traveling for years, had my girlfriends, and I was ready for getting married. I could tell that she liked me well enough, but I could see not to push things right away neither.

She and her mother, they picked cotton together. They had been doing that for years, but I don't think they had ever saved enough to head anywhere else. I think the Cartwright farm was as decent as anywhere else, but it was like that for a lot of people then. If all went well, what you made working barely kept you going. It didn't make for no choices, but nobody complained.

Her mama kept a tight rein on her and I wasn't too sure that her mother liked me, but I came up most weekends or days that I had off. After four months of getting to know each other, I just knew. Elzenia said yes.

After we were engaged, one day I just had to ask, "Elzenia, were you saying yes to starting a new life with me? Or did you just want to leave home and get away from picking cotton?"

She smiled and gave me a big kiss. "The answer is yes."

"To which question?"

"The answer is yes for both questions."

"Well, which question gets the bigger yes?" I asked.

"It's too soon to know yet," she said.

A month after I asked her, we got married. Up on the farm, there was a little church for all the people that lived there. We didn't jump the broom like the old folks used to do. The pastor married me and Elzenia right at the church. It was a nice, spring day in March. Our families and friends brought food and everybody had a good time.

By then I had moved to Dallas and I took

Elzenia home with me. Monday morning, I was back at work on the railroad. I had wanted to settle down and have a family. That's just what happened too. Amelia, the first of seven children, was born a year later.

CHAPTER 17

Scene 1: A crowd viewing the body of a man that has jumped from a skyscraper on Wall Street as police officers try to clear the street.

Scene 2: Squatters camp along the railroad tracks.

Scene 3: President Hoover talking: "Prosperity is just around the corner."

Narrator: "From the bankrupt executives in New York, to the Hoovervilles that are sprouting up across the country, this economic depression has hit hard. Families that have worked hard all their life are losing their homes, their farms, worried about their next meal. America has survived its trials in the past and we will again. We have elected the President to guide us and we must have faith in him."
—1930 newsreel

On another of his visits, Richard brought that movie machine again. As it was my night to cook dinner, I was back in the kitchen. I was trying to decide between cornbread and biscuits. I heard the television scraping across the living-room floor. I ignored that and decided to go with cornbread. My batter needed to be stirred so I ignored the comings and goings in the living room again. I like a cornbread batter to be stirred some so everything is mixed but not too smooth with all the lumps gone.

The batter was just the way I wanted it, when I heard him pacing around the living room. Since I was trying to find the right pan, I ignored it all again. If the pan is too wide then the batter gets too thin and the cornbread can burn. But if the pan is too small, then the batter is too thick and it might not cook in the middle either. After I got my cornbread in the oven, I noticed it was quiet. That made me wonder.

Out in the living room, Richard was sitting on the floor and glaring at the movie machine. "No luck?" I said.

"No."

I opened the little suitcase that it comes in. "You read the directions they got taped to the top?"

"Not really."

" 'Not really.' What does that mean? You read them or not?"

"Well, I read it last time and I figure it would be the same."

"Uh-huh," I said. "Well, I can read. I don't mind reading! Let me see."

When I got to step number 6, I read out loud: "If your VCR will not make audio connection, you may be using the old model that needs an adapter. Use the adapter in the compartment at the bottom of this case."

He just looked at me and didn't say nothing. I couldn't help myself and said, "Well, well, never hurts to read something a second time, now does it?"

He's pretty good about things and he laughed too when I said, "Now you finish up while I go check on my cornbread."

It's the same when my kids are around. Sometimes, I have to wonder how they can get along without me being there to help them. But that's okay. Even though I'm pretty busy with school these days, I don't mind helping people. It don't bother me none.

Too bad we don't have those newsreels anymore. Matter of fact, that's how a lot of folks got their news back then, especially people that couldn't read the newspapers. I remember President Hoover, people talking about him anyway. After times got tough, semed like the white folk didn't like him anymore. Course, it was mostly white folks that could vote then, so they should of blamed themselves if they didn't like him. For the colored folk, times was already tough and it wasn't so different than before.

A lot of squatter towns, Hoovervilles, was built on the tracks, I guess 'cause people got around by hopping the rails. Never saw a single person jump out of a window, though. In Marshall the tallest building was probably the hotel. When I moved to Dallas in 1928, most buildings there were nothing to speak of either. At least in the colored neighborhood, I don't remember no high-rises. I feel sorry that people would do that to themselves, though. Their families must have felt awfully bad. Myself, I've never lost any stock. I've never owned any in my life. Nobody that I knew owned any stock either.

I still didn't get it. I asked Richard, "Why did they have to kill themselves?"

Richard said, "They didn't have to, it's just what some people did when they lost all their money."

"So they was rich to start with?" I asked him.

"Some of them were very wealthy on paper, but when their stock value fell they couldn't pay their debts."

"Wealthy on paper, huh. Yeah, back in those days, when you could get them, I would always take a silver dollar over a paper dollar even though they was heavier to carry."

Richard said, "Well, I'm not sure how to explain it. Their paper wasn't even paper dollars. It was just pieces of paper that represented money. Their huge capital losses were really about losing money they never had."

I just looked at him.

"The more I think about it, I'm not sure that I understand it so well myself," he said.

I couldn't help myself from saying, "Tell me again how many years of schooling you've had."

Richard threw up his hands. "I never even took Economics 101."

"Well, I never did either, but I wouldn't go killing myself about losing some money that I never had in the first place."

Richard asked me what I remembered of the 1930s.

I was there in the thirties, all right, but I didn't know too much about a depression. Times was tough, but that's just how it was. I never gave it no thought and it never slowed me down. I had already started working for the railroad in 1928. That was a fine job. And when I wasn't doing a paying job like that, I still liked to break horses.

Once when I had a little time from the railroad, Elzenia, my brother, Johnny, and me went up north along the Oklahoma border before the first of our children was born. Johnny had just gotten a car. It was an older car, but we were ready for a trip. Back then, the way cars was and the way dirt roads was, you didn't need to go far for some adventure. There's not much up that way but lots of wide-open space. The ground is rocky and all dried out. That's not great for crops, but it's good for raising horses. Figuring it would be a good way to do some riding, we stopped by a ranch to see if they could use some help for a couple of days.

Right when we came into the ranch we spotted a crowd down around their corral. Cowboys were leaning against the rails and hollering all get-out. There was a little gap in the crowd and we worked our way to the rail to see what it was all about. The horse was a buckskin and as big as any I had ever seen before. Besides that, he was powerful: wide across the chest and real muscular. They was using two cowboys just to hold the reins while another one would hop on his back.

That horse was lightning quick. At the same time he arched his back, he would give a kick and send a cowboy sailing, all that in the time you could snap your fingers. That horse wouldn't stop there either. He was one of those that would charge a rider when he was on the ground. Those hooves could crush a man easy and that's what he wanted to do.

Some cowboys had a girlfriend with them and some just wanted to show off to the crowd. But when they hit the ground, you could read the panic in their eyes as they tried to scramble out from under those hooves. Even then, they only got away because a couple of cowboys were on the rail ready to jump in and distract that horse. The cowboy next to us said, "The boss pledged fifty dollars to anyone that can stay on, but it ain't going to happen."

Another cowboy said, "That's a killer horse. He knows what he's doing. It could be five hundred dollars but someone will get killed before they break that horse."

Funny thing was, just then that horse threw another cowboy. He came down hard and awkward like. Two more cowboys had to hustle in to drag him out. He couldn't get up and walk. Must of broke a leg or maybe worse.

That horse was intelligent, all right. If you ask me, he was smarter than some of those cowboys. At the same time, they was white and I knew enough to keep my mouth shut. There was already enough anger out there to heat things up good. After that man got hurt, they started hitting on the horse. The more it threw them, the harder they hit him. Of course, that only opened up the mean side of the horse and made him even wilder.

Pretty soon it took a group of men to hold the reins, and some of them would beat on the horse with a stick. I started to boil when I saw that. Elzenia could tell that and nudged me in the ribs. "Let it be," she said as she turned her head toward the crowd.

I knew what she meant. The crowd of cowboys had grown. They were two or three deep behind us. All of them were white. Without saying it, Elzenia meant, "Leave it where their anger is at the horse. One word could turn that kind of anger on a colored person."

She was right. With that type of crowd, there wasn't anything they wouldn't do to a colored person. And if that happened, there was nothing to be done. No judge would even listen to a colored man. We both knew it wasn't safe to show up a white man.

Even though I knew I could ride that horse, I kept my mouth shut. When a cowboy brought out an iron pipe instead of that old stick and started whaling away, the horse got a wild look in his eyes. He was dragging them all around the corral. The man got angry. He swung harder and harder. The pipe would hit with a thud and the horse would scream.

I jumped up on the first rail and shouted, "I can ride that horse."

Johnny tried to pull me down. I'm shorter

than him. But being up on the rail, I had some height on him and I gave him a good elbow in the chest. That sent him back a step and a white cowboy stepped in between us. There was quiet till another cowboy said, "The nigger boy thinks he can ride this horse. Let's just see him try."

I was pushing thirty, but that's how they talked to us then. By then, I was astride the top rail and I jumped down. The man with the pipe in his hands looked at me. I wondered if he was going to turn the pipe on me, but he just shrugged and headed toward the rail. I think the shrug meant, "Let the horse do you in instead of my iron pipe."

That was all right by me. The three other men in the corral still had hold of the reins. While we looked at each other, the horse calmed enough that they could start backing off. They took a few steps before he charged them. They hit the rails at a run. One of them was a little slower and he paid for it. It looked like his ribs were broken when he was pinned against the rails. But the men on the outside pulled him out of the corral. That was as much as I noticed.

There was all kinds of talk, but I didn't pay it no notice. I expect it was mostly trash talk though there may have been some cheers for me. Didn't matter. It was just me and the horse inside the corral. There was nothing else.

I stood still and looked at the horse. I was going to let him make the first move. He was looking at me too and I got ready to take his charge. No matter what, I knew not to back off. Forever came and went. When he charged at me, I planted my feet and looked him in the eye. He went to the side of me. He only wanted to scare me. I'm not sure why.

He waited for me to move but I just watched. I left myself open, but the second charge was the same, only to the left. This time, as he went by, with both hands I grabbed his reins. He was strong, all right; strong enough to jerk me off my feet. But my weight slowed him down a bit. My feet started to drag on the ground and my weight pulled down on the reins. His head came down toward mine. I don't think he liked it, but he went slower.

Besides my weight, I used all my strength to keep his head down so that we looked each other eye to eye. He still had the strength to crush me, but I slowly backed him into the fence. We were still squared off, eye to eye, but he wasn't going nowhere. When he finally dropped his head, I knew that we had an understanding. I climbed on his back and rode. He didn't try to throw me. I never hit him; didn't have to. When I climbed down, I tied him to the fence. He didn't mind.

All the while it was just me and that horse. There had been nothing else in the world. I felt so good, but it became awful quiet and I noticed the crowd along the rail. Right away, I knew I had done wrong. All my life, I had followed the code that told me to never show up a white man. To break that rule was unforgivable and could cost a colored man his life. Now here I had gone and shown up a whole crowd of white men.

Spinning around in a circle, I saw that the rails was packed. I made sure not to look at Elzenia for I didn't want to see how bad she would be feeling. I knew that I was going to pay for what I had done. What's done is done, though. Clenching my teeth, I promised myself I wouldn't plead with nobody, but I would take what I had coming. I knew there was no chance, but I wasn't going to make it easy neither. I decided I wouldn't be the only one hurt before it was done and I readied myself for what seemed like forever.

Odd thing. The colors became sharp. There was time to notice the clouds in a blue sky, the reddish-brown dust at my feet. Even the faces looking at me were so clear, I can still remember the details. Figuring that I would be jumped from the backside, I moved in a small slow circle to keep watching all sides of the corral. Even so, Johnny was there and up behind me just as I caught him in my sight.

He put his back to mine and then we did the slow circling together.

"What did you go and do that for?" I whispered.

He was half a head taller than me, but I was older and he said, "What else can I do? I just can't watch my big brother and not do nothing."

The men along the corral seemed a little startled. They had all the time they wanted and they seemed to set back and ponder what they would do next now that Johnny was there too. He was big enough to make them think first.

"You're a damn fool," I said.

Johnny gave a low laugh. "I'm a fool! I'd like to know who got in here first?"

"Well, that was my choice. It didn't involve nothing with you."

"Yeah, right," Johnny said. "You think I'm gonna go all the way home and tell Mama that I only watched the whole thing? I'll take my chances right here, thank you!"

"Hmm. Well, Johnny, your chances ain't too good," I said. "There's a lot of them."

"Think I don't know that? Maybe we can take a few with us anyway."

"That's the best plan you got?" I asked him.

"Hey, you started this, maybe you got a plan!"

I wished I did, all right. All we could do was get ready and take it as it happened. Meanwhiles, I looked over and saw that along the rail they were looking at each other. I think they were trying to see who was going to rush us first, figuring that the first couple might get hurt. There being two of us had slowed them down, but we was heading down the same road.

A cowboy right in front of me said, "That nigger acts like he can ride better than a white man."

Then another one said, "Maybe he thinks he is better than one of us by trying to win that fifty dollars that should of gone to a white man."

273

I had forgotten all about the money. "Hey, George, you gonna split that money with me?" Johnny asked.

"Hey, Johnny, you can have it all."

"No, I just want half."

With all that, I don't know why we were joking, but I said, "Oh, you'll get your share, all right."

I just knew that when the first one broke and made his move, we might take him down, but, for sure, there would be a crowd a coming behind him. Johnny and I became quiet, just watching to see where that break would be. I was concentrating hard when a man shouted, "Back off!"

I figure that he was talking to us, but some space opened at the rail. A different cowboy came up and said, "You boys won it. The money is yours."

He waved his arms and said, "The rest of you back off."

I didn't know he was the foreman, until everybody started to move away and someone said, "Okay, boss. We didn't mean nothing. We was just gonna have a little fun!"

He said, "You can collect your fifty dollars up at the big house. If you want to stay, you got a job breaking horses."

Elzenia had come up. Was she mad. "If you do, it's without me. You could of been killed on that horse."

Johnny butted in and said, "That's a big horse, but I think the cowboys was more dangerous than..."

She didn't say nothing but gave Johnny a look that shut him up good.

"All right, all right. I got my job on the railroad to go back to anyway."

"I don't want to see you breaking horses again anytime. I ain't gonna stay and watch you get yourself killed."

I thought I was the boss in our house, but I had never seen her like that before either. I figure if Elzenia loved me that much... Besides, she was pregnant and I guess it was time for me to be starting to think about more than just the two of us. That was the last time that I broke horses. Elzenia has passed away since then, but I ain't going to risk a broken leg at this point in my life. That would make it too hard to go to school.

CHAPTER 18

Bonnie and Clyde were apprehended and killed in a shootout in West Dallas in 1938. That brought to an end a crime spree that left several dead during their numerous bank robberies. They gave some of their money to the poor and their outlaw status gained a certain popularity and celebrity status.

—Caption accompanying photo of Bonnie and Clyde's bodies lying in the street, *Dallas Morning News*

Always Richard's bringing me articles to look at, but this time I had one for him. He looked closely at the news article that I had.

It was old, all right. I had been saving it all these years. The date in the corner was 1938. It was big news, but everybody knew Bonnie and Clyde. They traded at a gas station on the west side that was run by Clyde's father. People said that boy was always kind of wild. It was a bad thing for Bonnie to get hooked up with him. Folks said that she wasn't like that till she met Clyde—killing, shooting, robbing banks, and such things.

Nowadays, a lot of people say they were heroes. I hear there was even a movie about them. But I didn't see it; don't generally go to movies. I guess they gave some of that bank money to the poor, but they killed some people and scared a lot more. That's wrong. The Bible tells that straight off. They weren't no heroes. They were famous, all right, but they weren't no heroes.

Richard wondered if I remembered Al Capone from around that time. He wasn't from Dallas, but everybody knew of Al Capone. There was John Dillinger too. They killed a lot of people. They was famous, all right, but they did bad things too. They was gangsters. There was a lot of gangsters then.

Back then I was too busy with my own life to pay much attention. All that coming and going of them folks didn't have much to do with us. I was a father then and busy raising my own family. Besides that, I didn't rob nobody. I worked every day to earn a living.

When we moved to Dallas in 1928, I was working for the railroad. I did that for some years. That was a good job, but in the early thirties, I started working for the city. That was during the Depression. Times was tough, but I would take any job and I always had work. I've never been unhappy doing any kind of work. But every time I switched jobs it was to improve myself. I thought there might be more hours and maybe more pay. That's only what I thought might happen. But that's okay.

Junior was over visiting when I was talking about those times and he asked, "Daddy, didn't the city pay better than the railroad?"

I don't remember for sure, but all I knows is that if I had stayed with the railroad, I would be a rich man today. Since I been sixty-five, I got nothing but my monthly Social Security. Think how many paychecks I would of gotten by now if I had stayed and retired with the railroad. But it don't matter, I'm doing just fine.

I told Junior, "I just did what I thought would be the best thing for my family. With the city of Dallas, I worked on a road crew. We filled potholes and fixed roads."

He asked, "Daddy, was it easier work than the railroad?"

"Well, sometimes it could be. But on days when I had to stand over hot asphalt in the Dallas heat, nothing was ever easy. That would be when you were born, Junior. I had a growing family then, seven children to raise."

"They all did okay?" Richard asked.

Junior answered, "Yeah, we did. All of us graduated high school and all seven of us graduated from college too. Our school was just six blocks from here. I graduated fourth in my class."

"Elzenia and me wasn't going to have nothing less than their best work from the children."

"That's a lot of children," Richard said. "At least for today it would be."

"Yeah, that's true. It was pretty fair size even for them days."

Richard came back out of the bedroom with another one of those books he always brings. "Either of you ever seen this book before, called *Raising Your Baby* by Dr. Benjamin Spock?"

Sallie, Junior's wife, had just come in. It was a big, fat book, but not one I had ever seen.

Junior shook his head and Sallie said, "No, me neither."

"A lot of families in this country raised their children and used this book for advice or for directions on what to do."

"Nope. Never saw it," I said.

"Well, it sold millions of copies."

Sallie had it in her hand and started reading out loud. "You know more than you think you do. Your baby..."

It went on and on like that in the way that some books do. "Well, I don't suppose you had any books that you used for child raising?" Richard asked.

"Back then, I couldn't of read it anyway. We didn't need to read no book to raise our own kids."

Junior laughed. "That's right. My folks knew what they were doing."

"You bet we did. Raising you all was our job. So we just did it."

"The way everybody turned out, it seems they did a good job too," Richard said. "A lot of people haven't done as well. And you were successful with no formal education at all."

"Son, book-learning isn't everything. Common sense will go a long way. Me and Elzenia had plenty of that."

"That's it?"

"And love to. A family got to have a lot of that."

Richard set that book down and said, "Well, I guess that works." Then he said, "Junior, what do you remember about growing up in this family? What do you remember about your father?"

"Oh, we was always close. He took me fishing."

"Tell me about that."

"Well, Daddy would wake me about four in the morning. It was still dark then, but we would go down to the lake. It was about two miles away, but a lot of times we would walk there. We always caught fish too. When he wasn't off to work he took me everywhere, just the two of us."

Richard said, "That sounds nice, but there were a lot of children in your family."

"That's right," Junior said. "Thing is that Darrell, my only brother, wasn't born till several years after me. The girls would do things with my mother and I went with my father. That's how things were done then. For me and my brother and sisters, our childhood was great. Richard, if I could, I would give you the experience of my childhood as a gift. It was that wonderful for me."

"But from what I have heard, your family was very poor. You would definitely have been below the poverty level."

"You're right about that. Most of my childhood, Daddy had to work two jobs so we could get by. Still, if the Good Humor man came by after a payday, we would all of us get a nickel to get an ice cream. I still remember the excitement with that. We had all we needed and then some. There was no one that told us we were poor and I guess we just didn't know better."

"There must have been some moments things didn't go so well."

"Yeah, that's true too," Junior said. "My mother did most of the disciplining, and she was the one that always said no."

"I was mostly at work, but I was there when I needed to be. Junior, do you remember when I had to visit your principal at the high school?"

"Oh, yeah! I got in some trouble and got sent home early in the afternoon. I was sixteen and I guess that you could say I was feeling pretty full of myself. But I don't remember exactly what it was all about. I knew I was in some real trouble when my mother said, 'We'll wait till your father gets home.' "

"That's right. I did something I never done. I called in at work and said that I was gonna be late."

"Right there, that made me take notice," Junior said. "Daddy was never late and never missed work."

"Next morning I went to school with Junior and we went to see the principal."

"Yeah," Junior said. "But Daddy did all the talking."

"I told him, 'I got a job to do every day and I can't come in all the time. I expect my son to do his job at school. His work is at school. If Junior does something wrong, you don't need to call for my permission to punish him. That is your job to discipline him at school.'

"Both of us, me and the principal, looked over at Junior. He just nodded."

"That's pretty much it. I didn't get in any more trouble and I did well at school. We all did."

"That's right. Mostly I told them something and they listened. I only said something one time. See, I respected my own father and did what he told me. With my own children it was the same. We was the parents. It was our job to have the children ready to be in this world. A child doesn't learn so much by words as he does by watching. The children were always watching their mother and me. That's how they learn right from wrong, by watching what we do."

"Life wasn't easy then. You were still raising your children during the days of legal segregation," Richard said.

"They understood. It wasn't right, but that's how life was. Breaking the rules could be dangerous. In one way or another, every colored man had the same talk with his children: how to get along, how to survive in this world."

"Things was just that way. Daddy made it clear that there was no excuses; we would just have to work harder, that's all," Junior said.

"When we were raising our children, I worked on the city road crew, but in 1938, I got another job at the Oaks Farm Dairy, the place we visited on your last trip. I worked there almost twenty-five years."

Richard said, "I remember that dairy."

Junior said, "It's changed some. Since 1963, it's bigger but it looks pretty much the same. I used to drop Daddy off, sometimes at four in the morning, so I could use the car to go to work before school. Or I might come by at midnight to pick him up. There was different hours and different shifts, but I was over there a lot. Daddy was at the dairy a long time."

"Son, do you remember the room in the back with the big engines?"

Richard said, "Was that the room where they gave us earplugs to wear before we went in because it was so loud?"

"That's the room, all right. All the years I worked there, no one ever gave me no earplugs like we had on that tour. Things was different then. I know that's why my hearing isn't so good today."

"You never wore no earplugs?" Junior asked.

"No. No one ever mentioned them. Anyway, I kept things running. They counted on me. If I didn't come in to work, there wasn't no one to replace me. I always set the gauges right so they could pasteurize the milk. I did that without reading. I knew how the gauges should look. Sometimes, I was the only one that could fix the engines. I checked things ahead of time and kept everything running smooth."

"Up front in the lobby in that picture of all the workers, maybe forty or fifty men, none of them were black. I wonder if it was the photo or if they hadn't hired any back then?" Junior asked.

"That was in the late thirties. There was about four of us, maybe seven. That picture could have been right. I just might have been in the first group of colored to be hired there. I don't know, but it doesn't do any good to worry about those things."

"Well, how about that. You might have been one of the first, a pioneer," Sallie said. "Did people treat you right?"

"Oh, yeah. People was good to me."

Well, at the beginning I did have a few problems. See, I always paid attention and caught on to things quick. You don't always have to go to school to learn something. Just pay attention.

But there was a man named Luther wouldn't believe that I could know anything, me being a colored man. I hadn't been there that long when they put me to tending the boiler. I heard Luther tell the supervisor that they should send that nigger out back to dig a trench and send in somebody with some training for the boilers.

I didn't say nothing, but just went out back and started digging. Less than an hour later, the supervisor came out and said, "The boiler isn't coming up. Go back in and fix it."

That man didn't even know how to light it; that was the problem. I lit the boiler and got it up to temperature, but these other boilers were not running so well either. The supervisor asked if I could fix them all up.

"Sure, I can."

Luther said, "He can't do that. That boy ain't had no training."

I didn't say nothing, just got up to leave and go back to digging. The supervisor said, "Wait. I'm going to have Little Black George try."

I was short and that's what they called me. I went back into the boiler room. There were two pumps hooked up but only one working. I turned off the one that was working and took it apart to see what a good pump should look like on the inside. Then I took the other one apart and with a few small changes got it to running too. There was another pump still in the wooden crate. I got that out and hooked that up so that there wouldn't be as much pressure on the other pumps and there would be a backup if it was to be needed. That took all morning. After lunch, I cleaned the pipes, swept off the floor, and started the boiler.

I brought in a chair and just sat and watched the gauges. I would use the ejector for steam and oil so those gauges would swing back and forth but come back to the middle. About then, Luther and the supervisor came in.

"Look at him just sitting and doing nothing," Luther said.

The supervisor looked at me and raised his eyebrows, his way of asking a question.

I showed them what I did with the pumps and said, "Now I just be watching the gauges and the boilers running smooth."

That got Luther angry. He said, "This is a job for a white man with the right training."

The supervisor said, "Well, right now, we don't have anybody with the training for this job."

See, I could learn by watching. I would pay close attention and learn something every day. I would light those burners with a long fire stick. That's a stick with a flame on it. I always got the burners going with no problem and made sure my fire stick was out before I set it down. There were two rooms with boilers in them. Pretty soon, I was in charge of one and Luther, he was in charge of the other one.

One day, when I passed by, Luther was having a bad time. He couldn't get the burner to light. I could have done it, but if I had stopped to help, I only would have got him mad. I did say, "You shouldn't ought to leave your fire stick going when it's on the ground."

But he wasn't going to listen to me. He left his fire stick on and I went about my own work. Sure enough, about half an hour later, there was a loud "boom" and I went upstairs to see. He was all blackened. They took him to the hospital and he wasn't back to work for about three weeks. They sent me in to fix the burners. The burners were okay, though. He just wasn't being careful. I figured it was best not to say that. Instead, I spent some time cleaning up and then went back to my own work.

That was in the early forties. I was there for almost twenty-five years and didn't have no more troubles except for one time. A man named —— was always giving me a bad time. He would say, "George, do this" or "Boy, do that."

I didn't need that and I would get up and walk away. But he never let up on me, and it went on for weeks and months. I tried to stay out of his way, but one day we were both in the warehouse. There was a big load of sugar to be unloaded to be used for making ice cream.

I was up on top of three pallets cutting the hemp rope of the sacks of sugar. I heard the foreman say, "Help George here unload the sugar."

The foreman, he left straight off, but —— started going on and on. "They ain't gonna have me doing nigger's work."

We were the only ones there. He just kept talking, knowing that I couldn't help but hear. I'd heard it all before, but for some reason that was enough. It was a hot day, even warmer in the warehouse, and maybe that was it.

I jumped down from three pallets high. Somehow, I landed on my feet in front of him without losing my footing.

"Say what now?"

He just looked at me.

"You talking to me?"

In a more respectful tone, he asked, "You gonna use that knife?"

Till then, I hadn't realized I still held on to it. It was a dumb thing to jump with a knife, but there you have it. Shorter than a machete, it still had a good blade to it. Never would I have turned a weapon like that on anybody. But I just grinned and said, "The foreman, he handed me this knife and told me to use it."

He nodded at me, lifted a sack of sugar off a pallet, and set it on the handcart. We worked together just fine for the rest of the day and for many years after. I didn't even say his name for he changed a lot and we been friends for years. We even had us a joke just between the two of us. When we were eating lunch and I would bring out my jackknife to cut my sandwich, he would say, "You going to use that knife?"

I would say, "I might do that."

The two of us would laugh. Even when we was at a full lunch table, nobody else ever could figure it out. For a few people, my being there must have been an adjustment for them. Fact is, most people treated me just fine. I ain't got nothing to complain about.

They treated me fair on the job. See, I've always believed that you give a man a chance to work and then see what he can do. They did that. I did a good job and in almost twenty-five years I was never late or missed work. They could count on me and no one knew those machines better than I did. People were decent. I had no complaints. I was always just a working man. Nothing wrong with that.

Little by little things changed. I was there about two decades and some blacks became supervisors. I was a good worker and had my chance to move up too except I didn't fill out the application. I wasn't about to tell them that I couldn't read or write. I didn't know my letters and couldn't sign my name. No one was holding me back, but I couldn't fill out the application. Still, watching colored people hired more often and being promoted, that felt good. I had been one of the first and done a good, steady job. Maybe that might have made it easier for those that followed.

I stayed there all the way till retirement in 1963. I was sixty-five and they told me that government regulations said that I was too old to work any longer. I had just short of twenty-five years there so I don't think it was full retirement.

Junior laughed. "Tell him about the choice you had to make."

"I could collect a monthly check for the rest of my life or take a one-time cash payment. I took the cash payment. You never know about tomorrow."

Junior was laughing some more. "Daddy, I think you got to tell him how much money we're talking about."

They gave me $1,800 in cash. That's all gone now. If I knew I would be here talking about it at one hundred and one, I would have taken the monthly check. I get a Social Security check once a month, though, and that works.

CHAPTER 19

Picture: A civil rights march in the 1960s. An angry confrontation between police and demonstrators, being held at bay with large attack dogs.

—*Events That Shaped the Century: Our American Century,* by the editors of Time-Life Books

Zapruder film emerging from cold storage. A 26-second video of Kennedy's killing will be available and headed for video stores.

—*Seattle Post-Intelligencer,* July 8, 1998

Every day, we all did the best we could. The important thing, no matter what, was to keep our pride. I worked for a living and each day I did the best job that I could. When I had to quit my job in 1963, I didn't stop working. Even if I wanted to, I couldn't have done that. I did yard work and gardening for people.

No matter what the work or whatever the pay, I did my best. I remember one day I was at some lady's house. It was a nice big house, one of those older ones with the large porches, in a nice neighborhood and the grounds was big. There was nice plantings all over. In the early morning she laid out a ton of work for me to do. There was a day's work, all right, actually more than one. Once she showed me what she wanted, I never forgot and could work on my own without bothering her none.

It was already getting hot, so she was going back into the house.

"I don't know how you can stand this heat. I'm going to have to go back inside for the day. Thank God for air-conditioning."

"Yes, ma'am, it's gonna be a warm one."

"I guess the heat doesn't bother you people. You're fortunate that you can just keep working. It's too hard for us, especially when we get older."

Now, I was sixty-five and at least as old as she was. But since I was working for her she figured otherwise and didn't really bother to look at me. I guess she must have thought that since she could afford to retire, so could the rest of us.

I almost said, "We work in this heat because we have to work. We don't have no choices about it."

I could of got angry, but I could see that she meant no harm. Even though she had a lot of money, she was just ignorant. So, I nodded enough to show that I heard what she had said, but not a big enough nod to show that I agreed. She went on, "It's a warm day. Help yourself to some water. I'll have some lunch for you at noon."

"Thank you, ma'am."

Usually that's how it worked. Most often, at midday, someone had a lunch for me. At the end of each day, I got paid for the work.

291

Sometimes, if it went for two or three days, they might pay me at the end. I hadn't never worked for this lady, but I had done gardening for her neighbors. Because I did good work, one job always led to another. People would see me working hard at their neighbor's and then stop and tell me to come to their house next day when I was done. That's how I came to be there.

The pay wasn't much, nothing like the dairy, but it was usually the same at every house. I guess that was because they all knew each other. Matter of fact, my wife heard some of them talking once. They was all angry about some new lady that moved in and paid more for housework and yard work than they did. They didn't want someone to be making everyone look bad and be spoiling the colored besides. Me, I just let them pay me at the end of the day and what they paid me is what they paid me. If they paid me fair that was good. If they didn't, that was more their problem than it was mine.

Myself, I grow mostly vegetables. With the wealthy folk, it seems to me that they do flower gardens and big lawns. I guess they can buy their own vegetables. Now, when I say "them," it's mostly us that really does the gardening. When they talk about gardening, usually it means they give the directions and we do the work. That's how it ends up anyway.

One thing's for sure: These ladies all have their roses and it seems that one just has to outdo the other. To hear people talk, some of these roses are old, I mean really old. Their stock goes back to the Civil War and maybe earlier than that. The way I gather, with roses, the older the better. At least you got something to brag about. Like most of the ladies, this lady could be particular about her roses.

"Trim them along here, but not too short. Don't touch them on the other side of the house, not until I make sure that you're doing it right."

Now, thing is, I would nod and be all agreeable so as I could get to work. But I know for a fact that with roses, you could chop them off at the ground with an ax and next year they would probably come up all that much better for it. It only makes sense: If these roses have been around this long already, they are pretty sturdy. You baby anything, it doesn't help nothing. It's only going to make it weaker.

But I'm there to work for these people, not teach them. There was a regular rose garden and I started trimming in that. I finished the one section that she wanted and started digging out a new flower bed. The soil had a lot of clay and there were some sacks of chicken manure to add to it.

By midmorning, it was hot. Since she had mentioned water for me, I looked on the porch for a pitcher. I didn't see one and figured that she had forgotten. The water was warm, but I used the hose to quench my thirst and kept on working. Besides the garden, there was a pond to clean and a big tree with rotten limbs to come off. So, I got back to digging. This neighborhood was a long bus ride from where we lived. I left pretty early and didn't feel like a big breakfast at that time. So, by late morning, I was pretty hungry. I kept working, though, till the sun was straight up.

No one had called me so I walked to the back of the house figuring she was the type of lady that would want me to come in through the back door. We was still in those times when we was good enough to work at somebody's house, but not good enough to enter through the front door. I didn't see nothing happening and I didn't want to cause no problem either, in case she was just running late.

Since that side was in the shade, I picked up a saw that was leaning against a big shade tree just back from the house. Right then, I was too hungry to go back to digging. After looking over the tree good, I commenced to sawing off a limb that was rotted. Choosing a spot that was a couple feet above the rot, I cut at an angle so the rain wouldn't set right on it.

It was a big old tree with tight limbs and it was slow cutting. I was on a three-step ladder. The sawdust was falling into my eyes and as I was sweating pretty hard, it was sticking to my face too. At the sound of the screen door slamming, I looked up and was glad to see that she was coming out on the porch. She didn't see me from the shadow of the tree, but I watched as she put down two bowls on the floor for some dogs that had come out and were by her side. I walked toward the porch. The door slammed again, but she returned in a minute with another bowl. This one she set up on a shelf that was above the reach of the dogs. She waved as she saw me coming. Pointing toward that bowl, she said, "It's homemade."

The screen door slammed again as she went back inside. I climbed up on the porch and lifted the bowl off the the shelf. It was a big bowl of stew. Potatoes, big chunks of meat, and okra was all floating in some thick juices that almost made the spoon stand up. It looked good and, as hungry as I was, it smelled even better. In my other hand, I picked up a large biscuit that she had set to go with it. I was looking for a chair to sit in and a quiet spot to say grace when I looked down and saw the two dogs.

They were maybe a Lab-collie mix, black and brown with long hair and of a pretty good size, probably from the same litter. Their tails was moving double-time as they were eating their lunch. I saw it was more of the same that was there for me on the shelf. There weren't such a surprise in that. People didn't buy dog food in the sack like they do now. Dogs just mostly ate the leftovers from the table.

But what hit me was that she expected I would eat out on the porch with her dogs. I didn't have to eat in their dining room, but back in their kitchen would of been all right. I told myself that I was good enough to eat a meal with people, not dogs. I set the bowl back on the shelf. Being hungry, that wasn't so easy. It was even harder with the biscuit, but I set that down too.

I know she didn't plan to insult me, she just didn't know better. Still, she could believe what she wanted, but I weren't no animal and I wasn't going to eat with dogs. If I did, she would go on believing that way and maybe she would of been right. The stew was mighty tempting, though, and I carefully backed off the porch. My stomach had a problem, but my pride said, "No!"

I went down into the yard and got some water from the hose. The smell of the stew hung in the air, floated across the yard. The sawdust in my eyes bothered me more than it had before. I took a break to catch my breath, but my stomach started growling. When there wasn't much left of that limb, the saw got pinched.

I headed off to the toolshed for another saw. Thing was, that took me right by the back porch. I could see that bowl of stew, could even see the biscuit waiting for me. Might of just been me, but I swear that it smelled even better than before. It was all I could do to keep going. I was hungry, but I wasn't gonna give in and eat with dogs. I had to keep my pride. Without that, I had nothing.

It didn't take so long to bring down the limb even though it was a pretty good size. I cut off the branches and then started to cutting the limb into fireplace-sized logs. All the while I was working, it was hard to keep my mind off food. I thought about Elzenia being at home and maybe cooking dinner for us. Most of the children were gone by then. We was just down to a couple still in high school, but we always had dinner together as a family.

My mind wouldn't let go. I started trying to guess if there would be mashed potatoes and chicken. But each time I guessed, it was like I could almost smell the food. That sure didn't help me get by on an empty stomach! Sometimes, the mind is funny and just does what it wants. I tried to block out food and pretty soon that's all I could think of.

That sure made it more tempting to go over and get some lunch. I had earned it, all right, and nobody but me would know the way she treated me. I wasn't one that marched in Washington or joined the marches across the South. It just wasn't me. I was old by then and it wasn't the way I had been living all those years. But something told me, "George, don't go up on that porch. You must keep your pride. Those people have been marching for you and now you can't let them down. They will be counting on you. Do this for your children!"

I set to work, sawing harder than ever. That lady was gonna get her money's worth from me, all right! But the faster pace slowed the agitation in my brain. My mind let go of its anger and settled on other things. I had my pride to keep for me and for my children, who still looked to their father.

Pictures of my children went by. I remember my pride when Amelia, the first one, was born. From her first cry, I knew that I would always take care of her. I told myself it didn't matter what other people thought. I would carry myself so that she would have a father to be proud of.

Elzenia was a good mother. She just seemed to know what to do. In the way things were done then, she stayed home. I helped when I could, but also worked overtime whenever it was there. And a good thing too, because it wasn't so long before Novella was born. George Jr. was the first boy. He was followed by Dorothy, Cecelia, and Billie Jean. Darrell, the baby, is in his forties now.

From the beginning, family came first. No matter how many hours or even how many shifts, when I came home I left work behind. We were living in the housing project then, some government-built apartments for people without a lot of rent money. I was working full-time, but it didn't pay enough for both rent and food. It was a big help to us then. The projects were big apartment buildings. They were built of brick, and at the time they were brand-new. It was a nice place to live. It wasn't till later they got run down. We lived there till we moved to our first house.

We treated our children right. I hadn't been to school, but I made sure that all of them went. Every night, I listened when they showed me their work, but I never listened to any excuses. They had to take pride in themselves.

They got that pride from me and I wasn't about to let that lady take it away. I always told them, "Don't worry about what someone else thinks. Just do the right thing and take pride in yourself." I was hungry and my stomach was going to fight me on that, but I could see that I had to win. I listened to it growling but didn't give in. After cutting and stacking the wood for her, I went back and finished turning her new garden.

That was late afternoon and just when I was finishing, she came by. I hadn't even heard the door slam, but I nodded and tipped my hat when I saw her.

"You've been working hard."

"Yes, ma'am."

"I thought it might be too hot."

"No, ma'am. I'm all right," I said, though I doubt she really cared about my health.

"Good. My neighbor said you would do a good job."

We was walking back toward the house. She had seen the garden and took note of the wood I had stacked. I could see that she was pleased. She had some money folded over that she gave to me. Just then, in front of the porch, she looked up and saw the bowl of stew with the biscuit next to it.

She looked puzzled. "Didn't you see the lunch I left on the porch?"

I nodded. "I saw the dogs on the porch."

"Well, the lunch on the shelf was for you! It was a good lunch."

"Thank you. I'm sure it was. It's just that I don't eat with dogs."

As I said that, I looked her straight in the eye. I could tell she understood what I meant.

She got angry and red in the face. But I didn't turn away or look down.

"Fine, then. It's your choice to waste perfectly good food. I just hate to see that happen."

Despite what I was feeling inside, I kept a level voice. "I hate to see food wasted too, ma'am."

Her face softened a bit when I agreed with that. I went on, "But I eat with people. I am a human being."

At my words, her face tightened and her look changed to meanness and anger. From her mother and father and back through her grandparents, I could sense a hundred years of anger and fear coming out toward me.

I stood up to it and repeated, "I am a human being."

She was so angry, she couldn't speak. I waited. Finally, in a cold tone she said, "You don't need to come back anymore."

I said, "That's right. I don't need to."

Sometimes, it just wasn't going to be easy. And some folks were never going to change. But I could feel that things were getting better, even if it was slow. In our own way, we each of us did the best that we could do.

There was a lot happening in those times. Dr. King wasn't the only one assassinated. Some years earlier, President Kennedy was killed too right here in Dallas. Somehow, I think that's what might have started everything.

Something always keeps popping up about it. I've heard it said that everybody remembers where they were when Kennedy was shot. I was at the lake, fishing. A man came running over across the field. He said, "The president was shot."

We all crowded around a car with its radio on. "The president has been shot as his cavalcade went through downtown. Our own Governor Connally was also shot."

No one said anything and the next thing we heard was "We just have word: The president is dead."

We all stayed and shared the radio for a while. All the cars left at once. I think that everybody wanted to get home to their family. The site where the president was killed is still where everybody goes if they visit Dallas. There's a little park there now. For a long time there was nothing. But I guess they figured no one was going to let us forget it anyway.

Lyndon Johnson became president then. A lot of colored thought of Kennedy as a real friend and were sad to see him cut short. The white Southern voice scared some at first, but Johnson turned out to be okay.

CHAPTER 20

Faced with certain impeachment by the House of Representatives and likely conviction by the Senate, on August 8 Nixon announced to the nation in a televised speech that he would resign, becoming the first president in American history to do so. A pre-emptive pardon by his successor, Gerald R. Ford, spared him the further indignity of a possible criminal indictment.

—*Events That Shaped the Century: Our American Century,* by the editors of Time-Life Books

I looked at Richard's article. I remember Watergate, all right, but I wasn't one of those people that followed the hearings every day. I think that maybe Richard Nixon just wanted something too much. He worked too hard to get what he wanted and forgot the important things on the way.

It seems like he forgot what it was that made him want to serve his country in the first place. There was too much power and he just got lost in it. I've never had any power. I've always been watching from the outside.

I picked up a book about the presidents that was on the kitchen table. Each of them had their own page with their picture on it. I remember Jimmy Carter. He seemed like a nice man. Alongside a picture of Ronald Reagan, it says that he made people feel good about themselves.

Where I lived, I didn't see much changing then, but I didn't mind him. The one we have now, President Clinton, isn't in the book. A lot of people are upset with him. We even got impeachment hearings again. As I see it, it's all none of my business. That's what I think. Look at those people that do the accusing. I think the word for it is hypocrisy. Yeah, I think that's it. Black people understand that. Let the man do his job and I don't have to approve of the rest of his life. There been plenty of presidents and even enough wars in my time.

I missed World War I when my boss had me put an *X* on some kind of a paper. I was too old for the service in World War II, but the war did make for a lot of work. They was doing a lot of hiring at a munitions plant in California and people was saying that the pay was supposed to be good. My wife didn't want me to go, though. I didn't read then, but we had the radio and I followed as best I could. Hitler was doing bad things. I don't know why he was so mean inside. He had to be a crazy man.

Junior was drafted for the Korean War and was over there for three years. I asked him about that. He said, "I was in combat with soldiers from everywhere, white and black, different religions. We hung together. We had to. Life wasn't easy but we was all treated the same. That was a new experience.

"When I came home and our troop train got to the southern states, I had to leave and switch to the colored cars. We could fight together, but back home we still couldn't be in the same railcar."

I know that had to be true for all the colored boys when they came home, but I felt bad for Junior after all he had done. Still, I told him, "That's life and you just need to get settled back into things."

There ain't no sense on dwelling on things. I been around for lots of wars. Being younger, Richard asked me about the Vietnam War. I told him, "I didn't pay much attention to Vietnam or for that matter to all the protests either. Did have a great-nephew, Borice Stevens, that served and was killed there, though. Didn't see no need for that war."

All the presidents, I believe they had their points to make. They all wanted to do something in the way they saw fit. They didn't make a difference for me, though. Not knowing how to read then, I was on the outside. I could follow from what other people said or from the radio or TV later on. But I never read the papers for myself to know for sure.

After I retired I moved out of the projects and into a house. That was late in the 1960s. Just me and my wife then. The kids had left. That was my second wife by then. I met her at church. Thing is, I met my last three wives at church.

I was married four times. I've outlived them all. It's been twelve years since my last wife passed away. I took care of each of them to the end and gave them a proper funeral too. That's why I had no pension money left either. I tried to do the best I could for them.

People always ask me if I will ever get married again. I might. I might. There's lots of women that would like to marry me. That's because I treats them right and I am honest. I have never been unfaithful.

For me it's like fishing. Some folks, they go fishing and they keep reeling in, changing bait, and trying again and again. Me, I cast out and then I stick with it. I just wait and be patient. There's no sense in changing. I just take my chances and then that is that. There's no way to know that any change is going to make anything better. That's true with fishing and with women.

I once had plans to build a new house. I had the lot and everything. It was a nice, pleasant piece of ground. It was gonna be nice. For the first time in my life, I was going to live in a new house. But one of my daughters got cancer. That was seven years ago.

She ran out of money for treatment. The insurance wouldn't pay for all her treatment. I think they argued, but she couldn't get them to pay and she didn't have a lot of time. So, I sold the lot and used the money to help her. I think the treatment might of helped some. I don't know, but she didn't make it. Maybe it was too late. Watching my little girl die was the hardest thing. That was a good while ago and it still hurts. She was living in California. I flew out to see her. That was my first time on an airplane.

People ask me what did I do. Nothing to do. I just went on. Everybody has their time, and it ain't up to me when that will be. At those times, my faith helps me to keep going. I've been a member of the same church since 1928.

That's how it is that I'm still in this house. This little house has treated me fine, though. Someday, I should maybe give it a new roof. When it rains heavy, I might have to put some buckets in the living room to catch the water coming through. There's a room where the electricity don't come on anymore, and in the kitchen the linoleum is crumbling, but it's got everything I need.

My father died at the age of ninety-nine. My mother stayed on in the house in Kaufman. That's not far from here. One day, about a year after my father passed, my wife and I went out to visit her; no particular reason. My sister was there and then my brother came and pretty soon the other two sisters came. I asked them why they all came to visit at once like that, but nobody had talked about it and nobody knew. Just happened that way.

Mama had been fine, but suddenly my wife said, "Mama, put that broom down and rest yourself. You don't look so good."

My mother sat down. We went over to check on her. She said, "Everything will be all right." And then she died. Just like that. I don't know what it was exactly. We used to just call it old age. We didn't know it when we walked in, but that's why all her children was there.

Except for my son, Darrell, in Chicago, all my children live here in Dallas. So even when my last wife passed away, I've never been alone. I was doing yard work by then. I did that for more than twenty years. I was close to ninety when I stopped. I had to work all those years, but I was glad to work. A man is supposed to work and take pride in what he does no matter what the work is.

I've always treated everybody with respect and people have been good to me. There are always some that make life hard, though. Most people, when they show disrespect, they don't even know it. Don't mean nothing by it. It's not always big things. But I remember once when I was doing yard work, there was a lady getting ready for a garage sale the next day. She told me to stop working and help her son shuffle some stuff around in her garage.

When I worked for them, people would sometimes ask me to do just about anything and I didn't mind. We moved a big desk and behind that was a loom. It was nicer wood than the loom my grandma used with the thread we had made. We moved it against the garage wall. It was all polished wood and beautiful too.

The lady's son said, "I wonder what's this old thing that my grandma left us."

Made me feel just good to see one again after all those years and I said, "It's a loom for weaving cloth."

I started to show him where you tie up the

threads and said, "It's just missing a shuttle and then it be ready."

That boy looked at me but didn't, couldn't believe a word I said, and I shut up because he didn't even see me. He saw an old black man, a gardener. He didn't think I could know anything, especially something he didn't know. I stopped talking and he didn't learn nothing about his grandma's loom. He wasn't ready to learn.

I admit that bothered me a little, but not for long. What someone thinks about me is none of my business. He don't know me. I just keep moving and go my own way.

I had my own truck and got to where I had two men that I hired to help me. I was getting enough work to keep all of us going. They were a good bit younger than me and I was glad to give them some work. Problem was that one night, they broke into my toolshed in the backyard. They knew where everything was and stole my tools, even a chain saw and my shotgun that I kept back there.

I had to stop doing yard work. I was eighty-eight and really did retire then. I haven't just sat around for all those years, though. I went fishing just about every day. I fished for catfish at Hubbard Lake or some of the other lakes.

Hubbard Lake is a pretty good drive from my house, but I still owned a car then. I've been a Chevy man all my life. All these years, I've owned a fair number of cars. I always got my cars secondhand and did most of the work on them myself. I just learned it as I went along and as I needed to.

A couple of years ago, my car was parked out on the street and someone smashed into it. I got some insurance money but had some bills to pay before I was ready to get me another car. Thing is, I was supposed to renew my license last year on my hundredth birthday. But people made such a big deal about a birthday party that I forgot that my license was going to expire. I haven't been driving since then. Now I don't know if I can get another license. I don't really miss having a car, though. But every now and then...

One day when we were sitting on the porch, I asked Richard, "Is your car at home like the cars that you rent here?"

He said, "At home, I have a Ford."

"A new one?"

"Thirteen years old."

"That's pretty new. Does it have a radio?"

"Yeah, it does."

"That's good then. See that van you got parked in my driveway? I know what I would do if it was mine. I would load it up with some fishing gear. It's four hours to Galveston. We left now, we could be there before noon."

"What then?"

"We could go out on the dock and cast out. I would put on a heavy weight. See that house across the street? I would cast out that far, from this porch to that house, maybe two hundred feet out. Rent a chair for a dollar or maybe even bring a chair and then just wait. Cast out that far, it's deep and there is some big fish."

Now I got to plan when I go fishing and go with someone that can drive. When Richard has visited we've made it to a couple of lakes. But most days till I started school, you could find me at a lake. There's a lot of lakes around here. Even with fishing, I had a big garden that I worked on, grew my own vegetables.

Between the garden and fishing, I ate pretty well. I always caught fish, most of the time anyway. Sometimes I got buffalo fish. It's big like a catfish, and it's got a big head, a big ugly head. They ain't pretty, but you slice off some filets, and they cook just fine.

Since he had never had any, one night I was going to show Richard how to cook some buffalo fish. I was saying, "Put it in a pan with some—"

And Richard finished my sentence, "With some lard."

I asked, "How did you know that? You had buffalo fish before?"

"No. I've just been watching. That's how you cook everything."

I told him, "Good. You been paying attention."

I ate a lot of catfish, gave a lot away, and when I was fishing I would lay them out beside me. In the afternoons, some ladies that didn't catch no fish would buy some from me. No men ever did. I think their pride got in their way. If they didn't catch their own fish, then they would buy some hamburger for dinner.

I fished every day, all day long. But I'm not one of those fishermen that changes lures and checks their bait every five minutes. Lots of people fish that way. Not me. I put on some chicken livers or maybe some grubs and cast out from shore. I had a bobber up the line that would just sit out in the water. I carried all my gear in a big white bucket. When I was all set, the lid on the bucket was my seat.

I didn't just wait. No! I would be watching, always watching the water. I would look at the water. Most people look at the water but don't really see much. Not me. Every day, I be out there fishing. I look at the water. It's never the same. I just kept watching. That's when I saw what God does. Sometimes the water is so still, sometimes bubbles come up, sometimes the wind comes and the water's got ripples across the surface.

That's what God does. He moves the wind across the water or leaves it still. He can do all that. That's God doing that and He can do it on any lake that He wants to.

If they pay attention, everybody can see those things about God. But somehow there must be a hundred different churches that see God in their own ways. On Sunday, I took Richard to church, the Holiness Church of God, with me, not to convince him of nothing but so that he could see it my way too. Being the only Anglo, people could figure who he was, but when Reverend Williams introduced our visitor as "Brother Richard, the man who is

311

writing a book about the life and times of Mr. Dawson," I felt proud, for him and me.

It was a good service. Our preacher can get going and we was there for five hours. As our visitor, Richard even spoke. My granddaughter and great-granddaughter even sang a song special for me. It was mighty fine.

CHAPTER 21

The old man who could not read lives alone in a house that is small and square, in an area that some people call the ghetto.... The old man got by until 1996, when a young man knocked on his door and said he was recruiting people for the Adult Basic Education classes at the old high school.

"I've been alone for ten years," the old man told him. "I'm tired of fishing. It's time to learn to read."

—*Seattle Times*, Larry Bingham, February 1, 1998

I always had a dream that I would learn how to read. It was my secret, that I couldn't read. There was nothing I couldn't do and my mind was as good as anyone's. That's just how it was. All my life, I had been just too busy working to go to school. I kept it a secret that I couldn't read.

My mind worked hard. When I traveled somewhere, I could never read a sign. I had to ask people things and had to remember. I could never let my mind forget anything, never let my mind take a vacation.

I listened to the news and had to trust what I heard. I never read it for myself. My wife read the mail and paid our bills. I made sure that each of the children learned to read. When they came home from school, there was milk and cookies on the kitchen table. They would tell me what their classmates did and what the teacher said. I made sure they told me what they had learned that day. I always listened. I always asked if they had worked hard.

The answer was always yes, because they knew I would be waiting to find out. They knew what I expected: hard work. I would tell them, "School is important and there is a lot to learn."

To each of them I would say, "I'm proud of you."

I helped them with their homework.

"How could you do that," Richard asked, "if you couldn't read?"

Just then the screen door banged open and Junior came in. His jacket was dripping with water. "Tell Richard here how I helped you with your schoolwork. He don't believe me."

Junior laughed and said, "Every night, Daddy made us sit down at the kitchen table and do our homework. We had to show it to him when we were done. We didn't know he couldn't read. Daddy would say, 'Read back

313

what you got. You'll learn it better that way,' and that was probably true. I graduated fourth in my class! Daddy, and our mother too, they didn't want to hear about excuses. It was that simple," Junior said.

"When did you find out that your father couldn't read?"

"I was in high school when my father told me."

"What did you think?"

"He was our father and it didn't change anything, but we kept it a secret for him."

"Why?"

"Well, some folks don't understand things like that and we just wanted to protect him."

"So, it became more of a family secret?"

"That's a good way to put it."

"Back then, did you ever think your father would learn to read?"

"I knew he would have liked to. He thought reading was so important. But back then, there were more people his age that never learned to read than there is today."

"So it wasn't so uncommon?"

"I don't know for sure. It wasn't something people would talk about either."

I listened to the two of them talk, but I know that a lot of people still don't understand. They be thinking I spent my life just waiting to learn to read. That's not it at all. I didn't think about things I couldn't do nothing about. Things were just the way they were. And that's that.

People wonder why I didn't go back to

school earlier. After I retired, I finally had the time. I was proud to get my children through school and raise them properly. But I understood that school was there for the children. When I was young, I had missed my turn to go. I had never heard of these adult education classes. I've never had any extra money to hire a special teacher. People that been in my house have seen the sagging ceiling, the cracked window, the broken plaster on the wall and they know that. So I didn't expect nothing.

One day, out of the blue, a man came to the door. He handed me a piece of paper. Good thing I was home or I would have thrown it out like most fliers that I couldn't read. But he said there were some classes for adults. They taught reading. The school, the same one my own children had gone to, was close enough to walk to. It's maybe six blocks away.

Junior thinks that man might have thought there might be some of Daddy's grandchildren living in the house.

No matter. I live by myself now. I shook his hand and told him, "I will be coming to school!"

My turn had come. My first day of school was January 4, 1996. I was ninety-eight years old and I'm still going. Except for three funerals, I've gone to school every day for three years. School starts at nine. I can't wait and I'm up by five-thirty to make my lunch, pack my books, and go over my schoolwork. Since I started school, I'm always early. I haven't ever been late.

"I was just thinking," Richard said, "how hard it is to learn to read at any age. Not everybody succeeds. Mr. Dawson, were you a little afraid that you wouldn't make it? Didn't you have any doubts?"

"Son, I always thought I could drive a spike as good as any man and cook as good as any woman. I just figured if everybody else can learn to read, I could too."

"Was it hard to learn to read?"

"Sure, it was. But I been working hard all my life. I'm used to it and it don't scare me none. Mr. Henry, my teacher, he's a good man and he's a good teacher. Tomorrow, you come to class with me."

Richard came to school with me and I showed him my classroom. Since he teaches at an elementary school, I guess it would feel different to him. We're in the high school building, but my classmates are all grown up. They're mostly in their twenties and back to try it again at school.

At lunch, Richard asked Mr. Henry, "Are your students all high school dropouts that have returned?"

"Well, a large number of them dropped out of school and are back to get their GED, General Equivalency Degree. That's like a high school diploma."

"And the rest?"

"Oh, they graduated, but they can't read," Mr. Henry said.

"How is that?"

"Social promotion. Even if they didn't learn

they kept moving them up a grade and in some cases these kids actually graduated without being able to read. Now they've come back on their own to learn something."

Mr. Henry said, "I have been teaching thirty-three years with the Dallas schools. I taught music for fifteen years and then was an administrator of the music program in the Dallas public schools. I wanted to work in adult education and agreed to fill in for a young man that was just one course shy of getting his teaching credential. He got the credential and a job, so I'm still here. That was more than three years ago."

"Isn't that a long time for a temporary job?"

Mr. Henry laughed. "That's the truth. But since Mr. Dawson's been here I don't feel so old. Retirement was good for a few months, but I don't need it."

I had my schoolwork to do and left Richard to look around on his own. I've been coming every day for three years, but I still remember my first day at school. I came right in through the door and then Mr. Henry came over to talk with me. He asked me if I knew the alphabet.

"No, son," I said.

Mr. Henry tried to break it down into little bits, thinking six letters at a time would be good. But I said, "No, son, I want to see all the letters. I want to put them together."

Mr. Henry said, "So, that's what we did and by the second day, Mr. Dawson was set. He learned his letters in a day and a half. Then we moved on to phonics. You know, breaking words into small parts and sounding them out. Then Mr. Dawson said, 'I've waited too long, son, show me some words that makes sense.'

"A lot of teaching is usually built on repetition, but with Mr. Dawson, I show him a word and he knows and can spell it after the first time he sees it. But it's not just the way that he learns so fast. Having Mr. Dawson here has changed our class, has changed our whole program."

Just then P.J., one of my classmates, walked in. He's a tall man, taller than any of us three. Mr. Henry said, "P.J., come over here. This is Mr. Glaubman. Tell him how it's changed our class to have Mr. Dawson with us."

"Well, there's more of us now. That's for sure."

Mr. Henry said, "Mr. Dawson is like a magnet for this program. They look at him and say, 'No more excuses; if he can do it at niney-eight, so can I.' Our enrollment has doubled since he came."

Since I started to learn to read, I'm used to hearing people talk about me. It don't bother me. I just watch and listen. Now class was close to starting and people came wandering in. Someone else added, "The teachers and the mothers too, they tell the children, 'Honey, if Mr. Dawson can do it so can you. Just get to work.' "

Mr. Henry said, "He's inspired people. But that's not all. His work ethic and commitment help our younger students. Many of them never had that and didn't succeed in school. They see him coming to learn and that tells them something. These students get here early just to sit near Mr. Dawson, where before they were often late. At the same time he teaches us too.

"The other day we were talking about our presidents. Mr. Dawson started talking about the president that was assassinated in Buffalo. But down here in Dallas, a presidential assassination means John F. Kennedy. That's a part of our history."

"When Mr. Dawson talked about President Roosevelt taking over, we were really confused," Teresa, another classmate, said. "We had to go over to the library."

"Yeah, and that was different," P.J. said, "our wanting to go to the library like that."

Mr. Henry said, "Robin, tell Mr. Glaubman what we found out."

"President McKinley was assassinated in Buffalo, New York, in 1901 by an anarchist. Theodore Roosevelt took over for him."

"I assumed Roosevelt meant Franklin Roosevelt from World War Two," Mr. Henry added. "But it was Theodore Roosevelt and the war was the Spanish-American War."

"That war was in 1898," Richard said. "How can you remember about that? That's when you were born, Mr. Dawson."

I told him, "I remember my father telling me that people felt really bad about the president being killed."

P.J. said, "With Mr. Dawson here, history goes way back. History is real."

I came to school to learn something, but I'm happy to be helping people. Sure, it makes me feel good. You bet I like school! Every morning I get up and I wonder what I might learn that day. You just never know. I am so grateful to have this chance to go to school.

I have to admit, it's easier for me to do silent reading than it is for me to read out loud. To see how I'm doing, Mr. Henry has me read out loud to him, but I stumble a lot over words when I read that way. The day Richard was there, he was sitting at my table. Him being a teacher too, when I was done I said, "My reading is getting better and better, but when I read out loud it's harder."

Richard shrugged. "Probably, it's like when you first rode a bicycle. It was hard to keep your balance and then one day it just got easier. Do you remember how that felt?"

"No. I remember what it felt like the first time I rode a mule."

It's like we both speak English, but sometimes we just got to start over so we can understand each other. It's not easy for either of us, but we keep trying. I showed him the cafeteria where we have lunch. I unpacked my barbecued beef sandwich, and from a paper sack he took out a turkey sandwich.

I get hungry at school and besides a sandwich, I bring dessert. Pie is good and if I don't want it I can always trade a slice of pie with someone at my table for some cookies or cupcakes. I do that sometimes. Richard didn't bring any dessert.

I said, "See, if you don't have any dessert then you don't have nothing to trade."

"Next time."

Junior stopped by at lunch and he and Richard went over to my house when I went back to class. I followed later. When Richard comes, he rents these shiny little cars or a van and we drive around town in those. P.J. gave me a ride. He usually takes me home. P.J. has got a big old car. But nowadays cars are all the same to me. Thing is, it's hard to tell a Chevy from a Ford, plus there's all the other brands that people drive. One thing is they all got radios now. That's not so special like it used to be.

Junior and Richard were already at my house. Junior usually comes by after school anyway. I joined them at the kitchen table. Junior told Richard, "I used to come by almost every day. Now I come by after school. It's nice. It seems that it gives us more to talk about."

"I tell him about my classmates and what the teacher said."

Junior said, "He even tells me what they all had for lunch. I always ask, 'Daddy, did you work hard at school?' "

I said, "The answer is always yes."

Junior said, "I tell my dad, 'School is important. There is so much to learn. I'm proud of you.' "

CHAPTER 22

The old man who learned to read has touched the hearts of people who read about him.

After the Associated Press picked up our January 15 story about George Dawson, who learned to read at 98, hundreds of inspired readers wrote him cards and letters.

In fact, Dawson's life since then has become a story itself.

Dawson, the grandson of a slave, went to work instead of school. He was tired of fishing, and bored with retirement, when he set out to learn to read and write. When he turned 100 on January 17, he was reading on a third-grade level.

And the cards and letters keep coming. The latest came from California second-graders who sent the Dallas school system a donation of $157.10 in his honor. "It's been real nice," Dawson said.

How does all this attention feel?

"Far as I see it, it cheers you up," Dawson said. "It makes you feel good to know somebody's thinking about you."

He told a classroom of children, "I'm trying to get what you don't want [, the chance to go to school]." Dawson still goes to school, every Monday through Friday. He never misses.

—*Fort Worth Star-Telegram*, Larry Bingham, May 11, 1998

I got a stack of articles that I set out for Richard to look through since he always been bringing them to me. While he leafed through them, I said, "You ain't the only one that has questions. Since I turned one hundred, people have taken notice of me. But it don't bother me none."

I even have some pictures from when me and Mr. Henry went to NASA for something about pioneers of this century. There are some senators and politicians in the pictures with us. Nobody ever noticed me before, but everybody wants to see me now. They showed me and Mr. Henry around. We saw some big rocket ships like the ones that go into outer space. They say that someday people might even live up there. Not me. I don't think it's going to work for people. God didn't make us to have wings.

People fly in airplanes, but living on other planets, that's something else. They even gave me a picture of Mars. It's got poor-looking soil and it's too rocky to grow anything. Maybe they plan to bring food with them. Even so, I just don't see it. A man will come out on the front porch and there won't be nothing to do. There won't be no other people to mix with.

Of course, I didn't tell that to those folks at NASA. They have a good time there and like what they're doing. I wouldn't want to ruin that for them. If it don't hurt nobody else, I don't see no harm in it. But if they ever get up there to live, I think they're going to be disappointed. Still, they will have to figure that out for themselves.

We had a good time at NASA, must of walked ten miles going to see all the things they have there. It was something, all right. I think they had that on the news. Of course, I've been on the news a lot now. Dan Rather came down last spring too.

Ever since I turned a hundred and been in the news, life has been busy. After school, lots of days I'll go visiting. Mostly I go to schools and I talk to children. I talk about anything the children want to know and answer any questions they have. Usually, I go with one of my classmates or Junior comes with me.

"At the schools, the children love it. We were in a fifth-grade classroom last week," Junior said.

I said, "The children wanted to know what life was like."

Junior said, "They don't have any idea how rough it was."

"Or how good it was either! People forget that a picture ain't made from just one color. Life ain't all good or all bad. It's full of everything."

"Just the other day we went to a drug rehab center for teenagers," Junior said. "A counselor had seen Daddy on television and called. He thought Daddy might help those kids. Those children hung on every word. There were over a hundred of these kids, but they all listened and they had questions, all right."

One of them asked me if I get high! Another one asked me if I ever had a box of dope! I told them that I don't do that stuff. Life is good just like it is. You don't want to waste life, not even a minute of it. They act so tough, but those were just children. I could tell they were hurting. All of them were missing something inside. They so bad wanted answers from me. That counselor said that he hadn't seen them listen to anyone so closely before.

So many people are calling that Junior thinks I should limit those trips. But there's a lot of people that need some help. It started to slow down after my one-hundredth birthday but then I got to 101. There was a good party when I was one hundred. But at 101 we had two parties.

There was one at school with a big cake and some mighty nice birthday cards. I like them all because I can read them now. My whole family was there. The Dallas schools had some people come to make a few speeches. They honored me for being their oldest student.

Then we had another party. There were more people that wanted to celebrate with me. So we had to rent a hall on the weekend, a place at the community center. Maybe two hundred people came.

The people from the dairy had seen me on

the news. They got together and gave me a big television. It was a fine party. There was so many people enjoying themselves and having a good time. Everybody brought food. There was so much to eat. People was singing and dancing, having a good time. Some people came that I hardly knew and some I met for the first time. They just wanted to celebrate with me. My birthday was months ago and people still send me cards.

Junior wanted me to take a rest from it all. Not me. If I get tired, I can take a nap every now and then, but it don't wear me out. People are just trying to be nice. I appreciate that and it makes people feel good to do something nice. I wouldn't want to deny that to anybody.

People have been so good. And these good things just don't stop. Take last month. We went to a baseball game. Now I've played a lot of baseball in my day. I don't claim to have been that great, but it would have been nice to carry a childhood dream of playing in the majors that most children have. Still, I have always liked the game. I follow our team, the Rangers, whenever they're on television. When I played, I was a catcher and my nickname was Pudge. Our catcher, Ivan Rodriguez, has that nickname too. So, I root for him when he comes to bat. But I cheer for all of them.

I had told that to Richard. Sure enough if he didn't write a letter to the Texas Rangers. Now he didn't mention that to me, but one day I got a phone call from a man named Norm Lyons. He worked for the Rangers and he had some tickets for me to a baseball game against the New York Yankees! I have to admit that the Rangers haven't done so well against New York, but I still wanted to go.

I took Mr. Henry, Junior, and Richard. Matter of fact, on this visit, Richard had rented a minivan and we let him drive. Only thing is, he's not used to our freeways and traffic that we get nowadays. So we left early to be ahead of traffic. That got us to the ballpark early for batting practice, which was okay by me.

It's a pretty new stadium and folks around here are proud of it. At the ballpark, they treated us first class. We had valet parking. That means they take your car and do the parking for you! We had to walk a good ways to find Mr. Lyons's office on the other side of the stadium. He was waiting for us and each of us got a baseball cap. They are red with a big *T* on them. He had talked about some nice seats behind home plate. I figured we would get our tickets and be on our way. But he said, "Follow me. I'm taking you to a luxury suite instead."

We started walking back across to the other side of the stadium where our suite was. Let me tell you, it's a big stadium and I admit, I got a little tired. For me, that's not a problem; I just sit down and take a rest. But Mr. Lyons, he kept trying to be helpful in the way people do. He said, "We have wheelchairs. Let me get you a wheelchair."

I said, "Thank you, but I don't need no wheelchair."

Some people, when they want to help, they want to help, all right. He said, "We can just use a wheelchair till we get to the seats."

He pointed across the field. "We have to go all the way around to the other side. I can take the chair back with me from there."

Richard said, "I can use a rest for a minute. It's been a long day."

We all sat down in some empty seats. Mr. Lyons said, "I have a phone right here and..."

I waved my hands. I said, "I'll take a rest. If you want to order a wheelchair that's fine. You can use it. I don't need one. If I ever need one, that's the day I'll use one."

People are like that. You can't blame them for wanting to be helpful. But they should help someone that needs more help. Me, I do fine. It's not my fault I'm 101. We watched them start to take the tarps off the field. After a little rest, we walked around to the other side of the stadium before they had started batting practice. There wasn't just some seats for us.

It was like being in someone's living room, a nice living room too. Oh, yeah, we even had our own bathroom and kitchen with it too. Real nice. On the other side of these big glass doors, there was a deck with some chairs to sit on, kind of like a comfortable front porch. Or, you could watch the game from the living room if you wanted to be in the air-conditioning. Being a night game in the spring, it was just perfect Texas weather, 80 degrees or so.

Mr. Lyons showed us around and said, "Dinner will be served at six-thirty, in about an hour."

We all thanked him and said, "We could get used to this."

Mr. Lyons laughed and said, "That's not a good idea. We can't treat you to a corporate box each time you come to the stadium. So enjoy it tonight. I've got to go now, gentlemen."

"Oh, we will," I said. "You be coming back, Mr. Lyons?"

"Well, I'll try to stop by again during the game."

Junior was looking at all these warming trays on the counter and said, "There's going to be a lot of food. Come on back and have dinner with us."

He looked kind of surprised to hear that but said, "Hey, I'll try and do that."

We took some sodas out of the refrigerator and went out on the deck. Except for Richard we're all from Texas, but he was the only one that had been to the stadium. He pointed across to the bleachers. "See, that's where I sat when I was here before."

"When was that?" I asked.

"My first visit," he said. "I had to fly to Dallas on a Saturday, but I didn't have an appointment with you at your school till Monday morning. I had nothing happening and didn't know anybody then. I took in a Sunday-afternoon baseball game. I sat right over there in left field. See?"

"Out there in the bleachers?" Junior said. "Yeah, right along the foul line."

"Well," I told him. "Now you got friends in Dallas. You don't need to sit in the bleachers no more. You go with us. We do it in style."

Mr. Henry said, "Basketball is more my game, but I could get used to this. Fewer of our black children are doing baseball anymore. Which is something considering how Jackie Robinson opened it up and, really, that began to open all pro sports."

I said, "I don't think a lot of the kids today even know about him."

We watched batting practice while Richard went to get some T-shirts to take home for his kids. He always likes to walk around anyway, never sits still for very long. He came back with a little pile of them. I looked them over and asked, "Ain't this one a little big for your kids?"

He smiled. "I couldn't help it. I got one for me too."

Turns out that Roger Clemens was pitching for the Yankees and going for some kind of a record too. Now for a Rangers fan, it's enough just to try to beat the Yankees, but we don't need nobody coming down and putting themselves in the record book with us.

It was a sellout. What a game. The Rangers rocked Clemens in the first inning. They hit through the lineup: Pudge, Rusty Greer, Gonzalez, everybody got up to bat. We scored five runs in the first inning. Yes, sir. Clemens didn't last but a few more innings. The game settled down after that and in the middle innings, the Yankees scored a few runs to get closer. Trouble is, the Rangers can hit, but their pitching ain't so good. Some nights, no lead can be too big for the Rangers.

Just like they told us, dinner came to our living room. There were trays with spare ribs, coleslaw, sausage, and, of course, hot dogs since it was a ball game. It was mighty nice of them. Mr. Lyons stopped by to check on how we was doing. Pretty soon, he was sitting down and we was all first name. Besides Norm, some other people dropped by for "a minute" and then stayed: a baseball prospect with a broken wrist and some people that worked there—all kinds of people. There was enough food and drink for everybody and it got to be like a little party. We was all talking and eating and drinking and cheering for the Rangers.

A sports man from the television company came up to our box. He had us shuffle around in our seats so that he could sit next to me for an interview between innings. I'm used to it. That seems to happen everywhere I go. I don't mind. He asked me questions about school and baseball. I like them both.

It was a good game, but just like I told you, the Rangers' pitching couldn't hold a lead. They lost the game in the ninth. We got home past midnight. Next morning, I was up at five-thirty.

I had to walk through Richard's room to get to the kitchen and he said, "That was a late night. I think it would be okay to sleep in for a bit."

I said, "Nope. It's a school day."

At breakfast, I had my hot chocolate. He had his coffee. Same as every morning, I folded over my three slices of white bread to fit in my hand. That way I don't need to bother with a plate. Richard likes that brown bread. That's the first thing he gets at the grocery when he goes to the store, that and coffee. He puts butter on his bread. I eat mine plain.

When he visits, we just be two bachelors with different ways. But we get along fine. He looked at my hot chocolate and asked me, "Do you see that cup as half full or half empty?"

"I see it as being enough. So it's just fine."

Just then a mouse scurried along the floor by the counter. "Did you see that, Mr. Dawson? I think you've got mice."

"Yeah, I saw that. I got mice here. I know that."

"I could go get some mousetraps."

"I got some in the shed."

"I can help you set them up."

"No need for that, son. He was bothering my food, getting in the flour and such, but I got things worked out with him now."

"What do you mean?"

"See that potato in the corner? He goes and nibbles on that. I just leave it on the floor for him and he doesn't bother with nothing else. He's mostly out early in the morning, same time as I be eating my breakfast. Years ago I would have killed him in a trap. Now I just figure he needs to eat a little, but he ain't trying to cause me any harm. A potato lasts him a long time. When he finishes that, I'll just set out another if I have one."

"Well, how did you like the game last night, Mr. Dawson?"

I said, "I liked it fine except for the end. I tell you, it's not my job to manage that team, but Johnny Oates, he made a big mistake. He had the pitcher walk Tino to load the bases. Tino is a good hitter, but he's in a slump. That puts up Chili Davis, who already had four hits in the game. The scoreboard said he was hitting .393 for April. That man was hot. Of course, he gets the game-winning hit. What did you expect?"

Richard thought that maybe I was thinking of managing the team. I just like to second-guess the manager. That's what makes base-ball fun. But manager isn't a job that I would want. Besides, I'm happy to be in school. That was my first time at that stadium, but I would probably go to a game anytime. We had a good time.

Usually at breakfast, we got hours to talk. But Richard was going on a plane that day, going back to his family. He got up to pack his stuff. Now if it was me, I would have already been packed, but he does things at the last minute. That's fine for him, though, and I don't say nothing about that. But I did say, "You are planning on getting my television to run again before you leave?"

"Oh, yeah. Definitely. I'll do that right now. I'll just put my ticket in my rucksack first."

After he had hooked up the video, the television has been fuzzy. I don't watch it so much when he's here. Sometimes I watch the news, though if there is a newspaper around, I would rather see the news that way now that I can read. When Junior is over, we watch *Jeopardy!* And if the Rangers are on TV, I might watch them too. He got it fixed, though, and got to loading his suitcase.

On his last visit, he bought a new suitcase down here. He had to. He ripped the zipper in the other one because he filled it with so many books. I didn't say nothing, but from all the books I see he'll probably do it again. Though, I noticed, he put a lot of books in a rucksack now and that will help some.

It didn't take so long and I said, "That's good. I don't want to be late for school."

But before he hardly sat down, he bolted up. He patted his pockets and said, "My ticket's not there."

"Check your rucksack."

"No, it wouldn't be—"

"Check your rucksack."

"You think so?" he asked.

I nodded. It was there but at the bottom. I helped him haul his stuff out to the porch. It was early light with still some gray in it. There was the blinking lights of a big plane right over us.

"Hope that's not your plane," I said.

"Me too. Mine's in the afternoon."

"I'll be home then. They go right over my house. You should wave."

"I will."

"How many hours to fly?"

"About four."

"How about by car?"

"It must be over two thousand miles. It would be at least forty hours of driving time. Some pretty country to see, though."

"That's a lot of driving. If I visit you this summer, I think I'll go by plane."

"That's probably best."

"Son, school starts soon. We better load your stuff and you can drop me off or I'm going to be late."

School starts at nine. Usually, I'm there by eight-thirty. That morning we got there just before nine. When Richard and I walked in, my classmates cheered.

One of them said, "We count on you, Mr. Dawson. If you can make it, we can too."

Richard laughed. "I'm the one that almost made you late. I promise it won't happen again."

"That's good, son. Too many people count on me now."

CHAPTER 23

Food and Health: *Dr. Atkins' Diet Revolution, The Carbohydrate Addict's Diet, The 8 Week Cholesterol Cure, The New Beverly Hills Diet, Protein Power, The 5 Day Miracle Diet*

Personal Finance and Financial Planning: *Time Is Money, Money Dynamics for the 1990's, Your Money or Your Life, How to Retire Rich, Making the Most of Your Money, The Courage to Be Rich, Live Rich, The 9 Steps to Financial Freedom, Don't Die Broke*

B ooks was something missing from my life for so long. When Richard comes, the living room is full of them or the kitchen table is stacked up with books. I don't mind at all. Some of them were thin, but a lot of them were big, fat books. This time they were all about money or food. We looked in the back of them. I said, "People read these big, fat ones as much as the little ones. They been checked out a lot."

"Yeah, books about money or about cooking and diet are often out of the library. You have to put a hold on some of them for when they come back."

We sorted them into two piles: one about money and the other about food. I pulled one out of the food pile. Once I've seen a word for the first time, I usually remember it. But there's still a lot of words I haven't seen yet. I said, "What's this word here? There's a whole chapter about it."

Richard looked. "It's 'cholesterol.' "

We looked at the others in that pile, and that word was in most of them. "That's a big deal in these books, all right. Why?"

"A lot of people are worried about cholesterol these days and want to avoid it. But mostly they want advice on how to live healthier and longer. Matter of fact, people wonder how you do so well."

"You're going to ask for advice. It always starts with, 'You're doing so well' and then..."

"Well, it's just that people have questions. They are trying to sort things out for themselves."

"Like you are?"

"Yeah, I guess so."

We walked out on the porch and left those books behind us. "See that man across the street on his porch? That's my neighbor. We've lived across the street from each other for years. He seems like a nice man. Right now I can look at him and think maybe he could do better with his life if he would change it some. I've been around a few years and I could tell him some things that he might do that could maybe improve his life. But I don't do that."

"Why not?"

"He never asked me for any advice."

"So, you don't give advice unless someone asks?"

"See, I might think I know what's best for him, but I don't know what is really in that man's heart. I might think I do and tell him do this and do that. He might nod his head, but if in his heart he isn't ready to change, it won't make no difference, maybe even make for some bad feelings between us."

"Bad feelings, even though you would just be trying to help?"

"Unless a man asks for advice, he don't really want it. He isn't gonna thank you for something he don't need yet. That's right. No one ever asked me for advice. See, people looked at me and saw an old man, or saw an old colored man, or saw a man that can't read. They saw what they wanted to see. No one ever asked me for advice."

"But that's different now. People ask you for advice all the time."

"Now I am a man that can read and for some folks that makes a difference to them. For some folks, it made a big difference to them when I turned one hundred."

"So if someone asks for advice, then—"

"No, son, only if a man really means it when he asks. Most people ask a question when they got the answer in mind that they want to hear. That's not really a question. They just want you to help them prove what they already be thinking. I can't think of the word for that. Do you know what I mean?"

"To justify their idea?"

"That's the word for it. Sometimes, you're good with those words, son."

"But, Mr. Dawson, sometimes people need advice and they've got real problems to solve."

"Sure, people got their problems. See, if someone is being honest, I'm happy to listen. I'll listen, might even tell them what I think, but I can't solve nobody else's problems for them. It don't work that way."

We walked back into the living room and Richard said, "But people would like to learn more."

"And that's good. But look at all these books they buy just to figure what to eat. People worry too much. Look at this one. Carbohydrates, fats, vitamins, calories. You know what all that will do to you?"

"Improve your nutrition, help balance your weight?"

"Maybe. Most likely, though, it will just make a person worry."

"Well, a person has to eat something. It might as well be healthy," Richard said.

"Son, I'm healthy with what I do. I eat the common food, that's what I do."

"What do you mean?"

"I eat what I want and when I want. If it's two in the morning and I want some beans and potatoes, then I have beans and potatoes. If I don't feel like cooking the potatoes, I might eat them raw. You've been here a lot and seen what I eat. If I want fried chicken then I eat fried chicken. If I want to cook some ham hocks and cabbage then I will do that. Matter of fact, maybe I'll make us some cornbread right now."

Just then the door opened and Junior and Sallie came in. "Hey, it sounds like we're in time for lunch," Junior said.

"Nah, we're not eating anything, we're only talking about food."

"Oh, that again," Junior said.

"What do you mean?" Richard asked him.

"Oh, these days everybody wants to know what Daddy eats and what foods he grew up on."

"Same thing, I eat the common food, always have. Growing up, my mother always cooked just regular food."

"Like what?"

"Tell him about ash cakes."

"Your family did ash cakes?" Sallie asked.

"Why, sure we did. And they were good too. Right in the fireplace, when the flames had gone down some, my mother would lay out a flat rock. She would set a big ball of dough on that. As soon as it got a little crusty on top she covered the whole thing up with ashes."

"That's it?" Sallie asked me. "She didn't do nothing else to it?"

"Nothing. We just let it cook some more. When it cooked all the way through, we just scraped the ashes off the top."

"Wouldn't some of the ashes still be there?"

"Yeah, but it tasted just fine. We had it all the time. It was good."

"Eating all that ash, that would be hard on the intestines," Junior said.

"My intestines is just fine. I've never had a stomachache in my life."

"Well, it would be tough for me."

"I can eat anything I want. I still got all my teeth and my stomach never caused me no trouble."

"For breakfast, I always have three slices of white bread and a cup of hot chocolate. I never eat too much, just when I'm hungry. For lunch at school, I might pack a barbecued beef sandwich and get a carton of milk to go with that. For dinner, I'll just eat from whatever food there is. If I've been fishing, I would have some catfish. For that, I fill the frying pan with lard, let it melt down, and then throw a slab of fish in there to cook. I do my own cooking since my last wife died eleven or twelve years ago. These pots and pans that hang on the back door here, that's all I need."

"And that fire extinguisher on the counter?"

"That's for grease fires. They can be hard to put out. Anything about that in those cookbooks you brought?"

"I don't think so. What else did you eat when you were growing up?"

"We raised pigs and chickens and ate what was in season. We didn't get sick. Every morning my father gave each of us children a little shot of whiskey. He seen it as being like a tonic that's good for the system. It was only one small tumbler that we had, though my father would often do more than that for himself.

"I never really drank much in my life. Only once in my life did I ever drink too much. I went out and had a few beers after work with the fellas one time. It wasn't anything bad, but I came home late. We had our first child by then. Elzenia didn't say a word about it, but I could see as to how that was not the way to be an example for my own children. That was the last time I drank anything. I guess that would be over seventy years ago now. And coffee, I'm sure you remember about that."

On an earlier visit, Richard didn't believe I could stay so busy through the day and not be tired and not drink coffee. I said that I would just take a little nap and then be rested. I could tell he doubted that. In the chair I was in, I closed my eyes. Though he tried not to, Richard, sitting over on the couch, fell asleep too. Like I always do, I woke up in a short while. Richard kept dozing till someone came over and the screen door slammed. He jumped up and didn't know where he was.

"What does your doctor say about your health?"

"Don't have no doctor."

"Daddy, but you did see a doctor once."

"Oh, that. I wasn't feeling too comfortable and I let Junior talk me into seeing a doctor."

"Well, to me, it seemed like the best thing to do. Trouble was, Daddy didn't have a doctor or money so I took him to the hospital emergency room."

"Before you know it they got me about

naked except for some nightgown that don't even have any buttons in the back. Then he started in with questions, and with some questions that were none of his business. They acted like I couldn't have been alive without having seen a doctor before. More and more doctors and nurses kept coming in to meet me.

"They checked my heart and my ears and my knees and everything. And they gave me some pills to take."

"They said that he had an infection, but that he had the health of a very fit sixty-year-old man," Junior said.

"I threw the pills out and just got better. The old way works for me. I can go out in this back-yard and take some grasses or plants if I need to throw up or take some plants and make a tea to settle my stomach. I can do whatever it is that I need. Those things work just as well as any pill. My grandmothers taught me all that.

"I want for people not to worry so much. Life ain't going to be perfect, but things will work out. People come to visit and I always tell them not to worry. If you got something to eat, don't worry, be grateful. Just look at all those books. Those books aren't about food. They're to do with worrying about food.

"One of those stacks of books is about money. I bet people worry about money more than food, maybe more than anything. I think people buy these books to make enough money so they won't have to worry about tomorrow."

I set Richard's books down. Money just

isn't something to worry about. These books and such only get the brain working too fast. They only going to make people worry even more. A person can't always be thinking about tomorrow and still enjoy themselves today, right now. Nothing wrong with planning ahead, but wanting more than you have makes a person worry. A person only needs to manage with what they have. Be a good manager and there is no need to worry.

I looked at the calendar. It was only a few days to the first of the month, when my check would be coming. I figured that after school on Tuesday, I would take Richard with me to the grocery.

On Tuesday, Junior was at my house waiting for me and Richard. He had my monthly bills—phone, electric, and oil—on the coffee table. Junior had made up a list of those bills and said, "Daddy, your check came and here's a list of the money orders to get. Don't forget to buy three stamps. I need to catch my bus and I figured that Richard was going to go with you anyway."

We took my check down to the grocery. First of the month, there is always a long line at the cashier's office. I don't mind. While we waited, I showed Richard my check. It's the same every month, $520. The line goes back and forth between the ropes, but everybody in that line is happy to be there. It's payday for us.

When we got to the front, I handed the lady my money order list and set my check down on the counter. Then came the part I like. While she was watching, I signed my name in cursive.

She smiled and said, "Thank you, Mr. Dawson."

"It's my pleasure."

And it is too. After all those years of signing my name with an *X*, I am proud to sign my full name.

I pay my bills first and all the money I have left is for groceries. Usually I go shopping right then while I'm at the store. I buy my groceries once a month. When the money is gone, it's gone. I try to keep a little left over if I can. That way if a peddler come by selling vegetables I might get something fresh. Or if somebody has an emergency, I can help them out with bus money and such.

The money usually be mostly gone on one trip and I don't want to spend all my days shopping anyway. Fresh food goes first, but I got a garden. I might catch some fish. Besides, people come by to visit. They know that I like to eat a lot of fruit so they might bring me something. One day the cupboard is almost bare and the same afternoon, someone might bring some fruit or a cabbage or even a jar of honey. It's been that way for all these years now. It wouldn't have helped a bit if I had set to worrying about it. I don't worry. I know that things always work out. I just keep it simple.

Besides groceries, I don't go shopping. I don't need more clothes. In my closet there are a few shirts and a few pairs of pants and a suit and a tie for church. I got all that I need since I only wear one shirt and one pair of pants at a time. My daughter gave me a hat about eight or ten years ago and I wear it every day. It's still not worn out yet. So what would I do with another one? I know that to some folks, my clothes might look kind of raggedy, but I do the best I can.

I don't smoke cigarettes and I don't drink. So I don't have to be running off for cigarettes or to the liquor store. I told Richard, "If a man was to take that money when he was to go out and buy him a drink and invest it, then he would have something for himself."

"Invest it in what?" he asked me.

"Socks."

"Stocks?"

"No, socks."

"Socks?"

"Socks, that's what I said. If instead of buying a drink, you was to take that three dollars and buy a pair of socks, then you would have something. A pair of socks last a long time."

I've never owned stock. Probably a good thing too. I didn't lose a fortune when the Depression came. I don't have no checking account or bank account. My wife had one for us, but I get by without one. No charge card either.

I keep it simple. There's no need to worry that way.

CHAPTER 24

Dear Mr. Dawson,
   I am happy that you can read now. I'm glad
you like school. I do too. I am in fourth grade.
                          Your Friend,
                          Alexa

Dear Mr. Dawson,
   I am in second grade. I live in Wisconsin. I
am glad that your brain still works. Happy 100th
birthday.
                          From,
                          Jimmy

Dear Mr. Dawson,
   I hope that you got a new cane for your
birthday, because that's how I drew it in my
picture. You can keep the picture. My mom
keeps them on our refrigerator. You can do
that too if you want to.
                          Love,
                          Amanda

—From the grocery sacks of letters and
cards from schoolchildren and adults
all over the country

In my living room, I have grocery sacks full
of letters and birthday cards. There's even more
sackfuls in my bedroom. They're mostly from

schoolchildren. Sometimes I get a big envelope with cards from a whole class at once. I save them. Some people like to read them when they come over.

I guess that people been reading the newspapers or saw me on the television and knew it was my birthday. I read them all; for me that's the best part, being able to read them. I couldn't do that for the first ninety-eight birthdays.

Richard likes to read them. His favorite is the card that says he's glad my brain still works! That's one of my favorites too. Still, most people think that once I turned one hundred, I can't think well or I need a cane or I got to use a wheelchair. My mind is fine and I walk just fine. I've never used a cane in my life, but it seems everybody suddenly thinks that I should have one.

One night I was telling Richard that most people only know how old I am. They don't really know me.

He said, "Because of those articles, I guess that a lot of people know of you now."

"That's right. That's how I met you. You read about me in the newspaper," I said.

"Yeah, I read an article about you in the Seattle newspaper. It was in the Sunday edition, a reprint from the *Fort Worth Star-Telegram*. It stayed with me. I tried to understand what it would feel like to start school at ninety-eight, to learn to read, to do what you did. And I thought maybe it would be good for my students, most of whom only have celebrities for their heroes, to know what you had accomplished. The reporter Larry Bingham said to call."

"And then you did?"

"No, that was not the way I did things, just calling people that I didn't even know. I let it slide. About three weeks later, I was in my backyard, cutting the lawn. I got to thinking, cut off the lawnmower, and sat on the back steps. It was approaching a year since my father had died. I thought about him some, but at the same time, the images were fading."

"You got along all right?"

"Yeah, we got along and I know he loved me."

"Did you go fishing?"

"No, he didn't fish. When I was twelve, my whole family went on a camping trip to Montana and back. When he was sick, we talked a lot about that trip and how much fun it was. There were some good memories and we had always talked about going camping or on a trip, just the two of us, father and son. We didn't make it.

"He left me his car, his old Ford. The summer after he died, my son and I retraced that trip. We spent two weeks driving across the country, camping along the way. We even stayed in the same campground in the Bighorn Wilderness that I remembered from more than thirty years earlier. In Wyoming, we caught a lot of fish."

"I guess your father gave you a trip after all. Except on that trip, it turned out that you were the father and you were with your own son."

"I just never saw it that way until now. If I had seen what he gave me, I could have thanked him."

"It doesn't work that way most times. You got a son and daughter of your own and that's all that matters now. Son, I'm over a hundred and I'm still a father. The job never ends. It's a big job. I expect your father did the best he could. You came out okay."

"Thanks, I know. He was a nice man and I'm not complaining."

"I know you're not. Did you get to talk with him before he passed away?"

"I spent a few weeks with him. That was toward the end of his life and I helped to take care of him. He told me to watch closely and I could learn something. He was really sick then. But at the end, he told me it was the best visit we ever had. In a way it was. But still, I could see his life was ending and I wanted to talk about that. And I thought maybe there was something else he had been waiting to tell me. It didn't happen. Life went by too fast and we ran out of time. I was there to help him and maybe I wanted too much for me.

"I wanted to hear his life story. Maybe there were questions to be answered, but I don't even know what the questions would be."

"Son, I've seen death lots of times, but I ain't got no answers."

"I wonder if there was something that he had wanted to pass on to me. If so, I didn't know what it was. I guess we waited too long. It felt like it left a hole in me. I didn't want to wait too long anymore. I did remember that he had always encouraged me to write. So, I went in and made the call.

"I guess with any story the first step is the hardest. Still, I must of changed tickets two or three times. I had my doubts about flying all the way to Texas. Articles had already been done and by professional writers. I didn't see anything to add. It seemed like a long way to go to answer a few questions. I found a lot of excuses to stay home. But I'm glad I went anyway."

"I'm glad you came too. It all worked out after that."

"It has, but it didn't get any easier for me at first. I only focused on the story and I had a direction in mind for that. And at first, I asked the right questions and got just the answers that I wanted and expected. Then you gave me an answer that threw me off the track. I remembered that you had to leave your family at age twelve to work for less than a dollar fifty a week. I gave you the opportunity to tell me what you would do if you saw that man, Mr. Little, today. I was looking to give you the chance to voice your anger, to share your outrage about losing your childhood."

"Except that I don't have any anger."

"I know. Your answer wasn't what I expected and the rest of my questions didn't make sense anymore. I had come to record a life of hardship and was not prepared to hear of gratitude. I lost my story and had to start over and return for another visit."

"A lot more visits. I even fixed up the spare room where I stored my fishing gear so you would have a place to stay. Sometime, it's almost like you live here."

"That's right. I had to find different questions."

"Yeah, your questions got better. I guess you didn't quit on the idea of a book, though. How is that coming along?"

"Oh, the book. I'm still working on it."

"Someone going to print it, do you think?"

"I don't know. But if someone ever wants to publish a book about you, I found out that we both have to sign an agreement."

"Son, we already shook hands."

"I know, but an agreement would have to be in writing too for anybody else to look at publishing it."

"I guess that's how people are these days. We would be partners then?"

"That's right. You lived the life, I just helped to write about it. You might want to talk to Junior and Sallie and maybe Mr. Henry first."

"Oh, I already have. They think it's a good idea. We'll see Mr. Henry again on Monday. It's just that I like to think about things."

"It's fine with me either way. Who knows? Maybe there should be a movie. Do you see many movies, Mr. Dawson?"

"I've seen two movies in my life, one in California in the 1920s when I was traveling and the other was in the thirties. The second one had sound with it. I don't remember the names of them. You pay a nickel to watch something that isn't even real. That's just plain foolishness. The children went to movies, though. Their mother would give them a nickel or a dime to see a double feature on Saturday. They had to sit up in the balcony, the colored section, of course."

"Would you want someone to make a movie about you? Would you go to see it?"

"It don't bother me none, but I'm pretty busy with school and all. I don't know. I would rather go to a ball game like we did the last time you visited than watch myself in a movie. Then you are seeing something that is real."

Right about then Junior came over with O.J., his son-in-law, and Shetora, his granddaughter. Shetora is my great-granddaughter and just turned three, around when I had my own birthday. Junior and O.J. were going to head out looking for a radiator for O.J.'s car.

"Daddy, can Shetora stay here with you? Her afternoon nap be coming up pretty soon and she won't do so well at the auto parts store."

Shetora is here all the time anyway. She knows her way around my house. Richard and I got back to talking till Shetora tugged on my sleeve and said, "Read me a story, Jump Daddy. Story, Jump Daddy!"

"Why does she call you Jump Daddy?"

"All the little ones do. I don't know how many grandchildren and great-grandchildren I got now. But long time ago, when the first one was over, we were playing a game with her. I don't remember how it goes, but I joined in and some of my children said, 'Jump, Daddy, jump, Daddy!' Being that grandchild was just a little one, she was learning her words. She heard it all and called me Jump Daddy. Since then, they all do. I got grandchildren that are grown up that don't call me nothing but Jump Daddy."

"I like that."

"It don't bother me none."

Shetora climbed up on my lap and got settled. She had a little pile of picture books with big-print words in them. "You look kind of tired," I said.

"I'm not tired."

But before the end of the first book she was asleep. I lifted her off me and put her on the couch with a pillow under her head. "That's the best part of learning to read," I told Richard.

"What's that?"

"Reading stories to the little ones. Never read stories to my own children. That wasn't something I could do then."

We went back to talking in low tones, though the fact is that Shetora will sleep through just about anything. "She had fun at my birthday party, all right. Seemed like she was everywhere."

Richard had been reading the paper and I looked at the headlines: 15 CHILDREN DEAD AT COLUMBINE HIGH SCHOOL.

"Children killing children. That's a terrible thing."

"What do you think has gone wrong?"

"Its not just the children. It's the grown-ups too. Some people are growing children, not raising children, and there's a big difference."

"What do you mean?"

"Well, people grow hogs. You give them a place to live, give them all the food they need to keep growing, and make sure that they don't get sick on you. With children you got to raise them. Of course, you feed and clothe them. But a parent has to take the time to teach them right and wrong. A parent has to discipline them. And a parent got to be there to listen to them, help them with their problems. I think most people do their best, but there are some parents these days that are growing children, not raising children.

"It's a sad thing. These children have everything they need to grow up, but they are missing something inside. They must hurt awful bad and no one has shown them the way to live. Buying them their food or even fancy clothes or a car ain't going to help if a child is hurting inside. We all need the same things. Every person, black or white, has five senses: taste, touch, sight, hearing, and smell. We're all really the same, rich or poor.

"Well, son, there you go and got me philosophizing now!"

"Well, my fault. I asked."

"Yeah, you did. I think I'm going to turn in. Tomorrow is a school day."

When the house got quiet again, I actually stayed up thinking a bit. Almost always I look forward, look ahead. But right then I was looking back. When I was a boy, my father had told me, "Whites and colored ain't meant to mix. That's just the way it is. You go against that, you be asking for trouble. Somebody will get hurt."

He lived that way for ninety-nine years, and so far I followed his directions for 101. Between my daddy and me, that's two hundred years of living that got me all the way to where I am today. It's worked. I've stayed with what my daddy told me. Like he also told me, I don't judge nobody, but no reason ever came up to put my signature with a white man in any dealings before. Good thing in a way too, for I could only sign my name with an *X*.

Changes like that don't come in a day. I decided to sleep on it. Sometimes, morning is just a better time to make big decisions. Being able to sign my name is a new thing for me and brings choices I never had to make before. Richard be an honest man. It's not about him, though, it's just about a way of living that I've gotten used to, that's worked for me. He would understand if I keep my ways and don't put my name on nothing. I would just be doing what my daddy said. For my own children, I never gave them those rules. Things have changed and life has been different for them. I'm glad for that. For me, it's always been the old way, though.

Richard and me got to school early. Sure enough, Junior had come by and met us there too. Junior said, "This is a good thing. You both are like partners, Daddy, and if it does get published maybe there will be enough to fix your roof."

Carl Henry said, "I checked; it's a good agreement."

"I know," I said. "But what if I don't sign it?"

Richard shrugged. "That's okay, Mr. Dawson. I'll still finish the book. Nothing will change."

"Daddy, he can write, but then no one can print it."

I thought about what my father said. "Don't have no dealings with white people. That's the best way to live, the safest way."

I had to think on it some more. Nobody said nothing. I knew I was with friends and whatever I chose would be okay. Keep the old ways or make a change—a big change. It was quiet for a long time. It was for me to decide.

I put on my glasses and signed my name in cursive. I have my ways, but sometimes we all got to change.

It felt so good that besides Richard we told Junior and Carl they could be witnesses and sign it too. It was like a ceremony, something special for us. There may never be a book finished, but we went to celebrate what we did that day. We went out for lunch at Sweet Georgia Brown's. Richard said that they don't have food like that where he comes from, but he had the collard greens and baked okra like I did. They gave us so much food that we took some home for dinner.

That night, Richard asked what I remembered special about my life. Usually, I don't look back. I don't have time. But it's kind of funny to think what matters now and what mattered to me years ago.

"I remember when I got bit by a rattlesnake. I was out walking by the lake. I was along the shore and didn't have any shoes on. It came up and bit me on the ankle. I took up a stick and killed it. The ankle started swelling right quick. I hobbled home. My mother tied it off above the bite and then filled a pan with coal oil. I soaked my foot in that. Pretty soon it was filling up with blood that was seeping out. I guess the poison went out with it too. It still swelled up some. I couldn't walk for a couple of days, but it didn't kill me.

"I was only thirteen then. That was a long time ago. I'm glad that old snake didn't kill me. I wouldn't have known it, but think about all that I would have missed.

"I remember when I was twenty-one. My father told me, 'A man is born to die. You got to keep that in mind and don't do no wrong. Do that and you'll make me proud.'

"Funny how life works. That was eighty years ago that I heard that from my father. Finally, this is my time to pass that on. This is your time to listen and I give that to you. I guess that's how the world works."

"Someday, it will be my time to pass that on?"

"Or whatever it is that you've learned. First somebody has got to come with a question and be ready to listen, but at the right time someone will. It will be a long time from now, but till then you need to always be listening and watching, just like I have done all my life. That way you will have learned something and you be ready when the time comes."

"Do you have any regrets in life?"

"Only one. I hurt our mule, Blue. I lost my patience, but that didn't give me no cause to hurt that poor creature. I was sixteen then. That was a long time ago too, but I guess that everything a person does stays with them. I can't undo that, but I never hit an animal since then.

"But I don't look back, son. My next birthday, one hundred and two, I will have been alive in three different centuries. You and your family, you're invited to the party. Come celebrate with me. Right now, I just do what I've always done, just take it one day at a time."

I'm almost always up around five o'clock, but the next morning it was the phone that woke us. That's unusual. Actually, it was Richard that jumped up and got it. It was my nephew. Before he goes to work, he calls most mornings. He says that he just wants to make sure that I'm up and won't be late for school, but I think he's really calling to see if I'm all right.

Thanks to my nephew we wasn't running late at all. We got our breakfast: white bread and hot chocolate for me, brown bread with butter on it and coffee for Richard. He even cut up some cantaloupe for us that he got at the market. Even so early in the morning, not even light yet, he has questions in his brain.

"What do you see for the future, Mr. Dawson?"

"No way to know that, son."

"Do you think you'll stay here in this house?"

"Oh, yeah. I like living by myself, don't mind it at all. My children have asked me to move in with them. But I have my health and as long as that remains I'll stay here. Besides that I don't want to be a burden on no one."

"But they would be happy if you lived with them."

"That's true. They've even said that I could stay at one house for a few days in the week and then another. But I like it as it is. I do just fine living alone."

Richard smiled and said, "Except that you don't really live alone."

"What do you mean, son? You're here pretty often now, but besides that I am here by myself. Do you think there's some lady that I'm hiding from you all or something?"

He laughed. "No, but when you got that phone call this morning..."

"My nephew does that every day."

"I know. That's when I realized you don't live alone."

"Son, I don't know what he could have said to you, but it's just me here."

"I know, but I realized something this morning. You aren't really alone. People call and come by all day long. There is a community of people that cares about you. You live by yourself, but no, you're not alone."

"That's right. You figured that out. Yes, it is nice that people stop by like they do. But they do that because they want to. I have nothing to give them, but they always feel better when they leave."

"That sounds like a riddle."

"It does, doesn't it? I'll tell you the answer for that. All my life, I been good to people. In all those years, every person I met I have treated with respect. People do the same for me."

"What goes around, comes around."

"That's right. It all comes back, everything you do. Sometimes it might take a while is all. I tell people not to worry about things, not to worry about their lives. Things will be all right. People need to hear that. Life is good, just as it is. There isn't anything I would change about my life."

"People worry too much?"

"That's right. Be happy for what you have. Help somebody else instead of worrying. It will make a person feel better. It's good to be generous. It doesn't take much to make a difference. Even the poorest man can just take the time to say hello; that can be a help. Have some sympathy for someone's hard-luck story. It's not about money. Give what you can. And if you have nothing, at least pray for somebody. Have good thoughts."

"You're going to stay in school?"

"Like my classmates, I am working to get my GED. The reading is coming along. I work on my writing every day and that is getting better too. But I hear that there is a big essay on the final exam that I will need to write. Then besides that, I am going to have to study science and I got a long ways to go with my numbers."

"You got a late start."

"That's so."

"Because of the circumstances, maybe there might be a special degree, an honorary degree."

"No, what I get, I will work for and earn. Every now and then, I do get a little weary of school, though. I've been going every day for three years now, even in the summer. The brain needs a rest. Just like the body gets tired, the brain needs a rest sometimes too. It works better with a rest every now and then. I pulled my fishing gear out the other day, oiled the reels and cleaned the lines. I wouldn't mind doing a little fishing."

"Maybe you could take a vacation."

"You saw what happened with my classmates when I was almost late. They count on me and they aren't the only ones either."

"Who else?"

"Lots of people. I get letters all the time. Last week a lady sent me a letter. She is sixty years old and thought she was too old to go back to school. Then she read about me and changed her mind. She went back and told me that it was the best thing she ever did. Too many people need me so I can't do anything less than my best."

"So you're going to stay in school."

"I'll go fishing some weekend, maybe on your next visit. I'll get all the rest I need then. Son, I still got so much ahead of me to learn. What about you? Are you still going to keep working on our book?"

"Well, sure. Don't you want to see it finished?"

"That be fine if it is, and just fine if it's not."

"But I thought you said that we should work together on a book. I assumed you would want to see it completed."

"That's right. I did say that it would be nice, you've been working so hard and all."

"Wait, it's not for me. I remember you saying that the world only changes with one person at a time. Your story might be of help to someone that reads it and that might make a difference."

I could see his mind running in the way that it does sometimes. It can make him impatient and then he don't listen so well. I put up my hand to stop that. He waited.

"I did say that before. Things is different now. I will be happy if the only man who changes is the man that wrote it. If you needed to write a whole book to do that, fine."

I've never complained about it, but for once he turned his tape machine off. He gave me a hug and said, "The book is done then. I guess we're finished."

"No, son, we're not finished. We just don't

need us a book anymore. You can just come and visit anyway. I might go see your family too. I hear there's good fishing up your way. We did this book just like we said we would. We did our best. I don't care if nothing else happens with it or if somebody was to print a hundred copies. I'll have my own copy and I can read now."

"You've accomplished a lot."

"That's right. Yet, judge me not for the deeds that I have done, but for the life that I've lived. Son, people think one hundred years is a long time. Most folks just don't understand. My life hasn't been so long at all; seems short to me. It's all gone by so fast.

"Life is so good and it gets better every day."

ABOUT THE
AUTHORS

GEORGE DAWSON worked for more than seven decades. Some of his jobs have included breaking horses, driving spikes for the railroads, building levees on the Mississippi, and laboring on farms and in a sawmill. He is currently a full-time student and lives in Texas.

RICHARD GLAUBMAN is an elementary school teacher. He lives in Washington State.